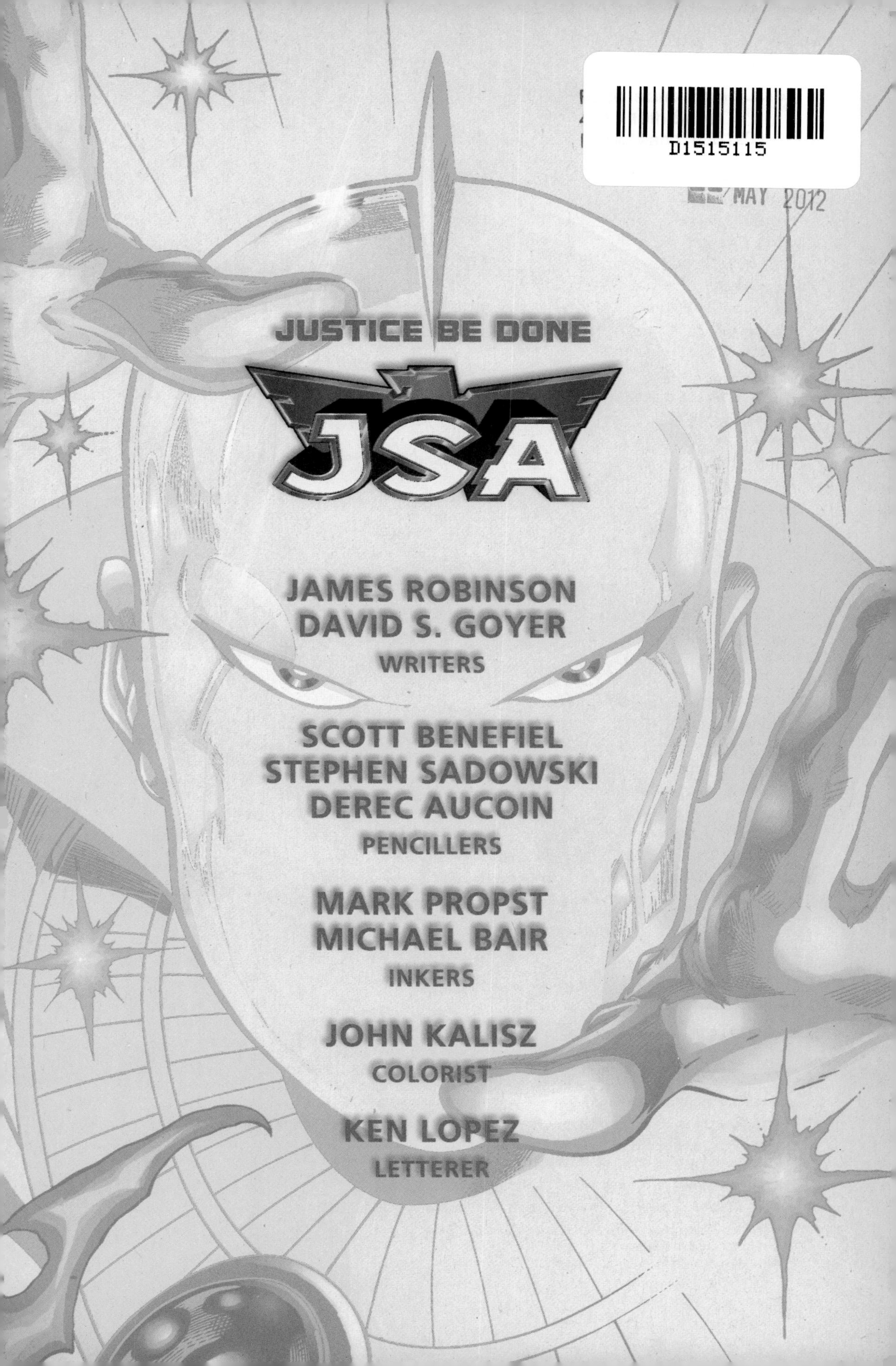

JUSTICE BE DONE

JSA

JAMES ROBINSON
DAVID S. GOYER
WRITERS

SCOTT BENEFIEL
STEPHEN SADOWSKI
DEREC AUCOIN
PENCILLERS

MARK PROPST
MICHAEL BAIR
INKERS

JOHN KALISZ
COLORIST

KEN LOPEZ
LETTERER

JSA: JUSTICE BE DONE

Published by DC Comics. Cover and compilation copyright
© 2000 DC Comics. All Rights Reserved.

Originally published in single magazine form as JSA SECRET FILES 1, JSA 1-5.
Copyright © 1999 DC Comics. All Rights Reserved. All characters, their distinctive likenesses
and related indicia featured in this publication are trademarks of DC Comics.

The stories, characters, and incidents featured in this publication are entirely fictional.

DC Comics, 1700 Broadway, New York, NY 10019
A division of Warner Bros. - A Time Warner Entertainment Company

Printed in Canada. First Printing.

ISBN: 1-56389-620-6

Cover illustration by STEPHEN SADOWSKI and MICHAEL BAIR.
Cover color by LEE LOUGHRIDGE.
Publication design by MURPHY FOGELNEST.

Forged in the fires of the second world war, they were the first to stand united against evil and injustice—giving birth to a legend that would never die...

It was the winter of 1940. Adolf Hitler, armed with the occult power of the mysterious Spear of Destiny as well as the assembled might of the Axis army, prepared to invade an unsuspecting England. Battling across two continents against forces both mythical and manmade, eight "Mystery Men" halted the invasion. At the behest of President Roosevelt, the eight remained together and formed the first super-hero team—the Justice Society of America!

Faithful defenders for the next several decades, the JSA eventually ceded the spotlight to the champions they had inspired. Rising once more to face the threat of the time-altering Extant, the JSA suffered their greatest loss as many of their number were killed in the battle. Among the fallen were HAWKMAN and HAWKGIRL—a reincarnated Egyptian prince and his bride, possessors of the secret of the gravity-defying Nth Metal—and DOCTOR FATE—a mystical agent of the forces of Order whose powers stemmed from a collection of magical artifacts.

Now, the survivors continue to serve as the teachers and advisors to the heroes of today. Of the eight founders, only three remain...

SENTINEL
Formerly known as Green Lantern, Alan Scott is the master of the green flame of the Starheart and can use its occult energies to create anything he imagines.

THE FLASH
The first in a long line of super-speedsters, Jay Garrick is capable of running at velocities near the speed of light.

WESLEY DODDS
As the gas gun-wielding vigilante THE SANDMAN, Wesley sought out the evildoers revealed to him in his dreams. Now, he has retired to a life of travel and discovery.

star-spangled kid

sandy hawkins

al rothstein

starman

obsidian

black canary

wildcat

hourman

Over the course of its long history, the JSA has called many heroes to join its ranks, including...

WILDCAT

A former heavyweight boxing champ, Ted Grant, a.k.a. Wildcat, prowls the mean streets defending the helpless. One of the foremost hand-to-hand combatants, he has trained many of today's best fighters — including the Batman.

WONDER WOMAN

During a time when she assumed the heroic guise of her daughter, Queen Hippolyta of the Amazons traveled back in time to join the JSA, offering them her warrior skills and tactical training. Now back in the present, she has reassumed her throne but remains ready to return to her comrades' side.

Among the JSA's proudest legacies are the heroes who have chosen to follow in their footsteps. Some are sons and daughters; others were simply inspired by their example.

STARMAN

Jack Knight, son of Ted Knight— the first Starman, carries on the family tradition and uses his star-powered cosmic rod and street savvy to protect his home, Opal City.

BLACK CANARY

A skilled detective and martial artist, Dinah Lance has idolized her mother and her JSA teammates all her life. Currently, she is partnered with the mysterious "Oracle" and travels the globe as a troubleshooter.

HOURMAN

An android from the 853rd century, his genetic software is patterned after the DNA of Rex Tyler—the original Hourman. Super-strong and able to fly, Hourman can activate a unique "Power Hour" that allows him to tap into the nigh-omnipotent power of the time-warping Worlogog.

SANDY HAWKINS

The ward of Wesley Dodds and nephew of Dodds's lifelong partner, Dian Belmont, Sandy was transformed through a bizarre experiment into a crazed silicon monster. Revived from a state of suspended animation and cured of his condition some years ago, Sandy is still deciding if he will continue the work started by his mentor.

AL ROTHSTEIN

Born super-strong and later able to increase his size and mass, Al assumed the alias of NUKLON to serve with Infinity Inc., and then the Justice League. Now on his own, Al searches for a way to better honor the memory of his godfather and JSA founder, the Atom.

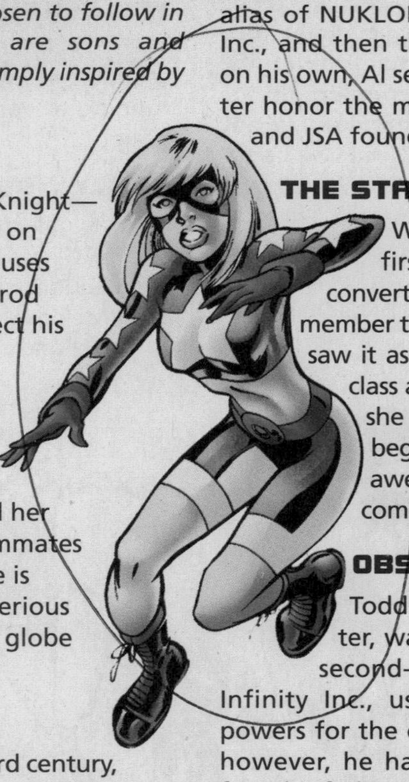

THE STAR-SPANGLED KID

When Courtney Whitmore first discovered the cosmic converter belt once worn by JSA member the Star-Spangled Kid, she saw it as an opportunity to ditch class and kick some butt. Now, she is slowly — very slowly— beginning to learn about the awesome legacy she has become a part of.

OBSIDIAN

Todd Rice, along with his sister, was also a member of the second-generation super-team Infinity Inc., using his shadow-based powers for the cause of right. Recently, however, he has begun to drift away from his father, Alan Scott, as well as the rest of his friends and family.

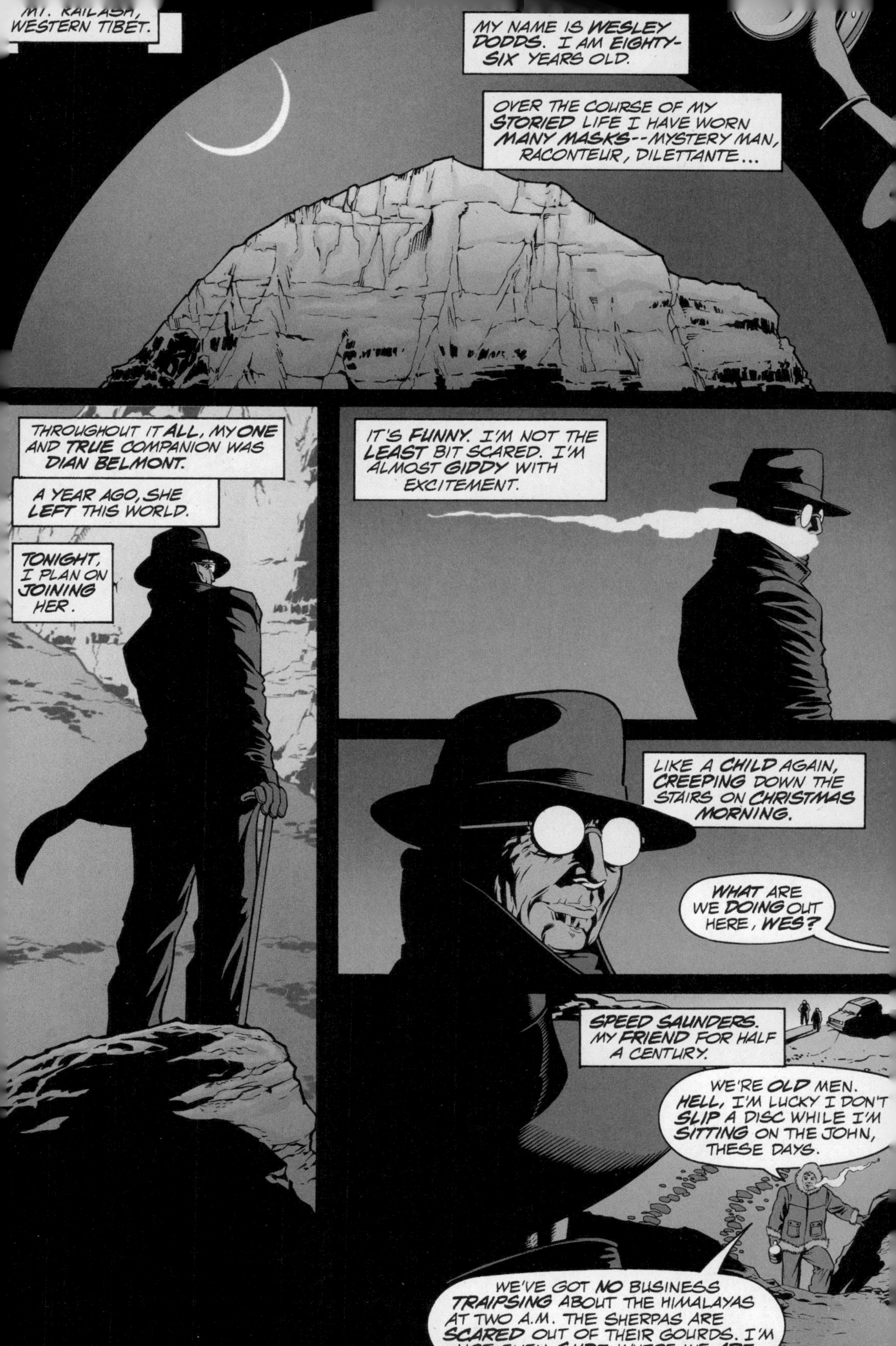
MT. KAILASH, WESTERN TIBET.
MY NAME IS WESLEY DODDS. I AM EIGHTY-SIX YEARS OLD.
OVER THE COURSE OF MY STORIED LIFE I HAVE WORN MANY MASKS--MYSTERY MAN, RACONTEUR, DILETTANTE...
THROUGHOUT IT ALL, MY ONE AND TRUE COMPANION WAS DIAN BELMONT.
A YEAR AGO, SHE LEFT THIS WORLD.
TONIGHT, I PLAN ON JOINING HER.
IT'S FUNNY. I'M NOT THE LEAST BIT SCARED. I'M ALMOST GIDDY WITH EXCITEMENT.
LIKE A CHILD AGAIN, CREEPING DOWN THE STAIRS ON CHRISTMAS MORNING.
WHAT ARE WE DOING OUT HERE, WES?
SPEED SAUNDERS. MY FRIEND FOR HALF A CENTURY.
WE'RE OLD MEN. HELL, I'M LUCKY I DON'T SLIP A DISC WHILE I'M SITTING ON THE JOHN, THESE DAYS.
WE'VE GOT NO BUSINESS TRAIPSING ABOUT THE HIMALAYAS AT TWO A.M. THE SHERPAS ARE SCARED OUT OF THEIR GOURDS. I'M NOT EVEN SURE WHERE WE ARE.

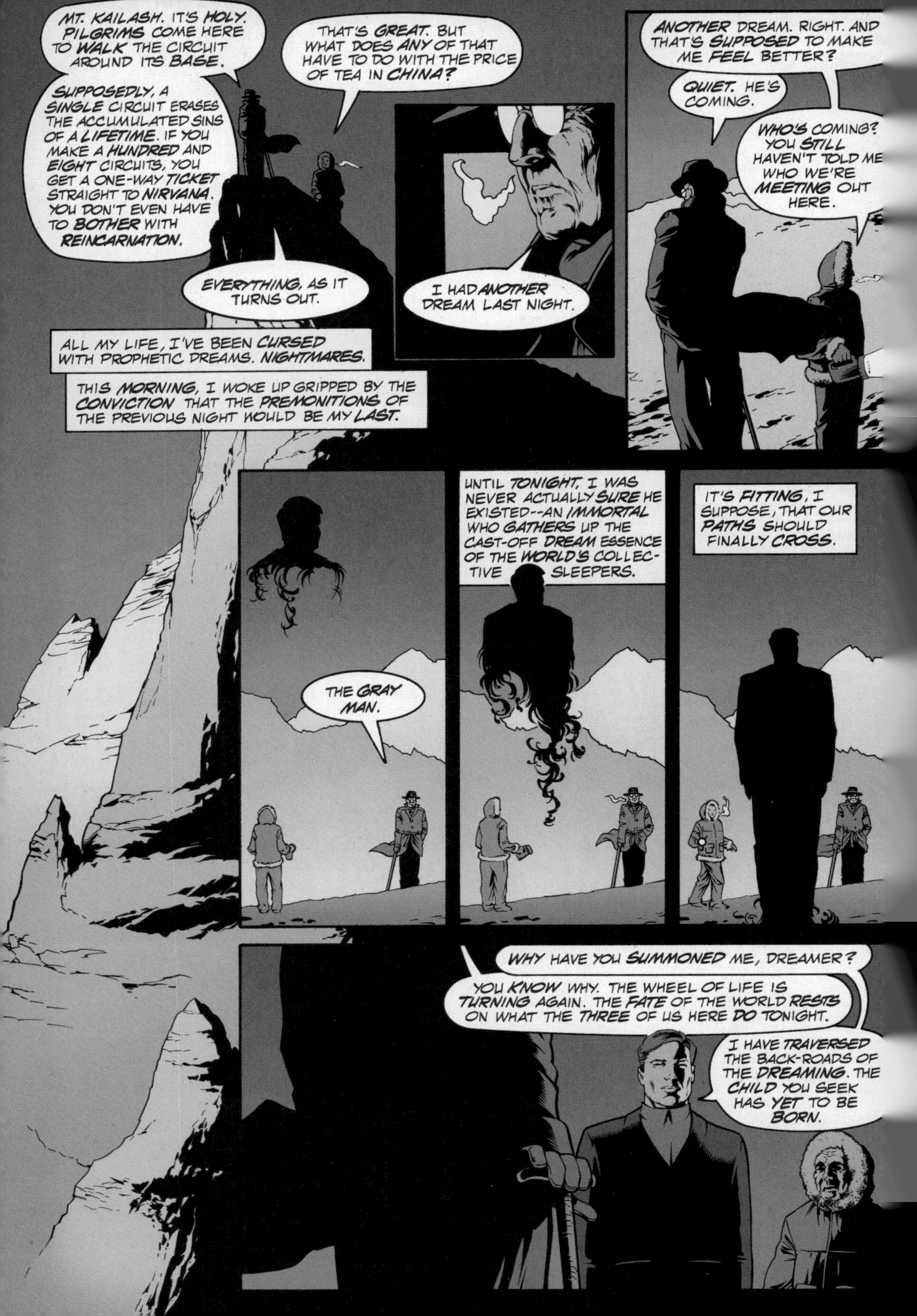
MT. KAILASH. IT'S HOLY. PILGRIMS COME HERE TO WALK THE CIRCUIT AROUND ITS BASE.
SUPPOSEDLY, A SINGLE CIRCUIT ERASES THE ACCUMULATED SINS OF A LIFETIME. IF YOU MAKE A HUNDRED AND EIGHT CIRCUITS, YOU GET A ONE-WAY TICKET STRAIGHT TO NIRVANA. YOU DON'T EVEN HAVE TO BOTHER WITH REINCARNATION.
THAT'S GREAT. BUT WHAT DOES ANY OF THAT HAVE TO DO WITH THE PRICE OF TEA IN CHINA?
EVERYTHING, AS IT TURNS OUT.
I HAD ANOTHER DREAM LAST NIGHT.
ANOTHER DREAM. RIGHT. AND THAT'S SUPPOSED TO MAKE ME FEEL BETTER?
QUIET. HE'S COMING.
WHO'S COMING? YOU STILL HAVEN'T TOLD ME WHO WE'RE MEETING OUT HERE.
ALL MY LIFE, I'VE BEEN CURSED WITH PROPHETIC DREAMS. NIGHTMARES.
THIS MORNING, I WOKE UP GRIPPED BY THE CONVICTION THAT THE PREMONITIONS OF THE PREVIOUS NIGHT WOULD BE MY LAST.
THE GRAY MAN.
UNTIL TONIGHT, I WAS NEVER ACTUALLY SURE HE EXISTED--AN IMMORTAL WHO GATHERS UP THE CAST-OFF DREAM ESSENCE OF THE WORLD'S COLLECTIVE SLEEPERS.
IT'S FITTING, I SUPPOSE, THAT OUR PATHS SHOULD FINALLY CROSS.
WHY HAVE YOU SUMMONED ME, DREAMER?
YOU KNOW WHY. THE WHEEL OF LIFE IS TURNING AGAIN. THE FATE OF THE WORLD RESTS ON WHAT THE THREE OF US HERE DO TONIGHT.
I HAVE TRAVERSED THE BACK-ROADS OF THE DREAMING. THE CHILD YOU SEEK HAS YET TO BE BORN.

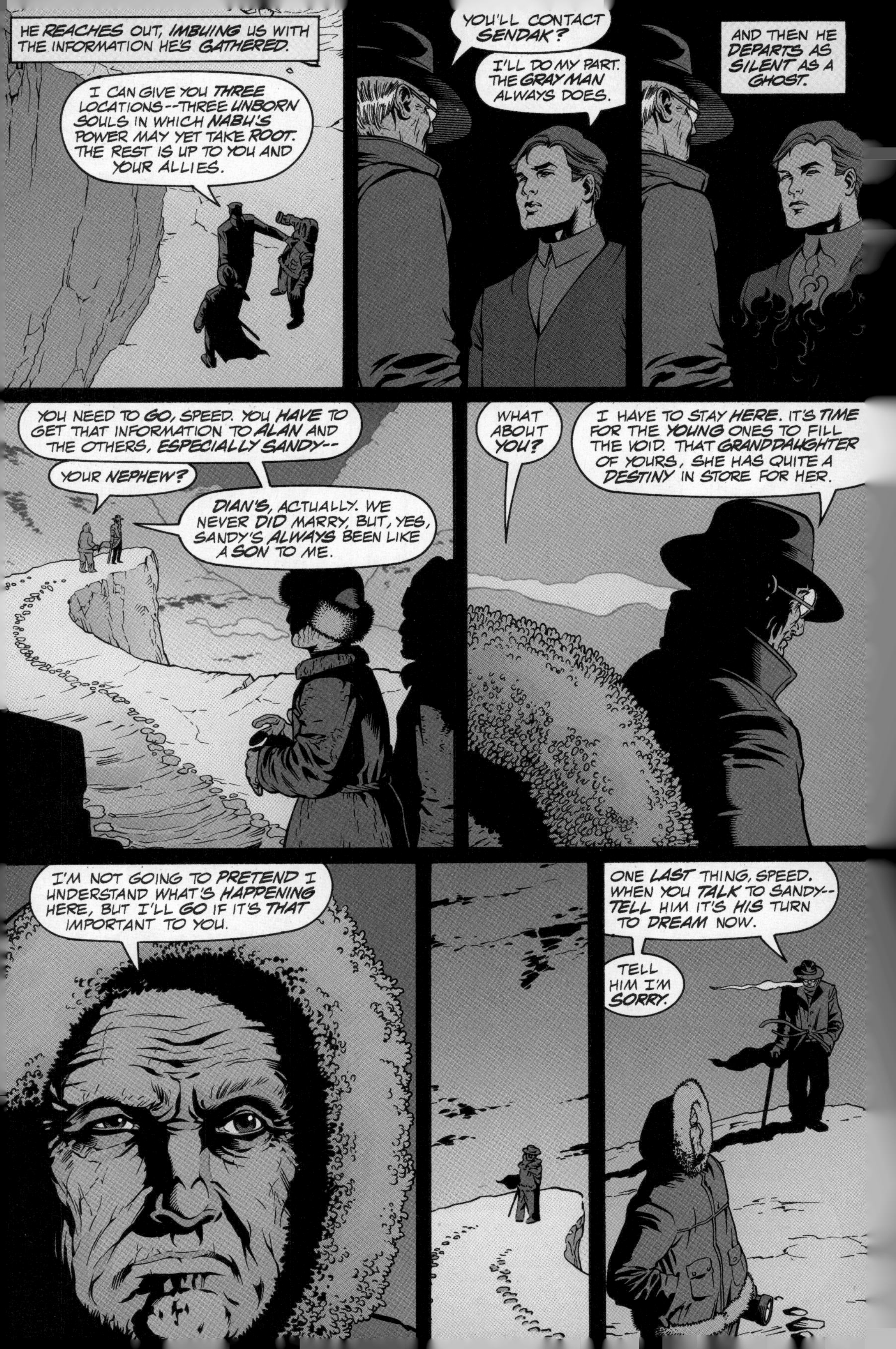

HE REACHES OUT, IMBUING US WITH THE INFORMATION HE'S GATHERED.
I CAN GIVE YOU THREE LOCATIONS--THREE UNBORN SOULS IN WHICH NABU'S POWER MAY YET TAKE ROOT. THE REST IS UP TO YOU AND YOUR ALLIES.
YOU'LL CONTACT SENDAK?
I'LL DO MY PART. THE GRAY MAN ALWAYS DOES.
AND THEN HE DEPARTS AS SILENT AS A GHOST.
YOU NEED TO GO, SPEED. YOU HAVE TO GET THAT INFORMATION TO ALAN AND THE OTHERS, ESPECIALLY SANDY--
YOUR NEPHEW?
DIAN'S, ACTUALLY. WE NEVER DID MARRY, BUT, YES, SANDY'S ALWAYS BEEN LIKE A SON TO ME.
WHAT ABOUT YOU?
I HAVE TO STAY HERE. IT'S TIME FOR THE YOUNG ONES TO FILL THE VOID. THAT GRANDDAUGHTER OF YOURS, SHE HAS QUITE A DESTINY IN STORE FOR HER.
I'M NOT GOING TO PRETEND I UNDERSTAND WHAT'S HAPPENING HERE, BUT I'LL GO IF IT'S THAT IMPORTANT TO YOU.
ONE LAST THING, SPEED. WHEN YOU TALK TO SANDY--TELL HIM IT'S HIS TURN TO DREAM NOW.
TELL HIM I'M SORRY.

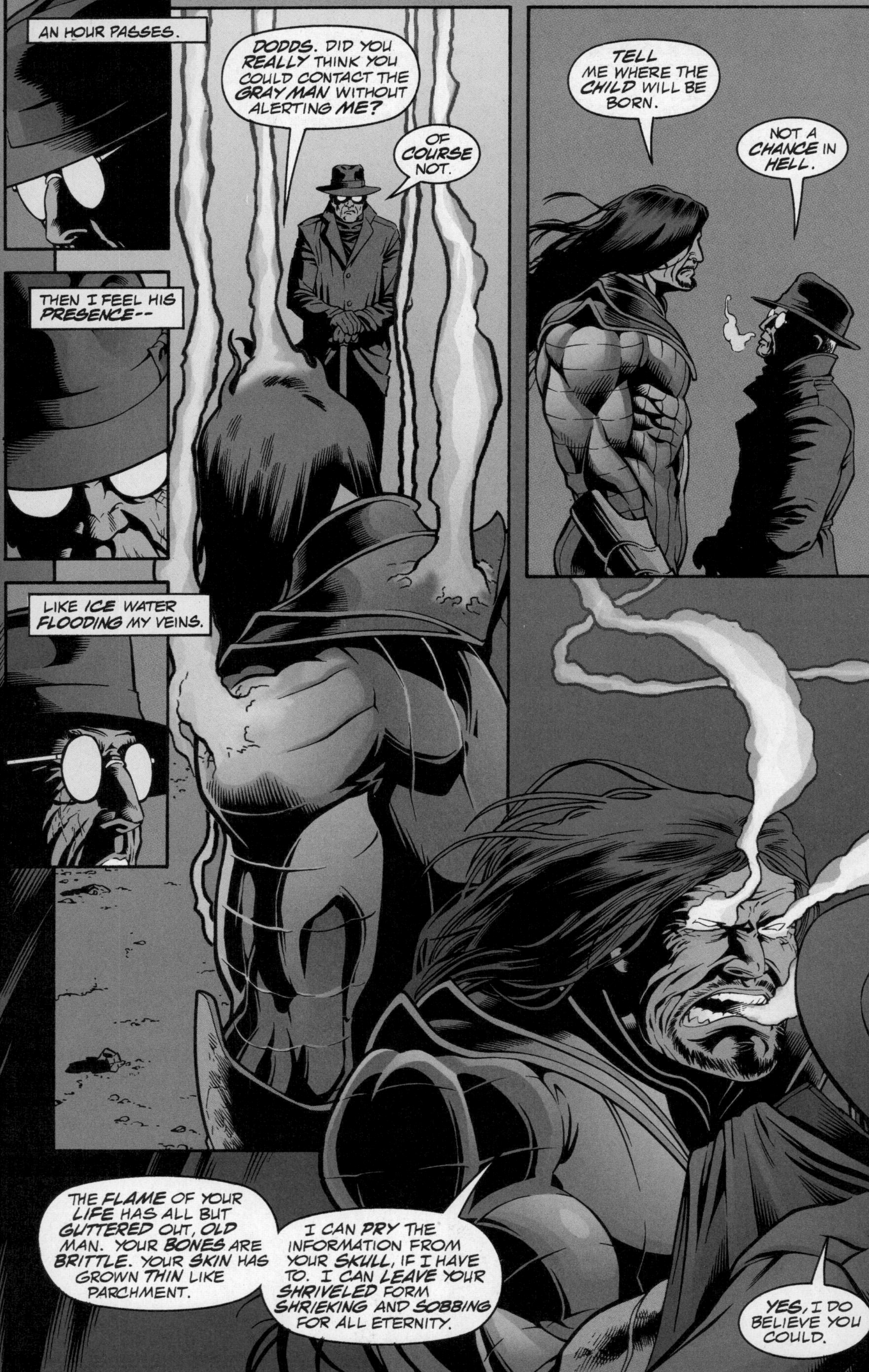

AN HOUR PASSES.
THEN I FEEL HIS PRESENCE--
LIKE ICE WATER FLOODING MY VEINS.
DODDS. DID YOU REALLY THINK YOU COULD CONTACT THE GRAY MAN WITHOUT ALERTING ME?
OF COURSE NOT.
TELL ME WHERE THE CHILD WILL BE BORN.
NOT A CHANCE IN HELL.
THE FLAME OF YOUR LIFE HAS ALL BUT GUTTERED OUT, OLD MAN. YOUR BONES ARE BRITTLE. YOUR SKIN HAS GROWN THIN LIKE PARCHMENT.
I CAN PRY THE INFORMATION FROM YOUR SKULL, IF I HAVE TO. I CAN LEAVE YOUR SHRIVELED FORM SHRIEKING AND SOBBING FOR ALL ETERNITY.
YES, I DO BELIEVE YOU COULD.

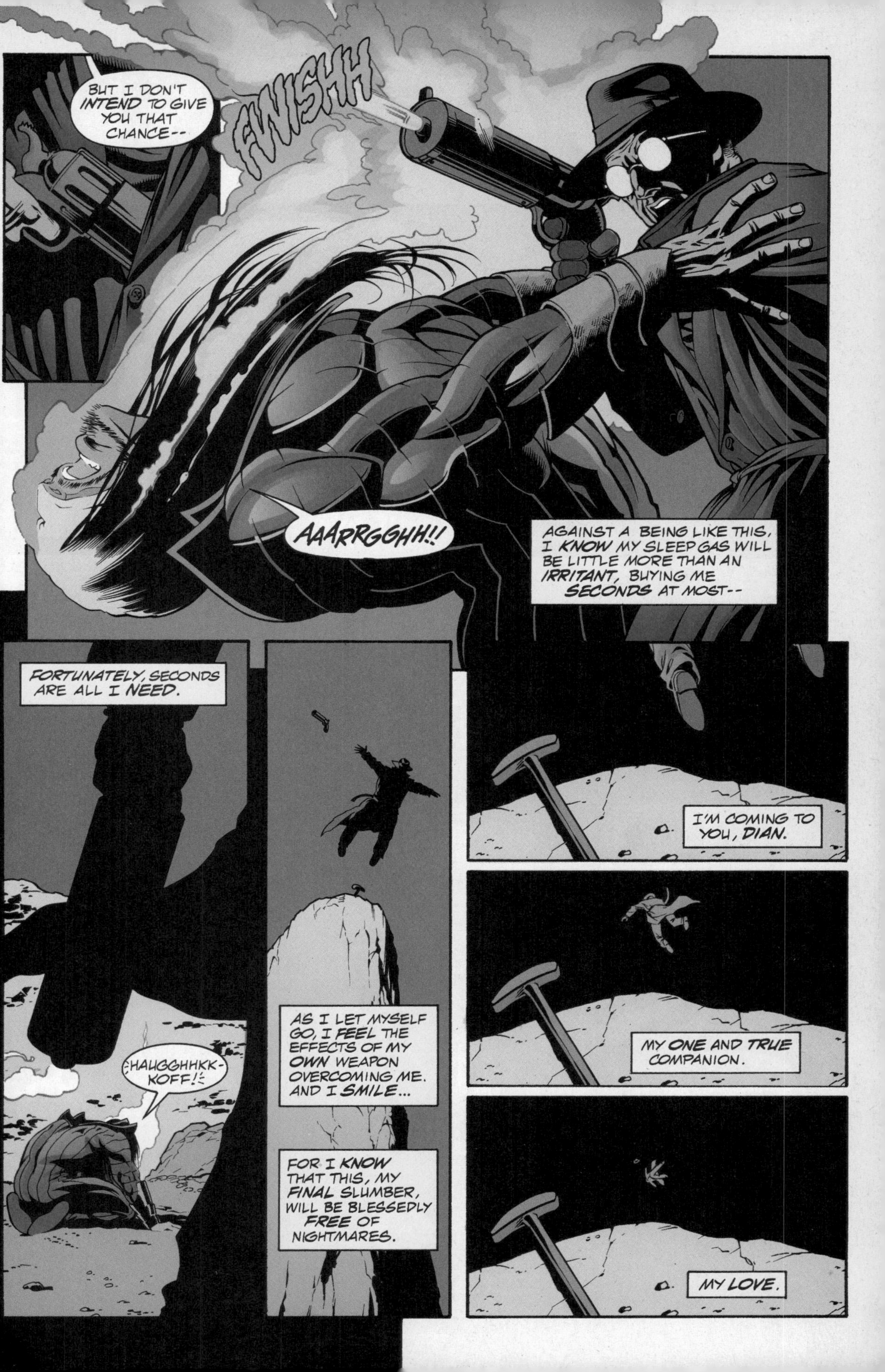
BUT I DON'T INTEND TO GIVE YOU THAT CHANCE--
FWISHH
AAARRGGHH!!
AGAINST A BEING LIKE THIS, I KNOW MY SLEEP GAS WILL BE LITTLE MORE THAN AN IRRITANT, BUYING ME SECONDS AT MOST--
FORTUNATELY, SECONDS ARE ALL I NEED.
HAUGGHHKK-KOFF!
AS I LET MYSELF GO, I FEEL THE EFFECTS OF MY OWN WEAPON OVERCOMING ME. AND I SMILE...
FOR I KNOW THAT THIS, MY FINAL SLUMBER, WILL BE BLESSEDLY FREE OF NIGHTMARES.
I'M COMING TO YOU, DIAN.
MY ONE AND TRUE COMPANION.
MY LOVE.

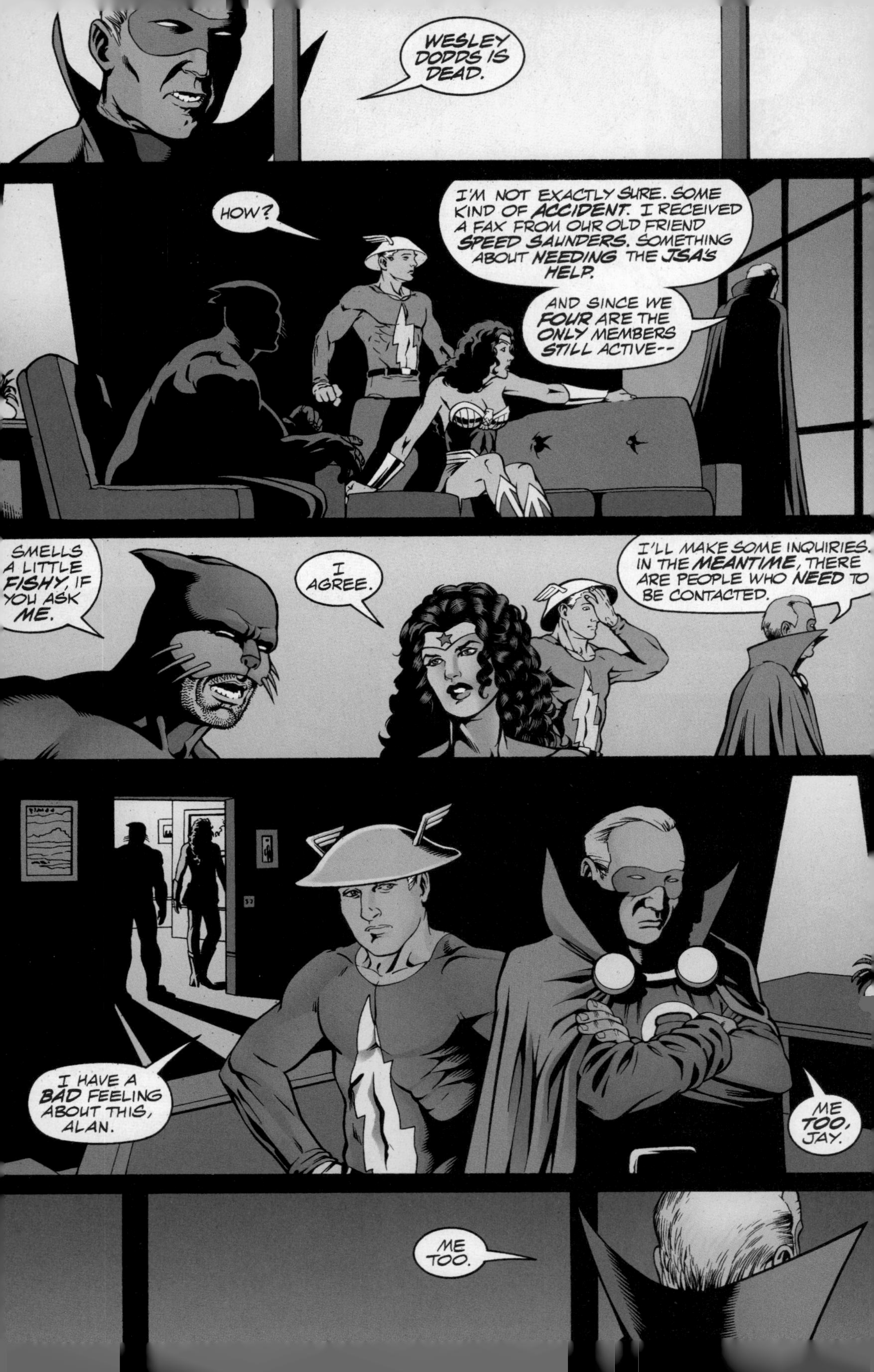
WESLEY DODDS IS DEAD.
HOW?
I'M NOT EXACTLY SURE. SOME KIND OF ACCIDENT. I RECEIVED A FAX FROM OUR OLD FRIEND SPEED SAUNDERS. SOMETHING ABOUT NEEDING THE JSA's HELP.
AND SINCE WE FOUR ARE THE ONLY MEMBERS STILL ACTIVE--
SMELLS A LITTLE FISHY, IF YOU ASK ME.
I AGREE.
I'LL MAKE SOME INQUIRIES. IN THE MEANTIME, THERE ARE PEOPLE WHO NEED TO BE CONTACTED.
I HAVE A BAD FEELING ABOUT THIS, ALAN.
ME TOO, JAY.
ME TOO.

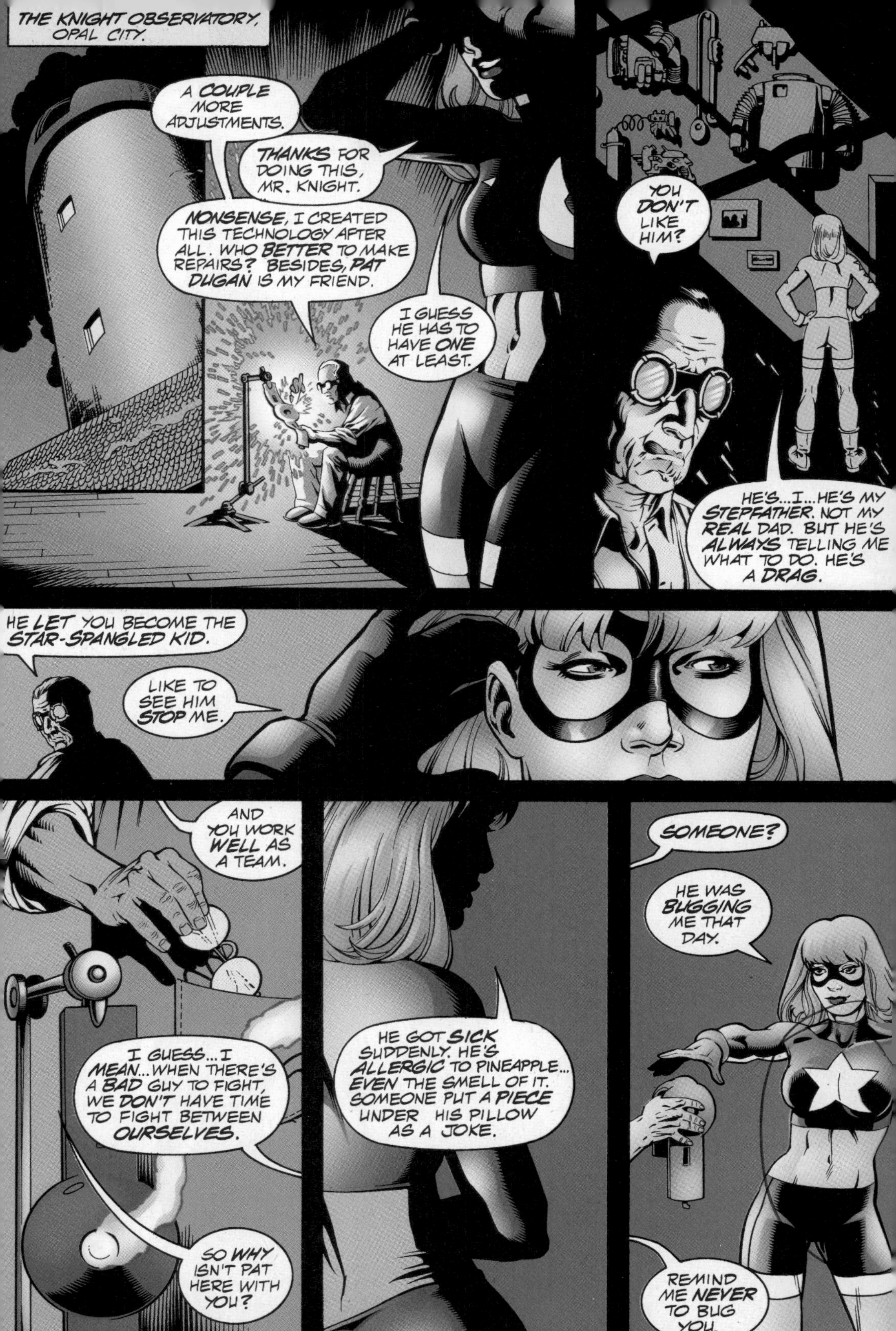
THE KNIGHT OBSERVATORY, OPAL CITY.
A COUPLE MORE ADJUSTMENTS.
THANKS FOR DOING THIS, MR. KNIGHT.
NONSENSE, I CREATED THIS TECHNOLOGY AFTER ALL. WHO BETTER TO MAKE REPAIRS? BESIDES, PAT DUGAN IS MY FRIEND.
I GUESS HE HAS TO HAVE ONE AT LEAST.
YOU DON'T LIKE HIM?
HE'S...I...HE'S MY STEPFATHER. NOT MY REAL DAD. BUT HE'S ALWAYS TELLING ME WHAT TO DO. HE'S A DRAG.
HE LET YOU BECOME THE STAR-SPANGLED KID.
LIKE TO SEE HIM STOP ME.
AND YOU WORK WELL AS A TEAM.
I GUESS...I MEAN...WHEN THERE'S A BAD GUY TO FIGHT, WE DON'T HAVE TIME TO FIGHT BETWEEN OURSELVES.
SO WHY ISN'T PAT HERE WITH YOU?
HE GOT SICK SUDDENLY. HE'S ALLERGIC TO PINEAPPLE... EVEN THE SMELL OF IT. SOMEONE PUT A PIECE UNDER HIS PILLOW AS A JOKE.
SOMEONE?
HE WAS BUGGING ME THAT DAY.
REMIND ME NEVER TO BUG YOU.

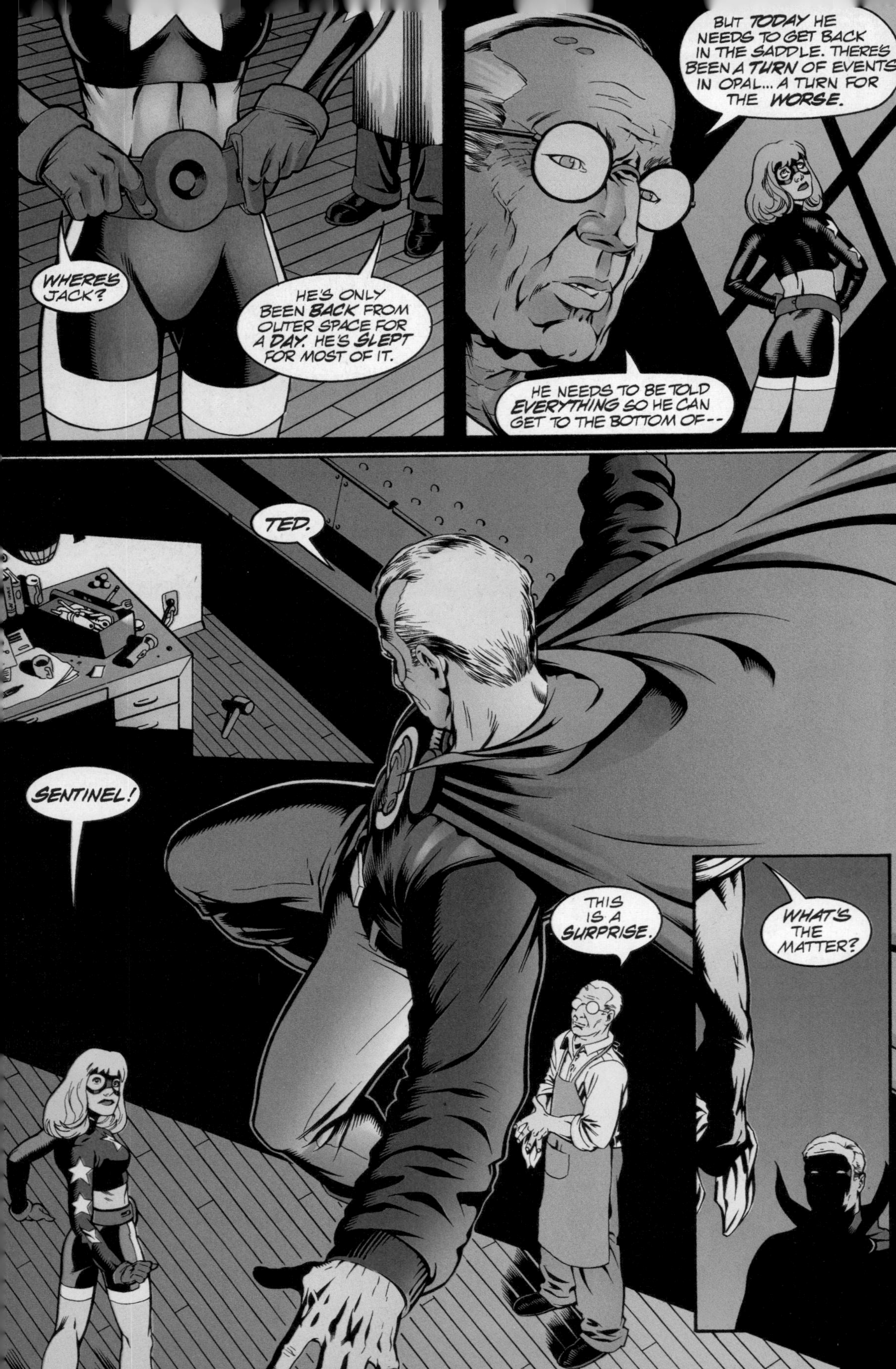
WHERE'S JACK?
HE'S ONLY BEEN BACK FROM OUTER SPACE FOR A DAY. HE'S SLEPT FOR MOST OF IT.
BUT TODAY HE NEEDS TO GET BACK IN THE SADDLE. THERE'S BEEN A TURN OF EVENTS IN OPAL... A TURN FOR THE WORSE.
HE NEEDS TO BE TOLD EVERYTHING SO HE CAN GET TO THE BOTTOM OF--
TED.
SENTINEL!
THIS IS A SURPRISE.
WHAT'S THE MATTER?

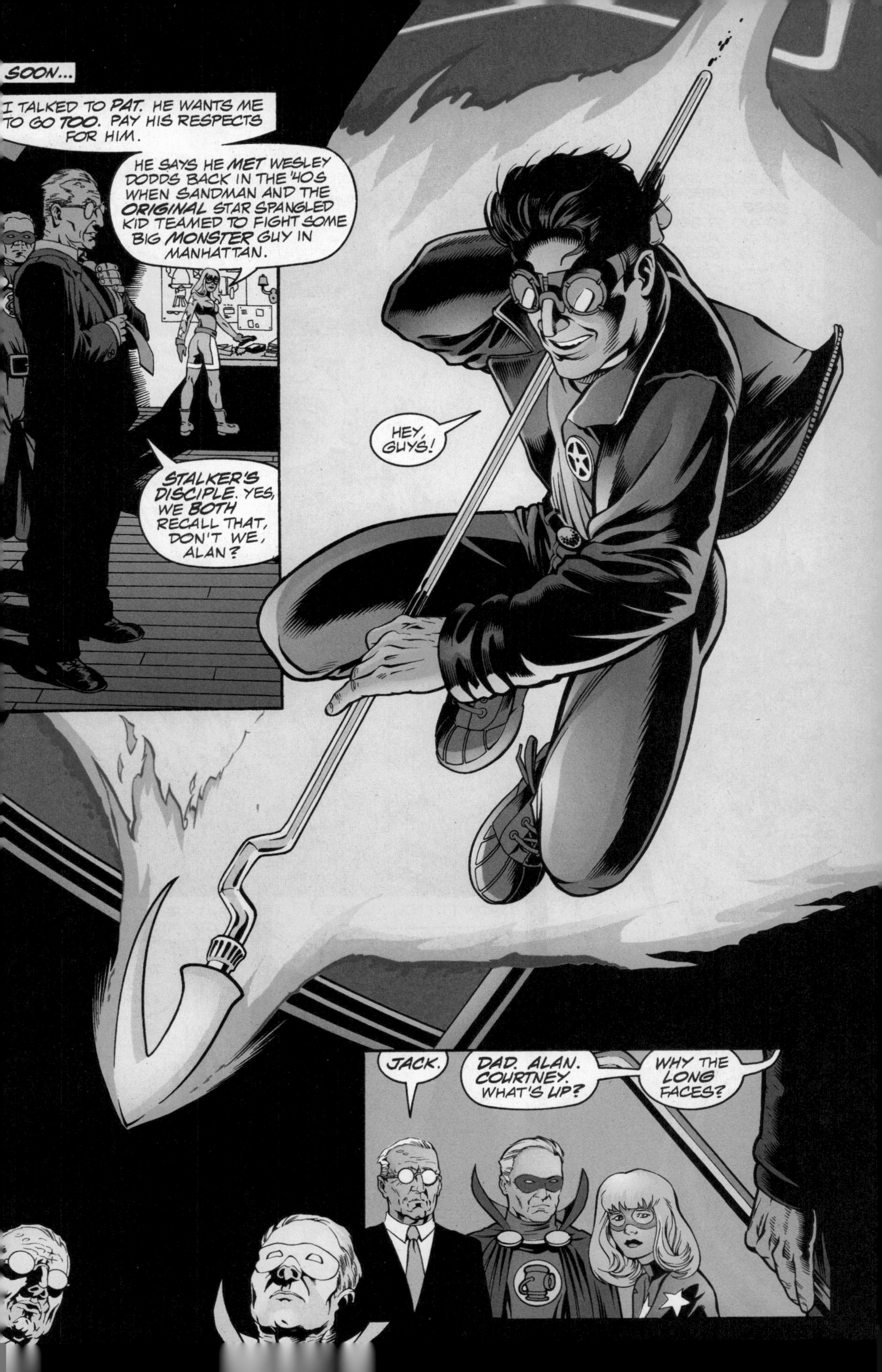
SOON...
I TALKED TO PAT. HE WANTS ME TO GO TOO. PAY HIS RESPECTS FOR HIM.
HE SAYS HE MET WESLEY DODDS BACK IN THE '40S WHEN SANDMAN AND THE ORIGINAL STAR SPANGLED KID TEAMED TO FIGHT SOME BIG MONSTER GUY IN MANHATTAN.
STALKER'S DISCIPLE. YES, WE BOTH RECALL THAT, DON'T WE, ALAN?
HEY, GUYS!
JACK.
DAD. ALAN. COURTNEY. WHAT'S UP?
WHY THE LONG FACES?

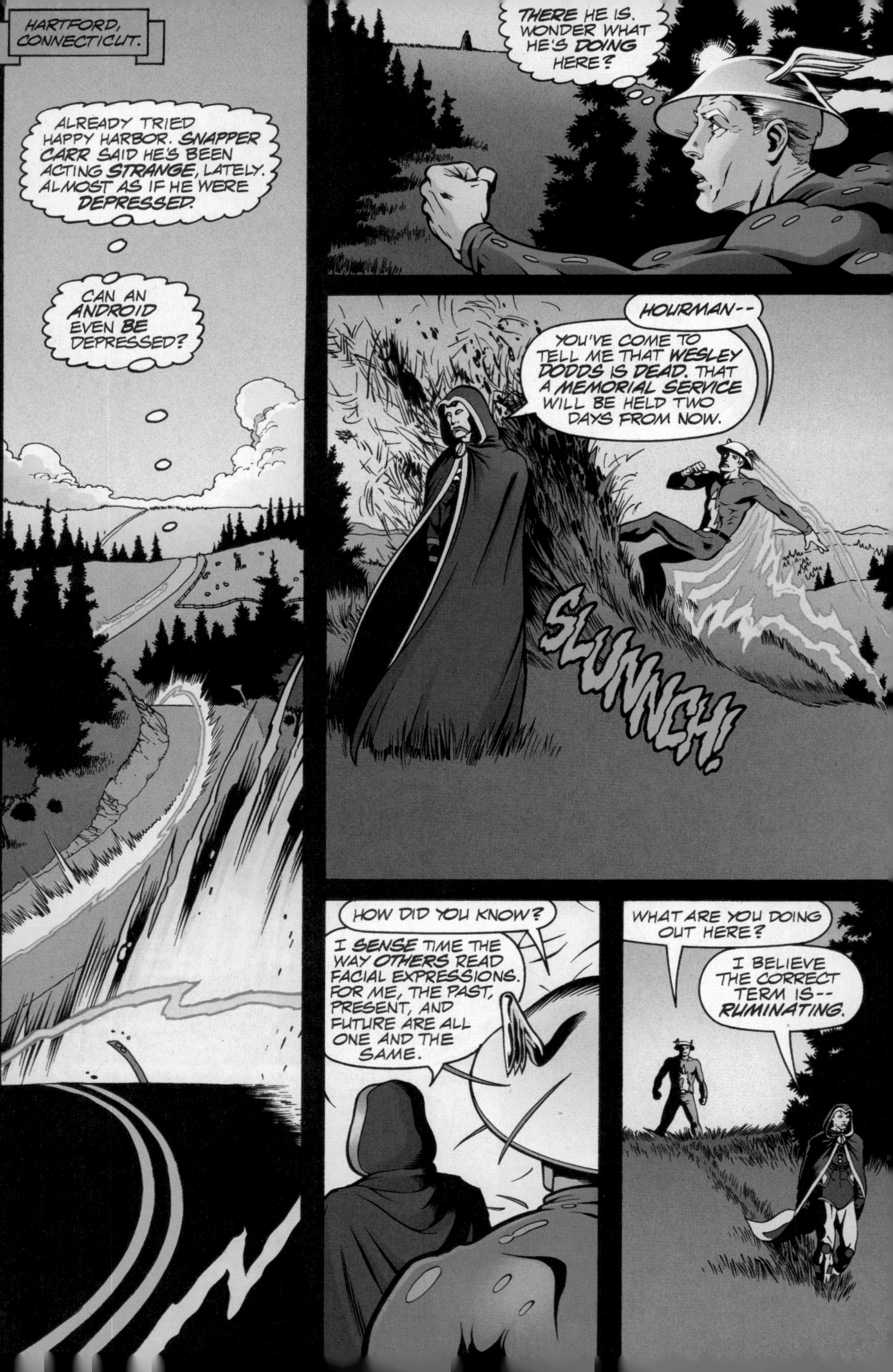
HARTFORD, CONNECTICUT.
ALREADY TRIED HAPPY HARBOR. SNAPPER CARR SAID HE'S BEEN ACTING STRANGE, LATELY. ALMOST AS IF HE WERE DEPRESSED.
CAN AN ANDROID EVEN BE DEPRESSED?
THERE HE IS. WONDER WHAT HE'S DOING HERE?
HOURMAN--
YOU'VE COME TO TELL ME THAT WESLEY DODDS IS DEAD. THAT A MEMORIAL SERVICE WILL BE HELD TWO DAYS FROM NOW.
SLUNNCH!
HOW DID YOU KNOW?
I SENSE TIME THE WAY OTHERS READ FACIAL EXPRESSIONS. FOR ME, THE PAST, PRESENT, AND FUTURE ARE ALL ONE AND THE SAME.
WHAT ARE YOU DOING OUT HERE?
I BELIEVE THE CORRECT TERM IS-- RUMINATING.

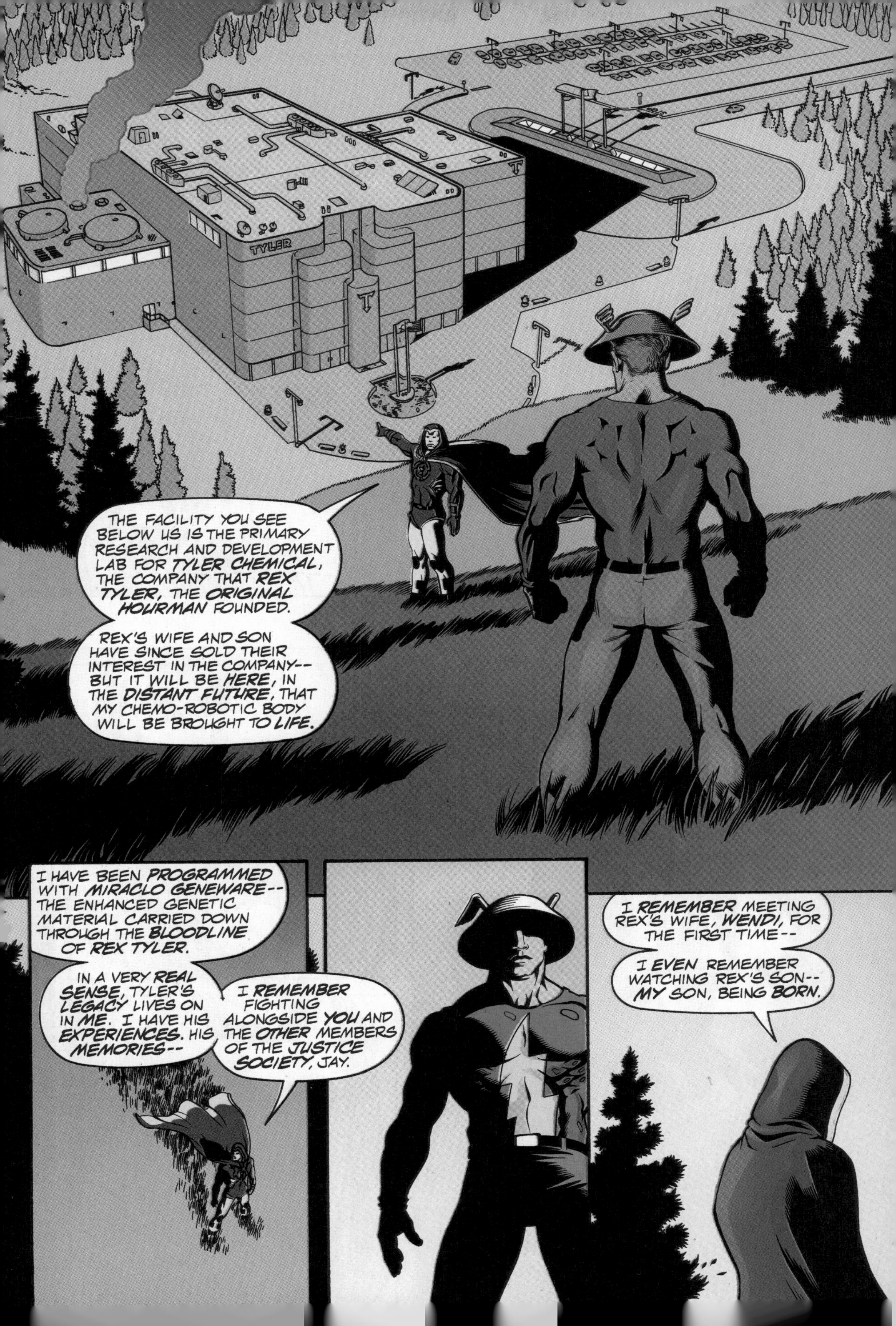
THE FACILITY YOU SEE BELOW US IS THE PRIMARY RESEARCH AND DEVELOPMENT LAB FOR TYLER CHEMICAL, THE COMPANY THAT REX TYLER, THE ORIGINAL HOURMAN FOUNDED.
REX'S WIFE AND SON HAVE SINCE SOLD THEIR INTEREST IN THE COMPANY-- BUT IT WILL BE HERE, IN THE DISTANT FUTURE, THAT MY CHEMO-ROBOTIC BODY WILL BE BROUGHT TO LIFE.
I HAVE BEEN PROGRAMMED WITH MIRACLO GENEWARE-- THE ENHANCED GENETIC MATERIAL CARRIED DOWN THROUGH THE BLOODLINE OF REX TYLER.
IN A VERY REAL SENSE, TYLER'S LEGACY LIVES ON IN ME. I HAVE HIS EXPERIENCES. HIS MEMORIES--
I REMEMBER FIGHTING ALONGSIDE YOU AND THE OTHER MEMBERS OF THE JUSTICE SOCIETY, JAY.
I REMEMBER MEETING REX'S WIFE, WENDI, FOR THE FIRST TIME--
I EVEN REMEMBER WATCHING REX'S SON-- MY SON, BEING BORN.

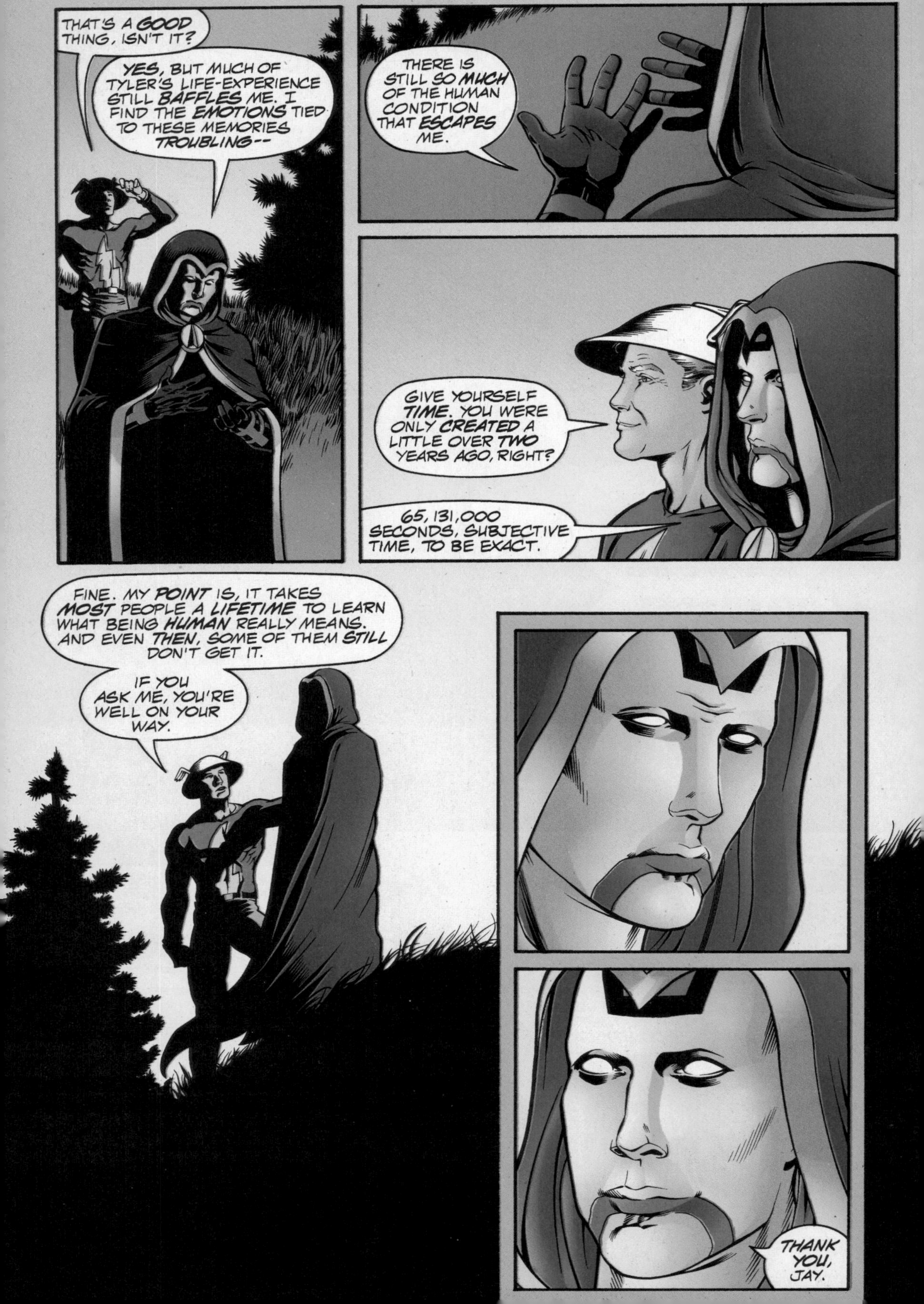
THAT'S A GOOD THING, ISN'T IT?
YES, BUT MUCH OF TYLER'S LIFE-EXPERIENCE STILL BAFFLES ME. I FIND THE EMOTIONS TIED TO THESE MEMORIES TROUBLING--
THERE IS STILL SO MUCH OF THE HUMAN CONDITION THAT ESCAPES ME.
GIVE YOURSELF TIME. YOU WERE ONLY CREATED A LITTLE OVER TWO YEARS AGO, RIGHT?
65,131,000 SECONDS, SUBJECTIVE TIME, TO BE EXACT.
FINE. MY POINT IS, IT TAKES MOST PEOPLE A LIFETIME TO LEARN WHAT BEING HUMAN REALLY MEANS. AND EVEN THEN, SOME OF THEM STILL DON'T GET IT.
IF YOU ASK ME, YOU'RE WELL ON YOUR WAY.
THANK YOU, JAY.

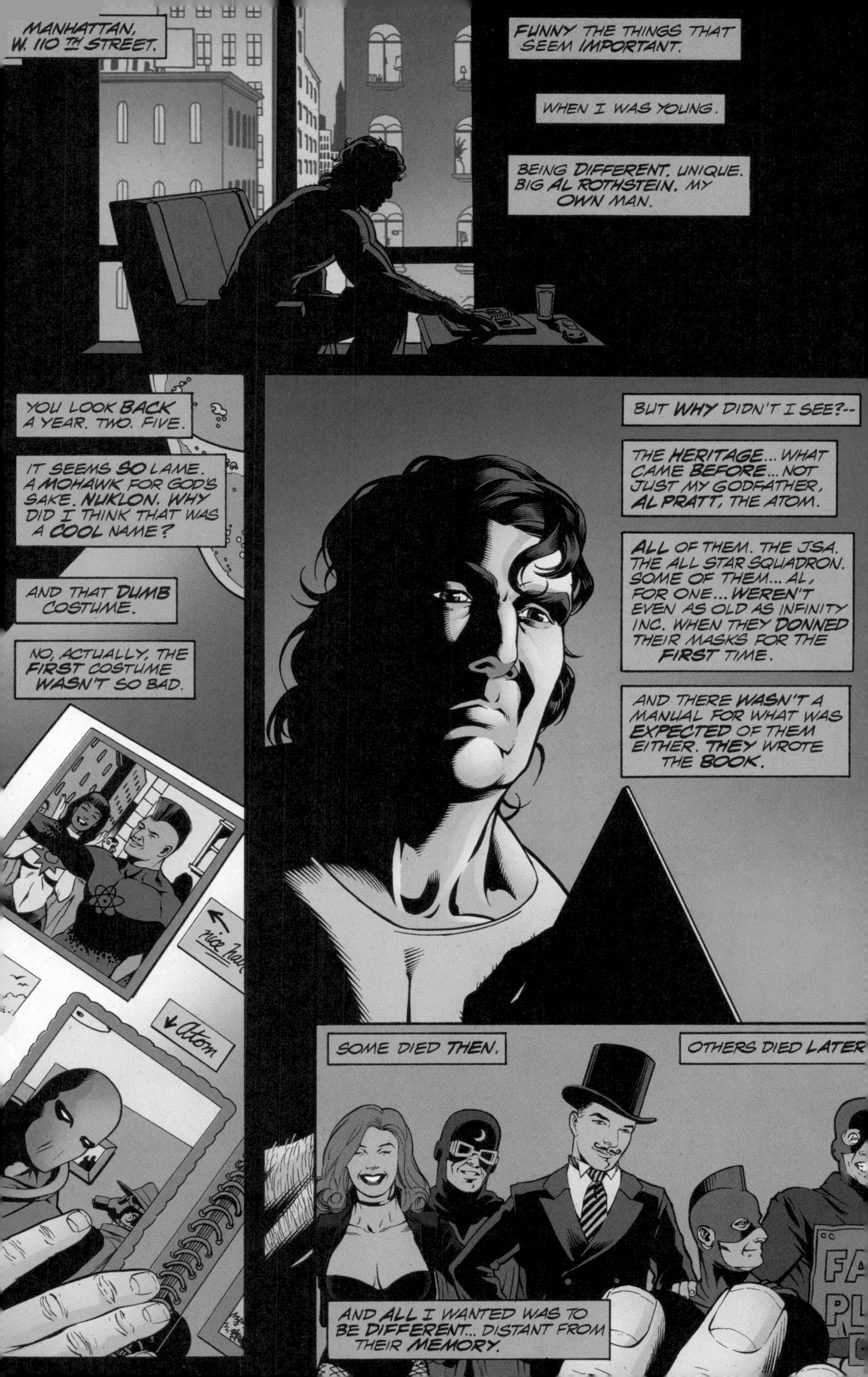
MANHATTAN, W. 110 TH STREET.
FUNNY THE THINGS THAT SEEM IMPORTANT.
WHEN I WAS YOUNG.
BEING DIFFERENT. UNIQUE. BIG AL ROTHSTEIN. MY OWN MAN.
YOU LOOK BACK A YEAR. TWO. FIVE.
IT SEEMS SO LAME. A MOHAWK FOR GOD'S SAKE. NUKLON. WHY DID I THINK THAT WAS A COOL NAME?
AND THAT DUMB COSTUME.
NO, ACTUALLY, THE FIRST COSTUME WASN'T SO BAD.
nice hai
Atom
BUT WHY DIDN'T I SEE?--
THE HERITAGE... WHAT CAME BEFORE... NOT JUST MY GODFATHER, AL PRATT, THE ATOM.
ALL OF THEM. THE JSA. THE ALL STAR SQUADRON. SOME OF THEM... AL, FOR ONE... WEREN'T EVEN AS OLD AS INFINITY INC. WHEN THEY DONNED THEIR MASKS FOR THE FIRST TIME.
AND THERE WASN'T A MANUAL FOR WHAT WAS EXPECTED OF THEM EITHER. THEY WROTE THE BOOK.
SOME DIED THEN.
OTHERS DIED LATER
AND ALL I WANTED WAS TO BE DIFFERENT... DISTANT FROM THEIR MEMORY.

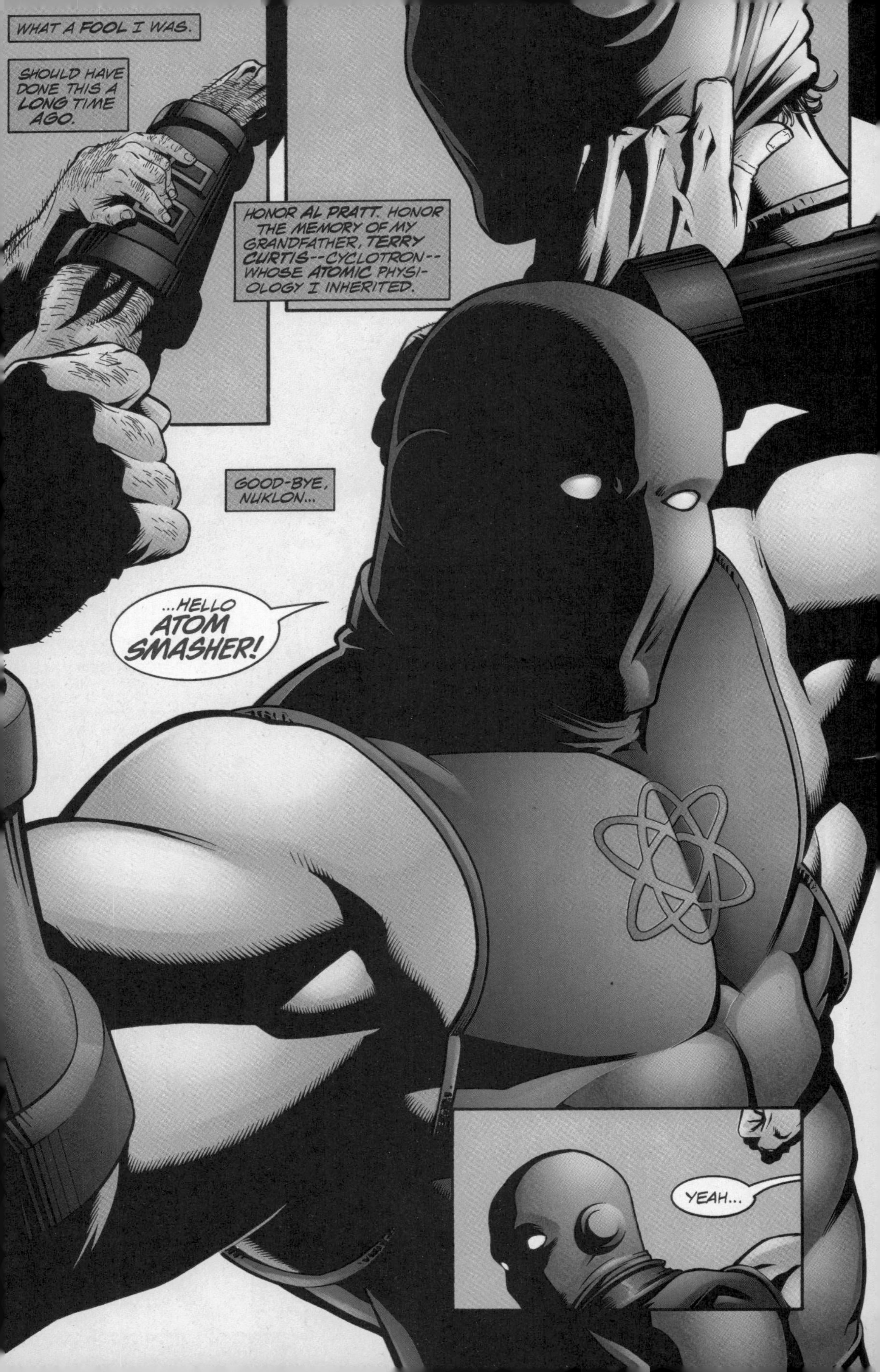
WHAT A FOOL I WAS.
SHOULD HAVE DONE THIS A LONG TIME AGO.
HONOR AL PRATT. HONOR THE MEMORY OF MY GRANDFATHER, TERRY CURTIS--CYCLOTRON--WHOSE ATOMIC PHYSIOLOGY I INHERITED.
GOOD-BYE, NUKLON...
...HELLO ATOM SMASHER!
YEAH...

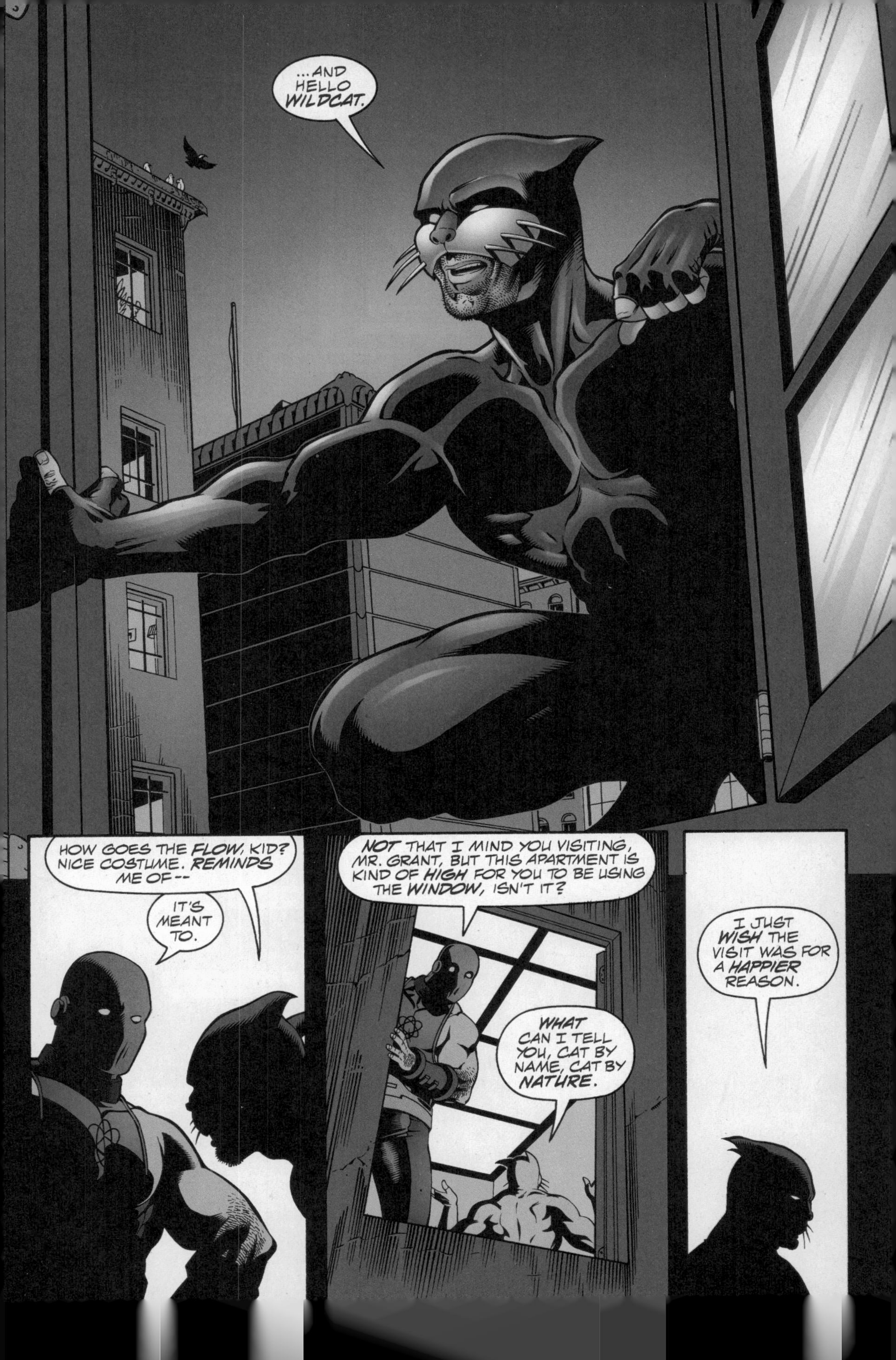
...AND HELLO WILDCAT.
HOW GOES THE FLOW, KID? NICE COSTUME. REMINDS ME OF--
IT'S MEANT TO.
NOT THAT I MIND YOU VISITING, MR. GRANT, BUT THIS APARTMENT IS KIND OF HIGH FOR YOU TO BE USING THE WINDOW, ISN'T IT?
WHAT CAN I TELL YOU, CAT BY NAME, CAT BY NATURE.
I JUST WISH THE VISIT WAS FOR A HAPPIER REASON.

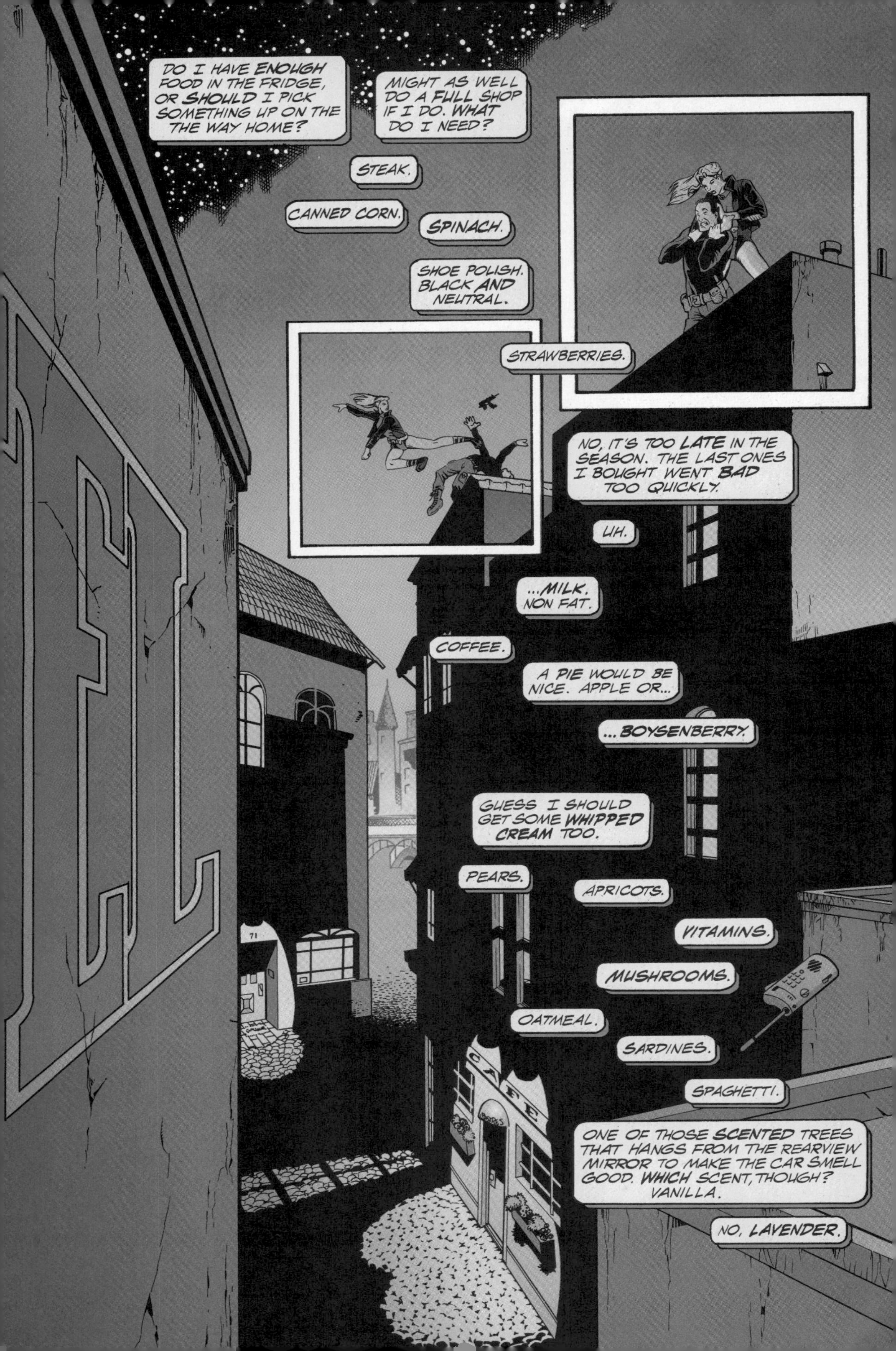
DO I HAVE ENOUGH FOOD IN THE FRIDGE, OR SHOULD I PICK SOMETHING UP ON THE THE WAY HOME?
MIGHT AS WELL DO A FULL SHOP IF I DO. WHAT DO I NEED?
STEAK.
CANNED CORN.
SPINACH.
SHOE POLISH. BLACK AND NEUTRAL.
STRAWBERRIES.
NO, IT'S TOO LATE IN THE SEASON. THE LAST ONES I BOUGHT WENT BAD TOO QUICKLY.
UH.
...MILK. NON FAT.
COFFEE.
A PIE WOULD BE NICE. APPLE OR...
...BOYSENBERRY.
GUESS I SHOULD GET SOME WHIPPED CREAM TOO.
PEARS.
APRICOTS.
VITAMINS.
MUSHROOMS.
OATMEAL.
SARDINES.
SPAGHETTI.
ONE OF THOSE SCENTED TREES THAT HANGS FROM THE REARVIEW MIRROR TO MAKE THE CAR SMELL GOOD. WHICH SCENT, THOUGH? VANILLA.
NO, LAVENDER.
CAFE

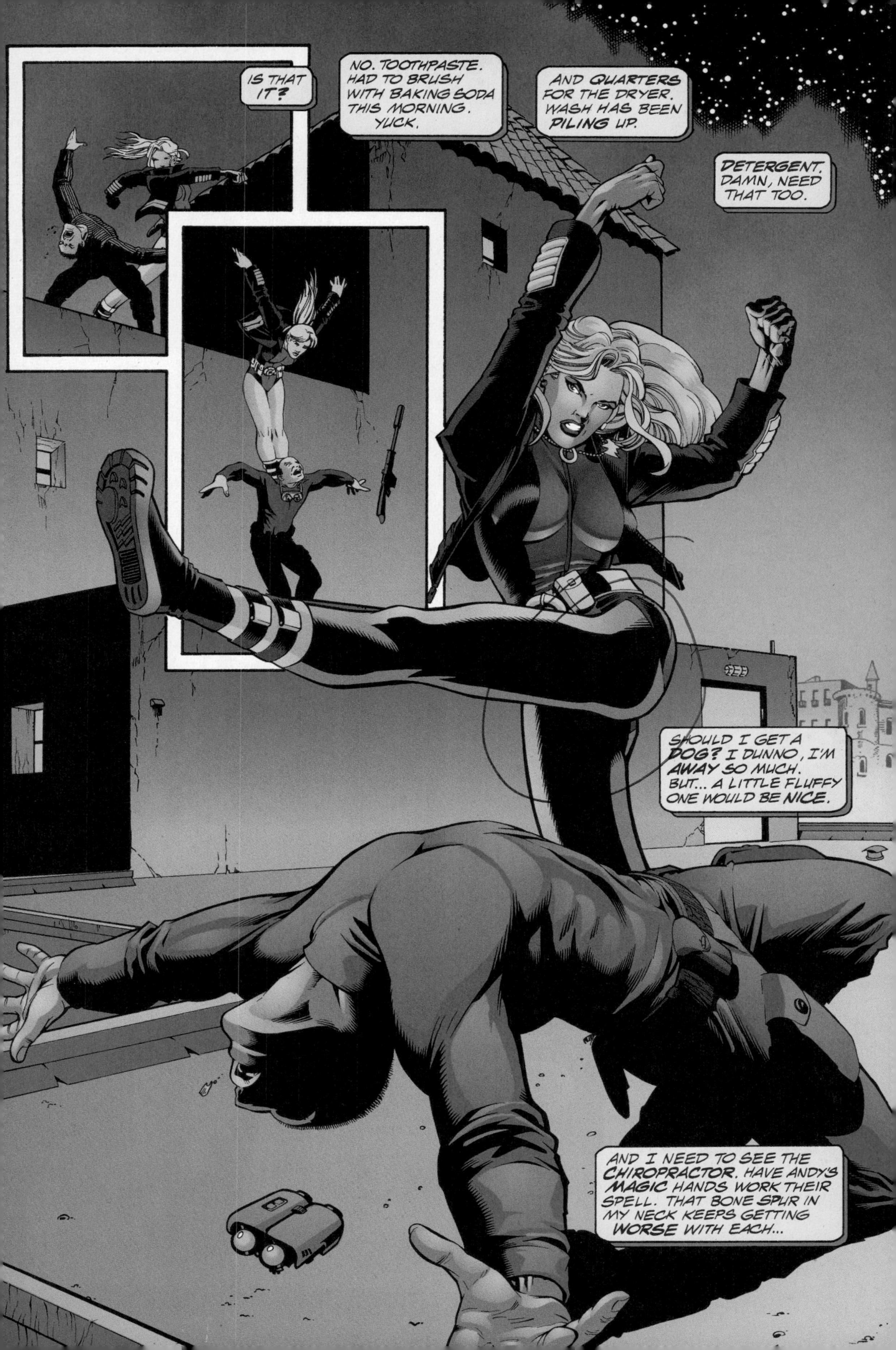
IS THAT IT?
NO. TOOTHPASTE. HAD TO BRUSH WITH BAKING SODA THIS MORNING. YUCK.
AND QUARTERS FOR THE DRYER. WASH HAS BEEN PILING UP.
DETERGENT. DAMN, NEED THAT TOO.
SHOULD I GET A DOG? I DUNNO, I'M AWAY SO MUCH. BUT... A LITTLE FLUFFY ONE WOULD BE NICE.
AND I NEED TO SEE THE CHIROPRACTOR. HAVE ANDY'S MAGIC HANDS WORK THEIR SPELL. THAT BONE SPUR IN MY NECK KEEPS GETTING WORSE WITH EACH...

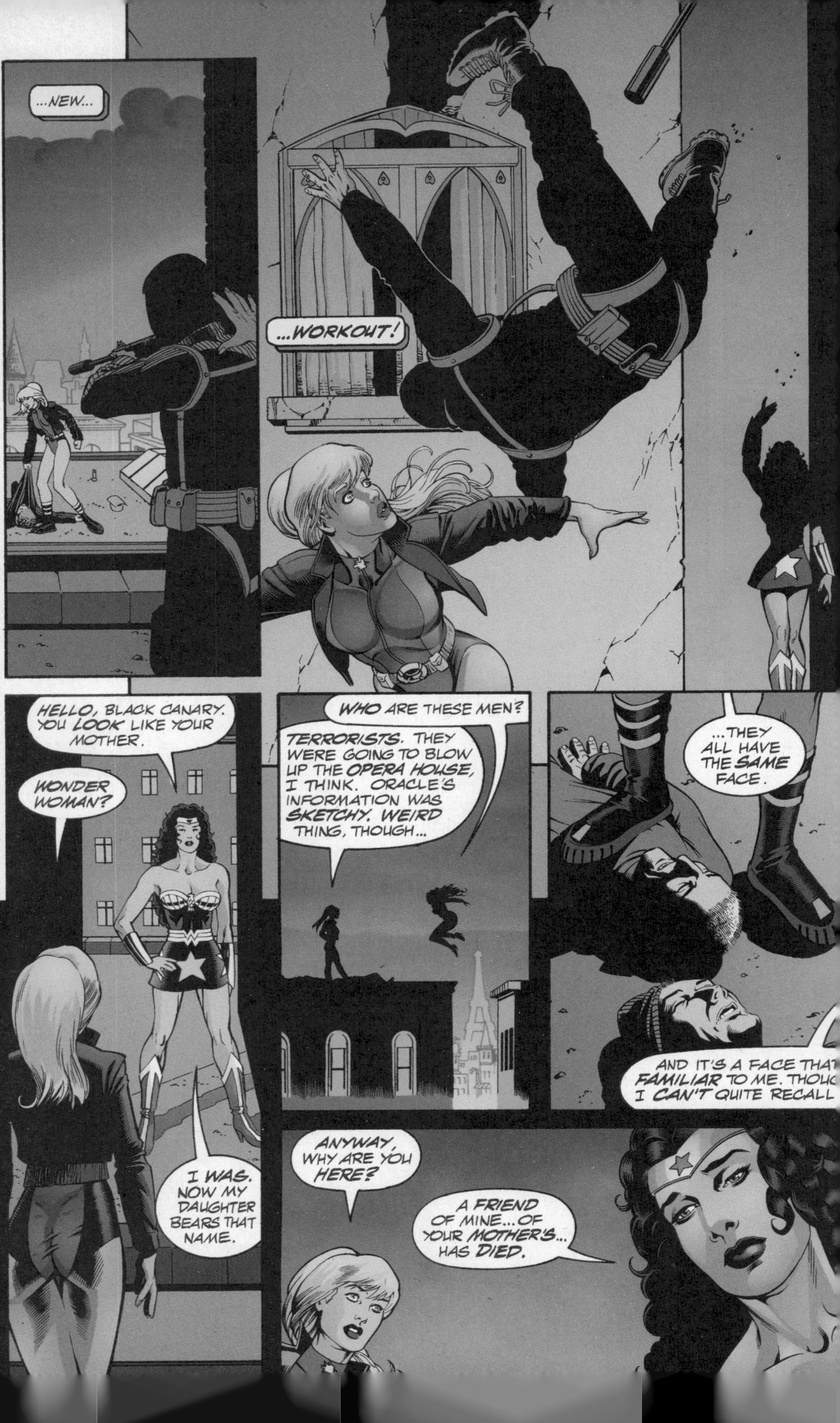

...NEW...
...WORKOUT!
HELLO, BLACK CANARY. YOU LOOK LIKE YOUR MOTHER.
WONDER WOMAN?
I WAS. NOW MY DAUGHTER BEARS THAT NAME.
WHO ARE THESE MEN?
TERRORISTS. THEY WERE GOING TO BLOW UP THE OPERA HOUSE, I THINK. ORACLE'S INFORMATION WAS SKETCHY. WEIRD THING, THOUGH...
...THEY ALL HAVE THE SAME FACE.
AND IT'S A FACE THA
FAMILIAR TO ME. THOU
I CAN'T QUITE RECALL
ANYWAY, WHY ARE YOU HERE?
A FRIEND OF MINE... OF YOUR MOTHER'S... HAS DIED.

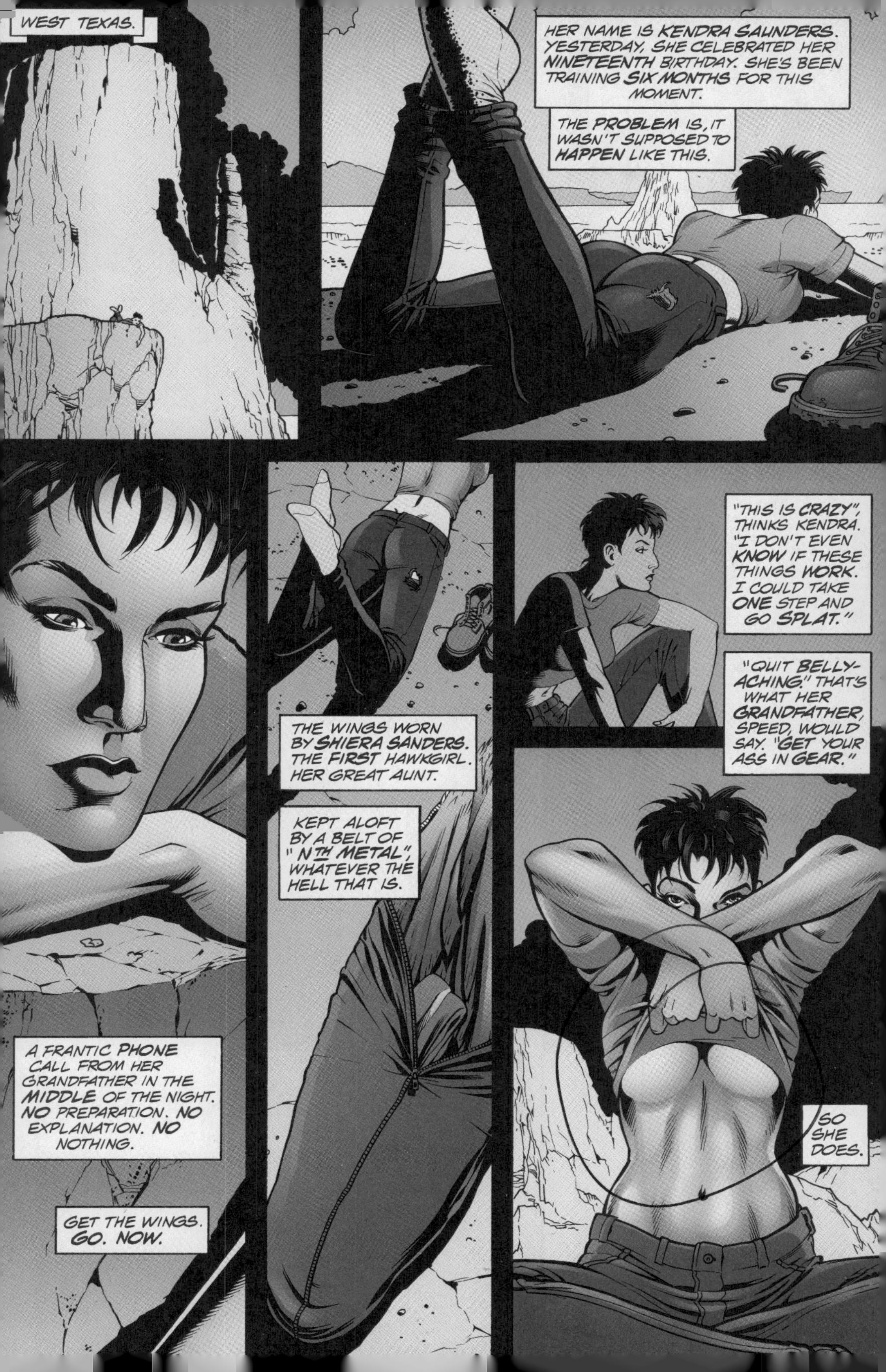
WEST TEXAS.
HER NAME IS KENDRA SAUNDERS. YESTERDAY, SHE CELEBRATED HER NINETEENTH BIRTHDAY. SHE'S BEEN TRAINING SIX MONTHS FOR THIS MOMENT.
THE PROBLEM IS, IT WASN'T SUPPOSED TO HAPPEN LIKE THIS.
A FRANTIC PHONE CALL FROM HER GRANDFATHER IN THE MIDDLE OF THE NIGHT. NO PREPARATION. NO EXPLANATION. NO NOTHING.
GET THE WINGS. GO. NOW.
THE WINGS WORN BY SHIERA SANDERS. THE FIRST HAWKGIRL. HER GREAT AUNT.
KEPT ALOFT BY A BELT OF "NTH METAL", WHATEVER THE HELL THAT IS.
"THIS IS CRAZY", THINKS KENDRA. "I DON'T EVEN KNOW IF THESE THINGS WORK. I COULD TAKE ONE STEP AND GO SPLAT."
"QUIT BELLY-ACHING." THAT'S WHAT HER GRANDFATHER, SPEED, WOULD SAY. "GET YOUR ASS IN GEAR."
SO SHE DOES.

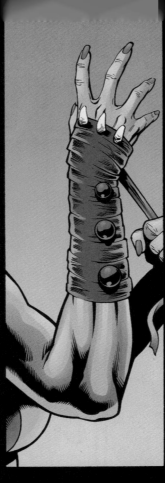

WELL.

HERE GOES NOTH--

--IIIIIII!!!!

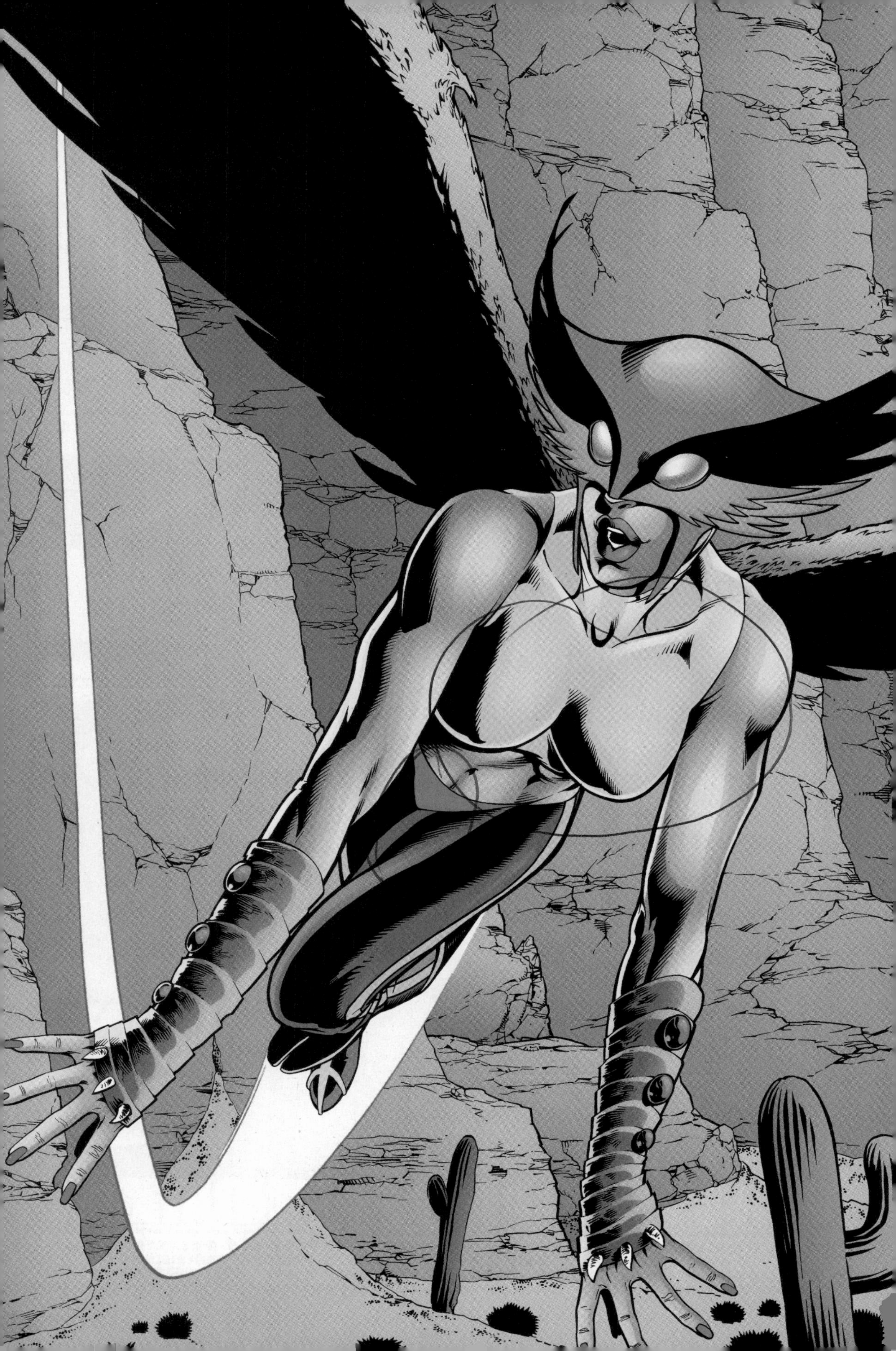

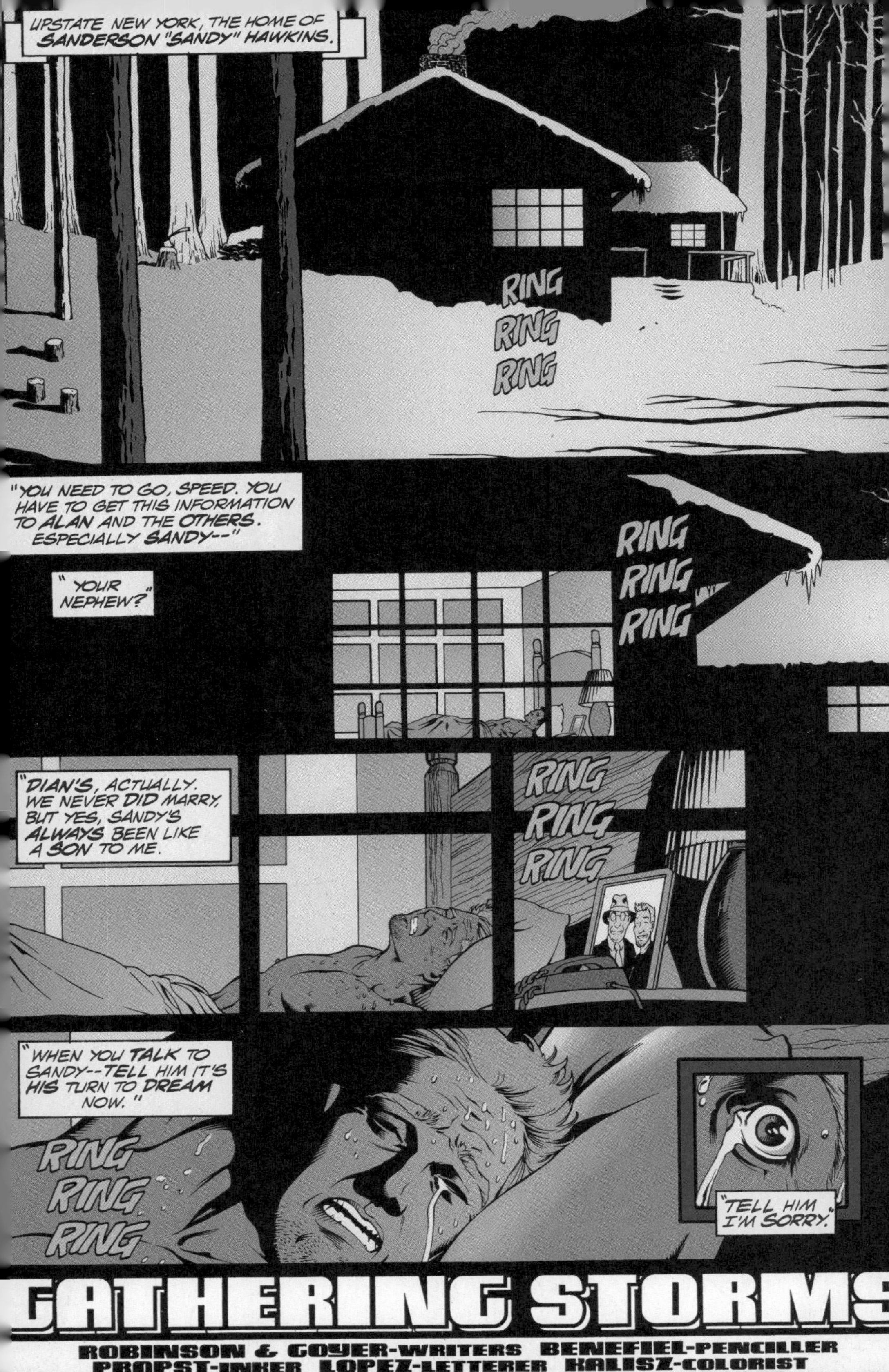
UPSTATE NEW YORK, THE HOME OF SANDERSON "SANDY" HAWKINS.
RING RING RING
"YOU NEED TO GO, SPEED. YOU HAVE TO GET THIS INFORMATION TO ALAN AND THE OTHERS. ESPECIALLY SANDY--"
RING RING RING
"YOUR NEPHEW?"
"DIAN'S, ACTUALLY. WE NEVER DID MARRY, BUT YES, SANDY'S ALWAYS BEEN LIKE A SON TO ME.
RING RING RING
"WHEN YOU TALK TO SANDY--TELL HIM IT'S HIS TURN TO DREAM NOW."
RING RING RING
"TELL HIM I'M SORRY."
GATHERING STORMS
ROBINSON & GOYER-WRITERS BENEFIEL-PENCILLER
PROPST-INKER LOPEZ-LETTERER KALISZ-COLORIST
DIGICHAM-SEPARATOR WILLIAMS-ASS'T ED. TOMASI-EDITOR

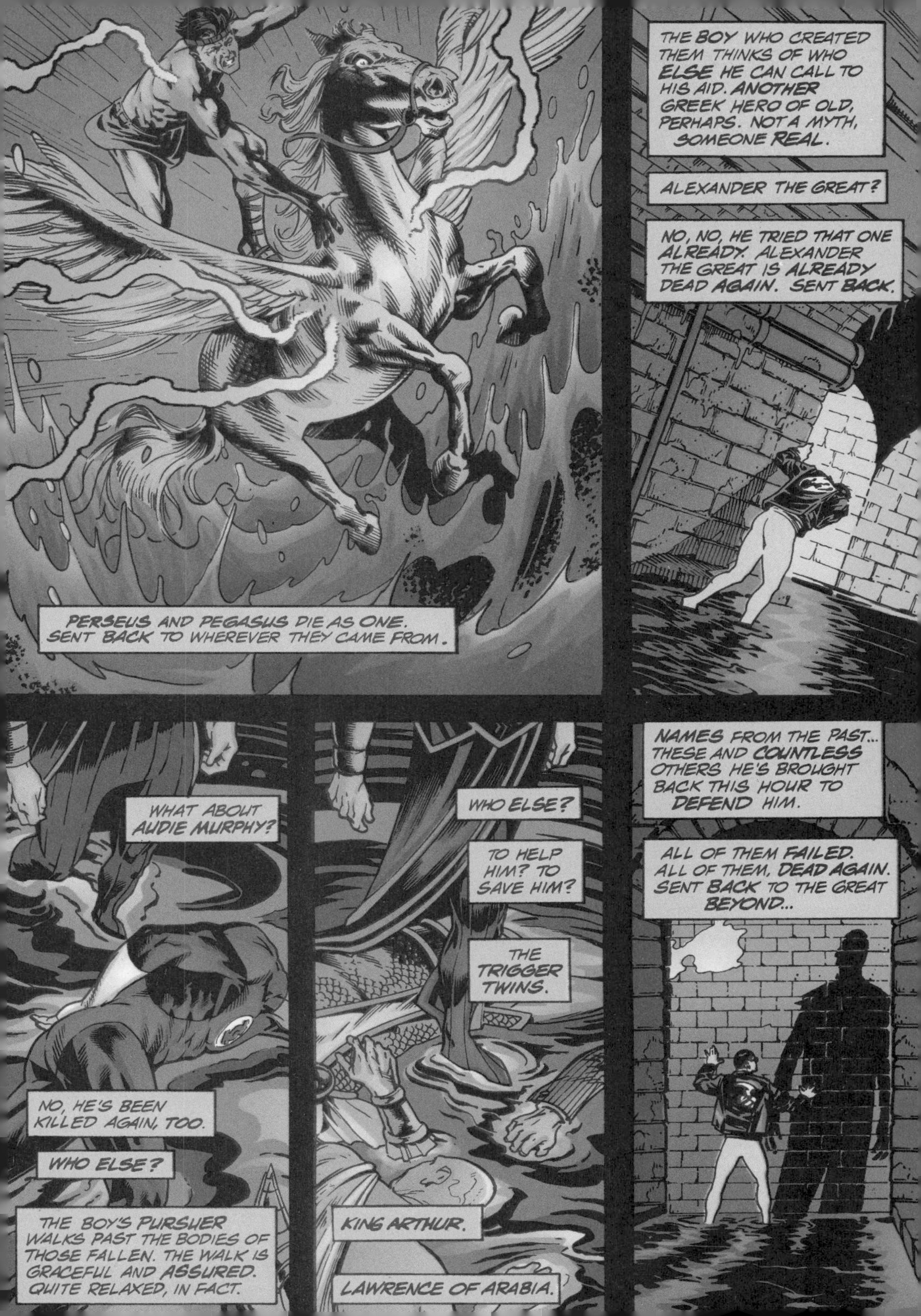
PERSEUS AND PEGASUS DIE AS ONE. SENT BACK TO WHEREVER THEY CAME FROM.
THE BOY WHO CREATED THEM THINKS OF WHO ELSE HE CAN CALL TO HIS AID. ANOTHER GREEK HERO OF OLD, PERHAPS. NOT A MYTH, SOMEONE REAL.
ALEXANDER THE GREAT?
NO, NO, HE TRIED THAT ONE ALREADY. ALEXANDER THE GREAT IS ALREADY DEAD AGAIN. SENT BACK.
WHAT ABOUT AUDIE MURPHY?
NO, HE'S BEEN KILLED AGAIN, TOO.
WHO ELSE?
THE BOY'S PURSUER WALKS PAST THE BODIES OF THOSE FALLEN. THE WALK IS GRACEFUL AND ASSURED. QUITE RELAXED, IN FACT.
WHO ELSE?
TO HELP HIM? TO SAVE HIM?
THE TRIGGER TWINS.
KING ARTHUR.
LAWRENCE OF ARABIA.
NAMES FROM THE PAST... THESE AND COUNTLESS OTHERS HE'S BROUGHT BACK THIS HOUR TO DEFEND HIM.
ALL OF THEM FAILED. ALL OF THEM, DEAD AGAIN. SENT BACK TO THE GREAT BEYOND...

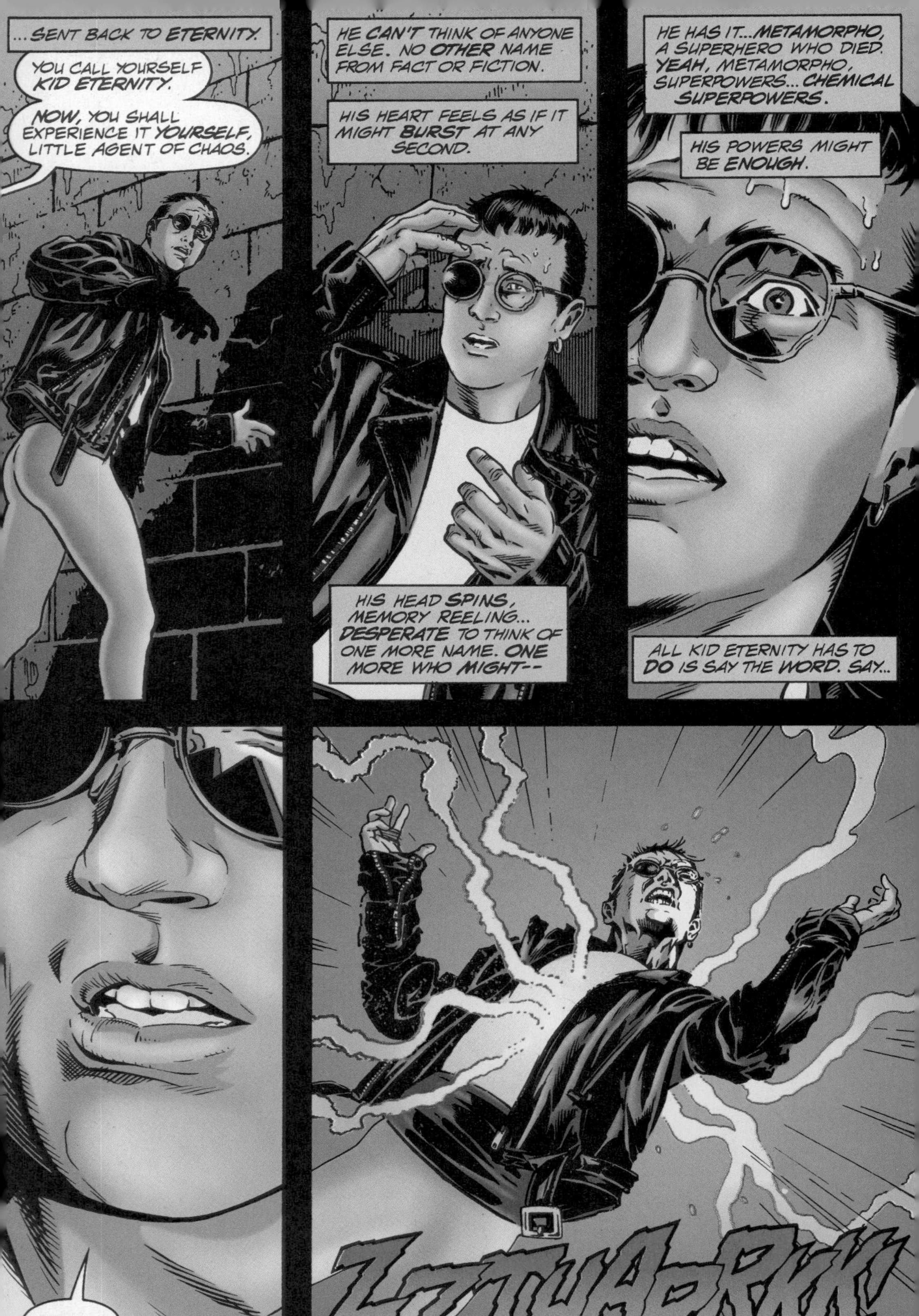
...SENT BACK TO ETERNITY.
YOU CALL YOURSELF KID ETERNITY.
NOW, YOU SHALL EXPERIENCE IT YOURSELF, LITTLE AGENT OF CHAOS.
HE CAN'T THINK OF ANYONE ELSE. NO OTHER NAME FROM FACT OR FICTION.
HIS HEART FEELS AS IF IT MIGHT BURST AT ANY SECOND.
HIS HEAD SPINS, MEMORY REELING... DESPERATE TO THINK OF ONE MORE NAME. ONE MORE WHO MIGHT--
HE HAS IT...METAMORPHO, A SUPERHERO WHO DIED. YEAH, METAMORPHO, SUPERPOWERS...CHEMICAL SUPERPOWERS.
HIS POWERS MIGHT BE ENOUGH.
ALL KID ETERNITY HAS TO DO IS SAY THE WORD. SAY...
ETERN--
ZZTHARRK!

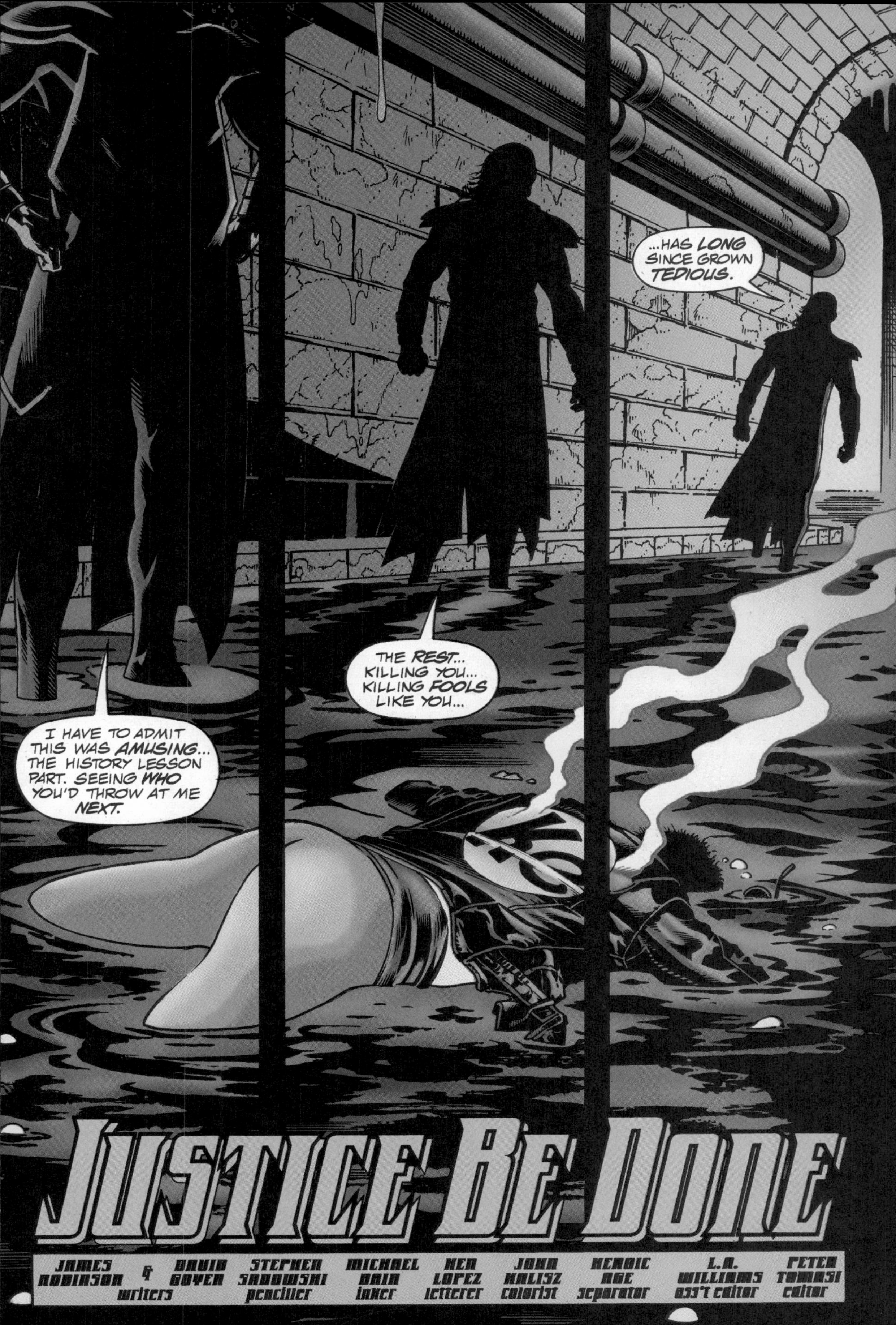
I HAVE TO ADMIT THIS WAS AMUSING... THE HISTORY LESSON PART. SEEING WHO YOU'D THROW AT ME NEXT.
THE REST... KILLING YOU... KILLING FOOLS LIKE YOU...
...HAS LONG SINCE GROWN TEDIOUS.
JUSTICE BE DONE
JAMES ROBINSON & DAVID GOYER writers
STEPHEN SADOWSKI penciller
MICHAEL BAIR inker
KEN LOPEZ letterer
JOHN KALISZ colorist
HEROIC AGE separator
L.A. WILLIAMS ass't editor
PETER TOMASI editor

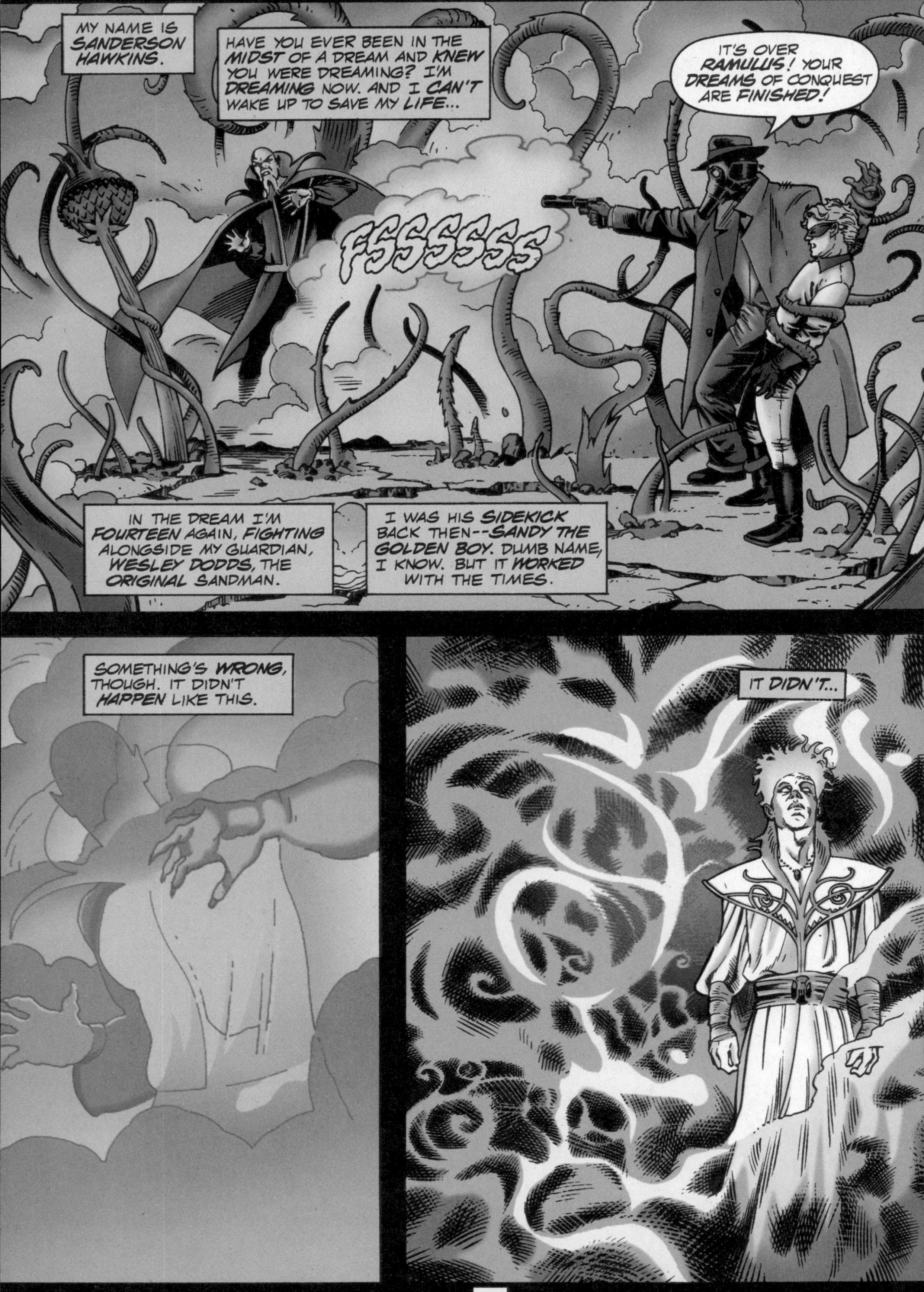
MY NAME IS SANDERSON HAWKINS.
HAVE YOU EVER BEEN IN THE MIDST OF A DREAM AND KNEW YOU WERE DREAMING? I'M DREAMING NOW. AND I CAN'T WAKE UP TO SAVE MY LIFE...
IT'S OVER RAMULUS! YOUR DREAMS OF CONQUEST ARE FINISHED!
FSSSSSS
IN THE DREAM I'M FOURTEEN AGAIN, FIGHTING ALONGSIDE MY GUARDIAN, WESLEY DODDS, THE ORIGINAL SANDMAN.
I WAS HIS SIDEKICK BACK THEN--SANDY THE GOLDEN BOY. DUMB NAME, I KNOW. BUT IT WORKED WITH THE TIMES.
SOMETHING'S WRONG, THOUGH. IT DIDN'T HAPPEN LIKE THIS.
IT DIDN'T...

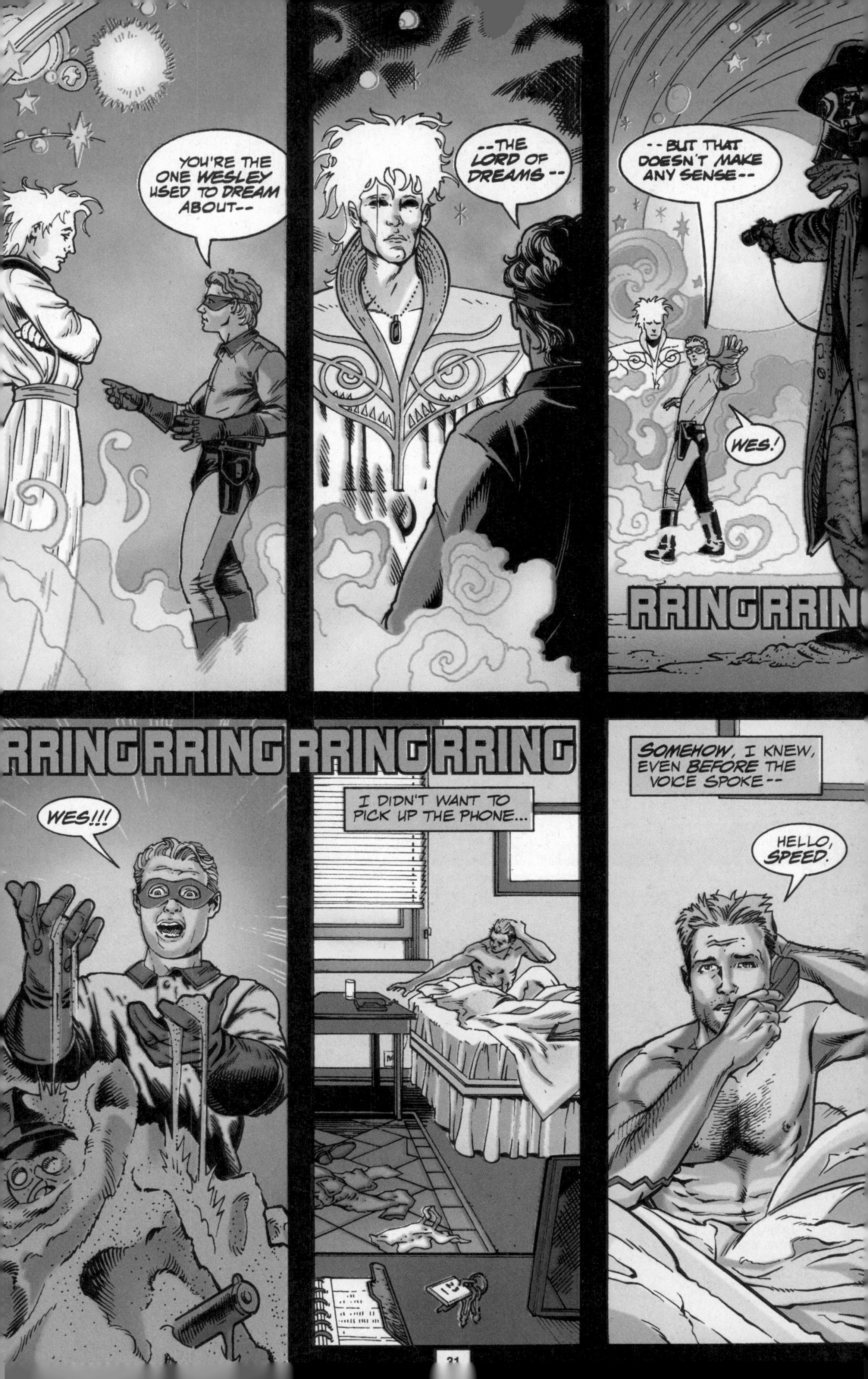
YOU'RE THE ONE WESLEY USED TO DREAM ABOUT--
--THE LORD OF DREAMS--
--BUT THAT DOESN'T MAKE ANY SENSE--
WES!
RRINGRRIN
RRINGRRINGRRINGRRING
WES!!!
I DIDN'T WANT TO PICK UP THE PHONE...
SOMEHOW, I KNEW, EVEN BEFORE THE VOICE SPOKE--
HELLO, SPEED.

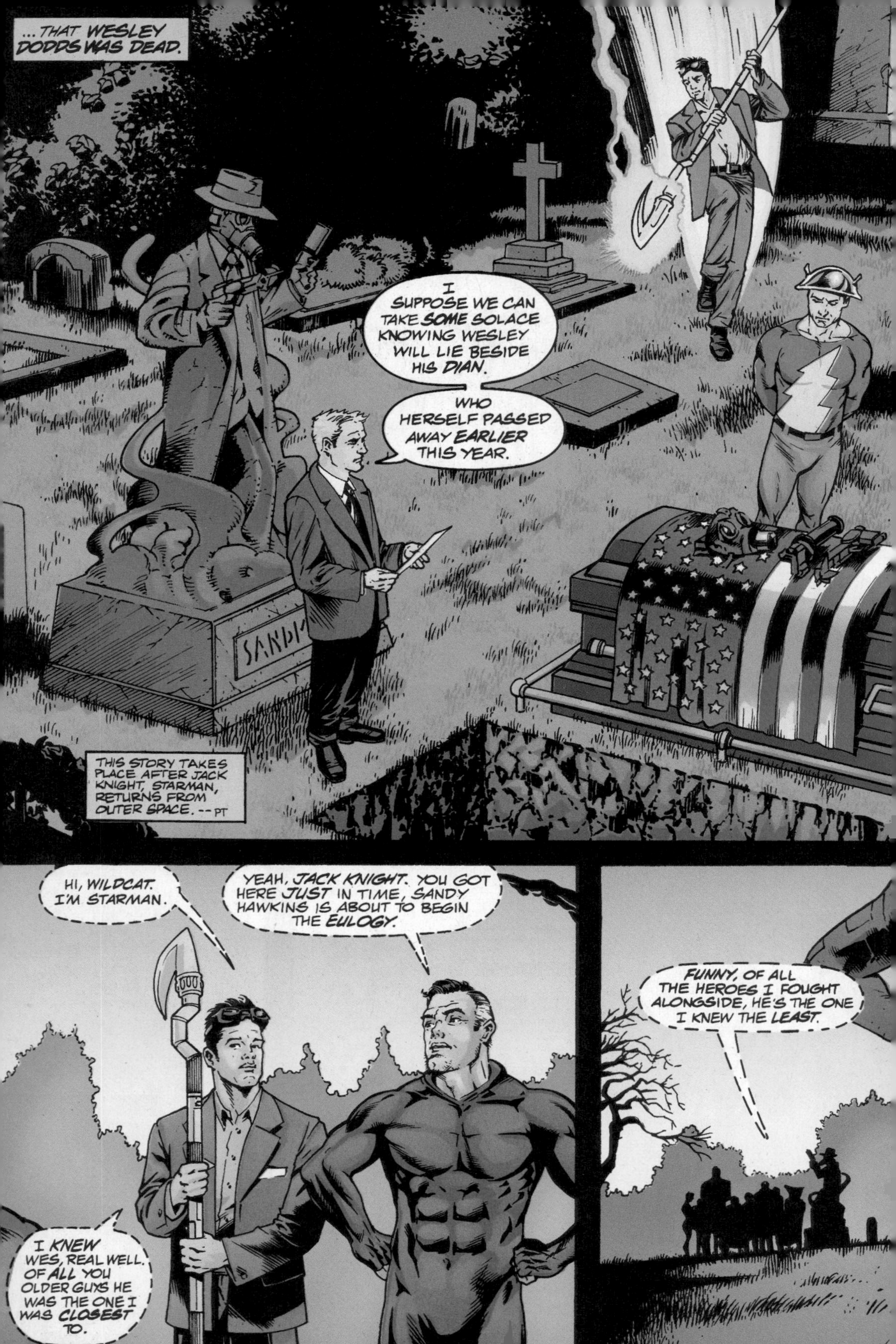

...THAT WESLEY DODDS WAS DEAD.
I SUPPOSE WE CAN TAKE SOME SOLACE KNOWING WESLEY WILL LIE BESIDE HIS DIAN.
WHO HERSELF PASSED AWAY EARLIER THIS YEAR.
SANDM
THIS STORY TAKES PLACE AFTER JACK KNIGHT, STARMAN, RETURNS FROM OUTER SPACE. --PT
HI, WILDCAT. I'M STARMAN.
YEAH, JACK KNIGHT. YOU GOT HERE JUST IN TIME, SANDY HAWKINS IS ABOUT TO BEGIN THE EULOGY.
I KNEW WES, REAL WELL. OF ALL YOU OLDER GUYS HE WAS THE ONE I WAS CLOSEST TO.
FUNNY, OF ALL THE HEROES I FOUGHT ALONGSIDE, HE'S THE ONE I KNEW THE LEAST.

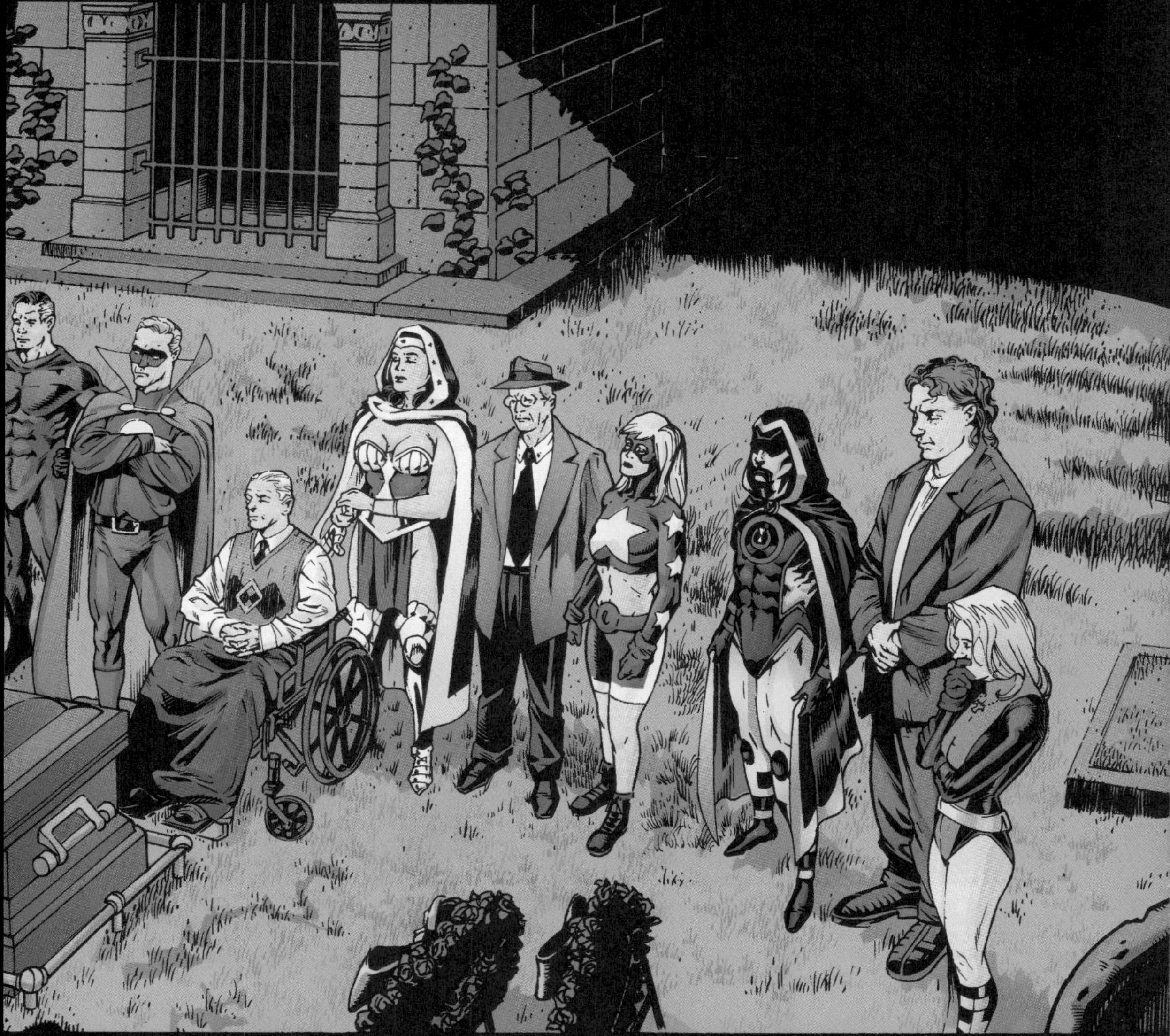

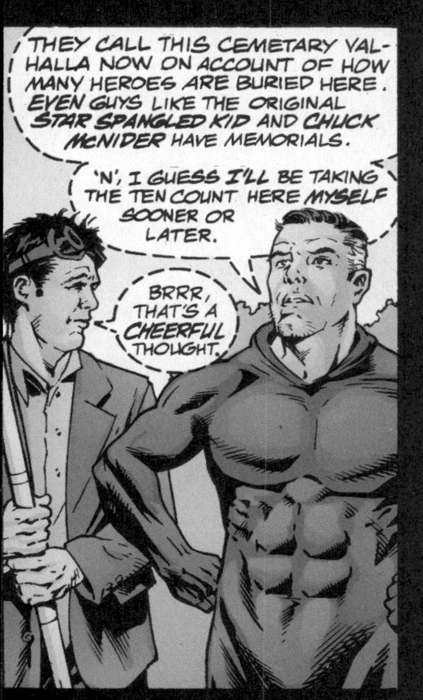
THEY CALL THIS CEMETARY VALHALLA NOW ON ACCOUNT OF HOW MANY HEROES ARE BURIED HERE. EVEN GUYS LIKE THE ORIGINAL STAR SPANGLED KID AND CHUCK MCNIDER HAVE MEMORIALS.
'N', I GUESS I'LL BE TAKING THE TEN COUNT HERE MYSELF SOONER OR LATER.
BRRR, THAT'S A CHEERFUL THOUGHT.

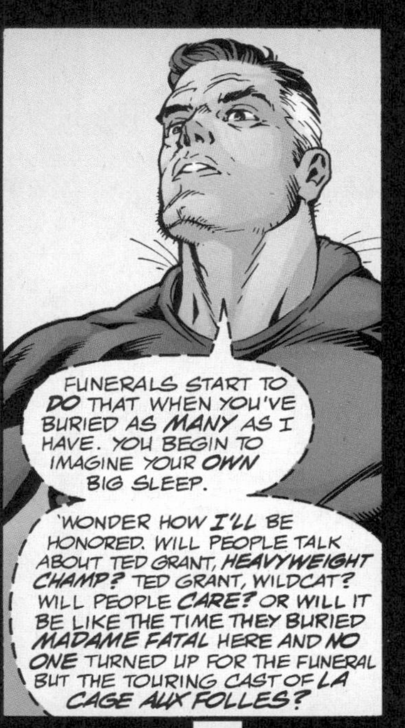
FUNERALS START TO DO THAT WHEN YOU'VE BURIED AS MANY AS I HAVE. YOU BEGIN TO IMAGINE YOUR OWN BIG SLEEP.
'WONDER HOW I'LL BE HONORED. WILL PEOPLE TALK ABOUT TED GRANT, HEAVYWEIGHT CHAMP? TED GRANT, WILDCAT? WILL PEOPLE CARE? OR WILL IT BE LIKE THE TIME THEY BURIED MADAME FATAL HERE AND NO ONE TURNED UP FOR THE FUNERAL BUT THE TOURING CAST OF LA CAGE AUX FOLLES?

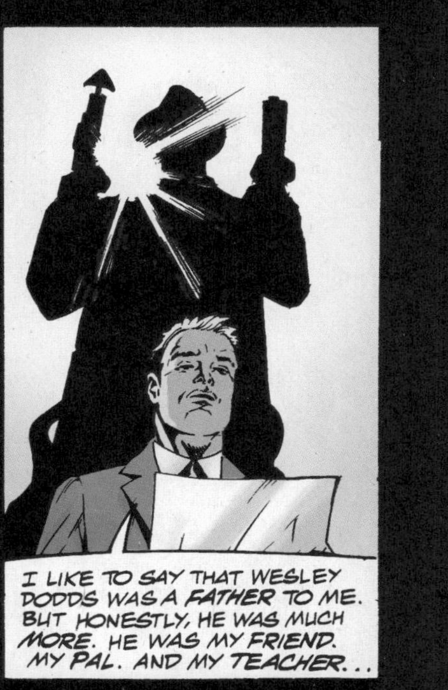
I LIKE TO SAY THAT WESLEY DODDS WAS A FATHER TO ME. BUT HONESTLY, HE WAS MUCH MORE. HE WAS MY FRIEND. MY PAL. AND MY TEACHER...

THE GANG'S ALL HERE AT LEAST, AND NO ONE ELSE LOOKS LIKE THEY'RE GONNA CHECK OUT JUST YET.

...NOT *JUST* SUPERHEROICS, LIFE *OUTSIDE* OF THE MASK, TOO.

JAY. HELL, JAY STILL RUNS ABOUT AS THE FLASH MORE TIMES THAN NOT.

ALAN. THE SAME WITH HIM... HE'S AGED *BACK* CLOSER TO HIS *REAL* AGE, BUT HE STILL FIGHTS THE FIGHT AS SENTINEL.

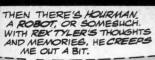

THEN THERE'S *HOURMAN*, A *ROBOT*, OR SOMESUCH. WITH *REX TYLER'S* THOUGHTS AND MEMORIES, HE *CREEPS* ME OUT A BIT.

AL ROTHSTEIN. THE GODSON OF *AL PRATT*, THE ORIGINAL *ATOM*.

I GUESS HE'S RECALLING WHEN HE LAID AL IN THE GROUND.

YEAH, I IMAGINE *BLACK CANARY* FEELS THE SAME WAY. IT *WASN'T* THAT LONG AGO WE BURIED HER *MOM* IN GOTHAM.

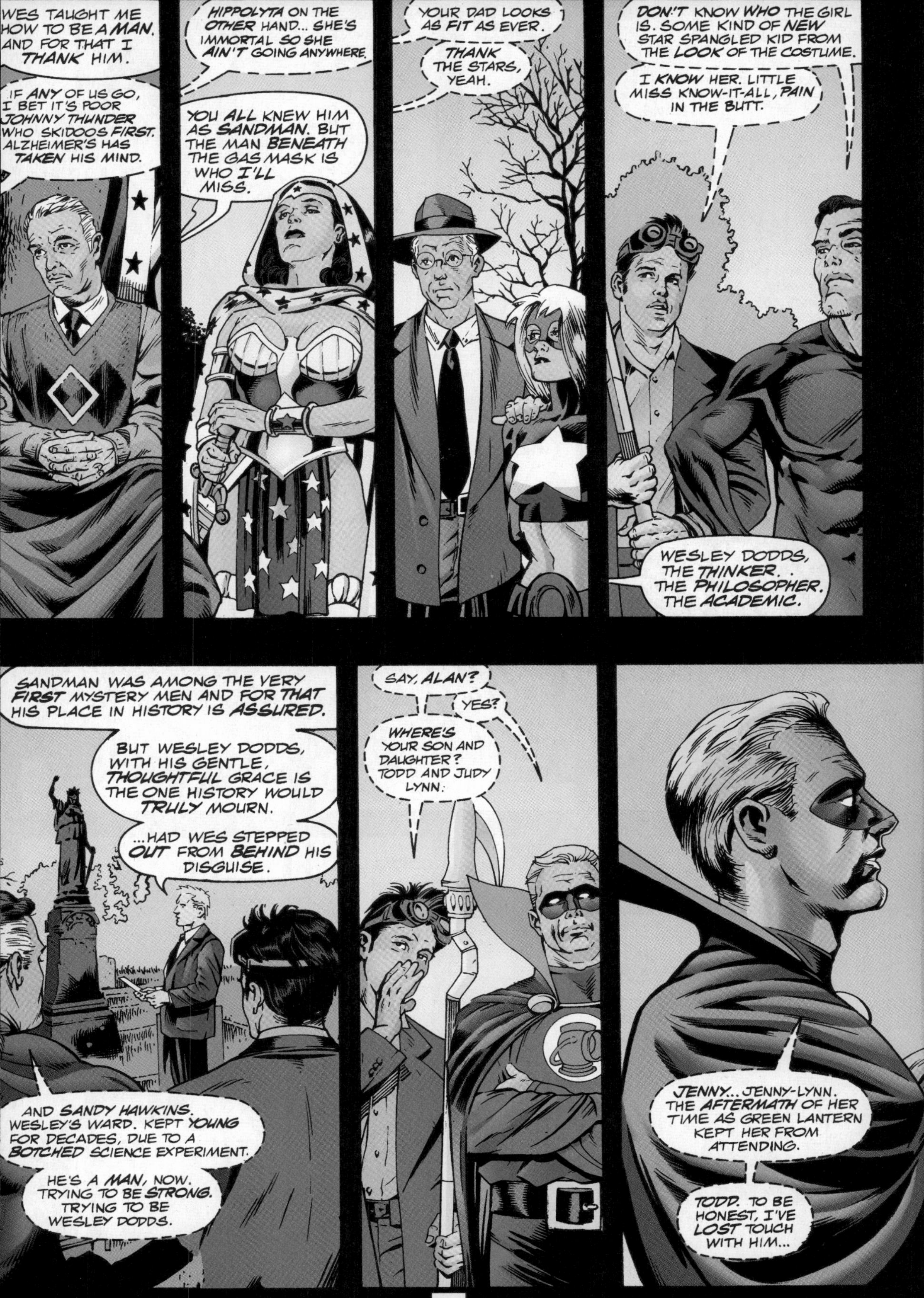
WES TAUGHT ME HOW TO BE A MAN. AND FOR THAT I THANK HIM.
IF ANY OF US GO, I BET IT'S POOR JOHNNY THUNDER WHO SKIDOOS FIRST. ALZHEIMER'S HAS TAKEN HIS MIND.
HIPPOLYTA ON THE OTHER HAND... SHE'S IMMORTAL SO SHE AIN'T GOING ANYWHERE.
YOU ALL KNEW HIM AS SANDMAN. BUT THE MAN BENEATH THE GAS MASK IS WHO I'LL MISS.
YOUR DAD LOOKS AS FIT AS EVER.
THANK THE STARS, YEAH.
DON'T KNOW WHO THE GIRL IS. SOME KIND OF NEW STAR SPANGLED KID FROM THE LOOK OF THE COSTUME.
I KNOW HER. LITTLE MISS KNOW-IT-ALL, PAIN IN THE BUTT.
WESLEY DODDS, THE THINKER. THE PHILOSOPHER. THE ACADEMIC.
SANDMAN WAS AMONG THE VERY FIRST MYSTERY MEN AND FOR THAT HIS PLACE IN HISTORY IS ASSURED.
BUT WESLEY DODDS, WITH HIS GENTLE, THOUGHTFUL GRACE IS THE ONE HISTORY WOULD TRULY MOURN.
...HAD WES STEPPED OUT FROM BEHIND HIS DISGUISE.
AND SANDY HAWKINS. WESLEY'S WARD. KEPT YOUNG FOR DECADES, DUE TO A BOTCHED SCIENCE EXPERIMENT.
HE'S A MAN, NOW. TRYING TO BE STRONG. TRYING TO BE WESLEY DODDS.
SAY, ALAN?
YES?
WHERE'S YOUR SON AND DAUGHTER? TODD AND JUDY LYNN.
JENNY... JENNY-LYNN. THE AFTERMATH OF HER TIME AS GREEN LANTERN KEPT HER FROM ATTENDING.
TODD. TO BE HONEST, I'VE LOST TOUCH WITH HIM...

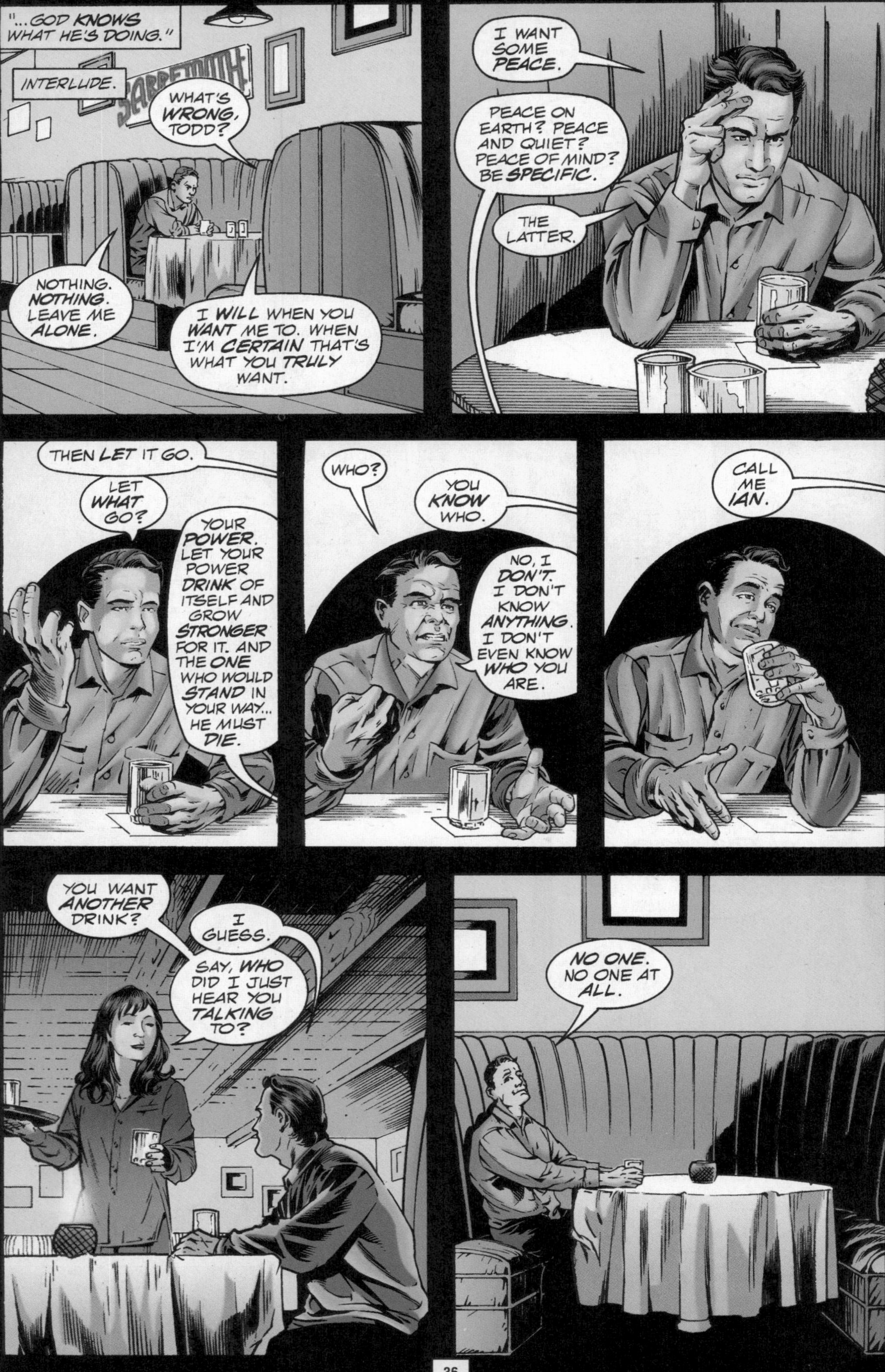
"...GOD KNOWS WHAT HE'S DOING."
INTERLUDE.
WHAT'S WRONG, TODD?
NOTHING. NOTHING. LEAVE ME ALONE.
I WILL WHEN YOU WANT ME TO. WHEN I'M CERTAIN THAT'S WHAT YOU TRULY WANT.
I WANT SOME PEACE.
PEACE ON EARTH? PEACE AND QUIET? PEACE OF MIND? BE SPECIFIC.
THE LATTER.
THEN LET IT GO.
LET WHAT GO?
YOUR POWER. LET YOUR POWER DRINK OF ITSELF AND GROW STRONGER FOR IT. AND THE ONE WHO WOULD STAND IN YOUR WAY... HE MUST DIE.
WHO?
YOU KNOW WHO.
NO, I DON'T. I DON'T KNOW ANYTHING. I DON'T EVEN KNOW WHO YOU ARE.
CALL ME IAN.
YOU WANT ANOTHER DRINK?
I GUESS.
SAY, WHO DID I JUST HEAR YOU TALKING TO?
NO ONE. NO ONE AT ALL.

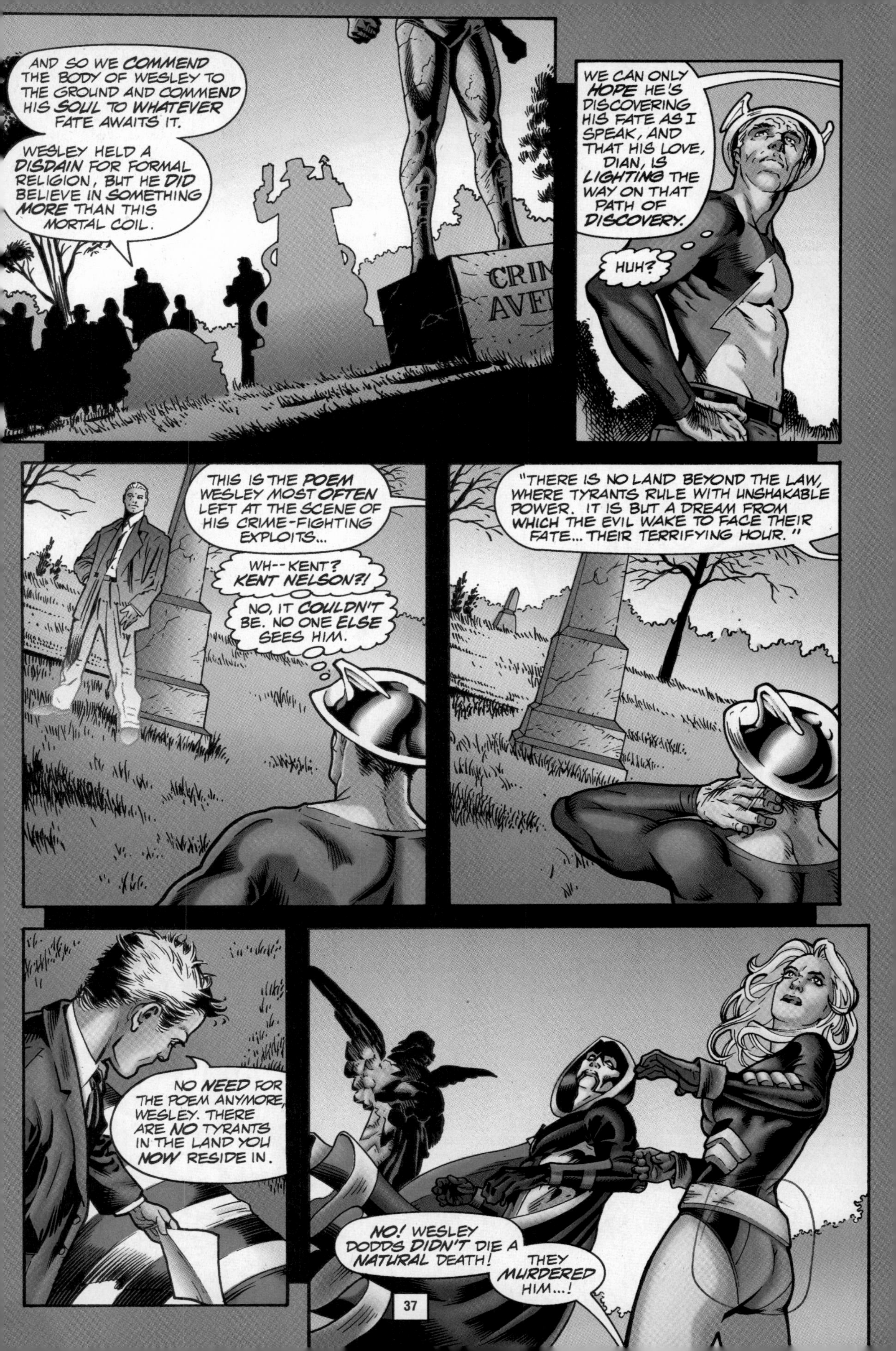
AND SO WE COMMEND THE BODY OF WESLEY TO THE GROUND AND COMMEND HIS SOUL TO WHATEVER FATE AWAITS IT.
WESLEY HELD A DISDAIN FOR FORMAL RELIGION, BUT HE DID BELIEVE IN SOMETHING MORE THAN THIS MORTAL COIL.
CRIM
AVE
WE CAN ONLY HOPE HE'S DISCOVERING HIS FATE AS I SPEAK, AND THAT HIS LOVE, DIAN, IS LIGHTING THE WAY ON THAT PATH OF DISCOVERY.
HUH?
THIS IS THE POEM WESLEY MOST OFTEN LEFT AT THE SCENE OF HIS CRIME-FIGHTING EXPLOITS...
WH--KENT? KENT NELSON?!
NO, IT COULDN'T BE. NO ONE ELSE SEES HIM.
"THERE IS NO LAND BEYOND THE LAW, WHERE TYRANTS RULE WITH UNSHAKABLE POWER. IT IS BUT A DREAM FROM WHICH THE EVIL WAKE TO FACE THEIR FATE... THEIR TERRIFYING HOUR."
NO NEED FOR THE POEM ANYMORE, WESLEY. THERE ARE NO TYRANTS IN THE LAND YOU NOW RESIDE IN.
NO! WESLEY DODDS DIDN'T DIE A NATURAL DEATH!
THEY MURDERED HIM...!

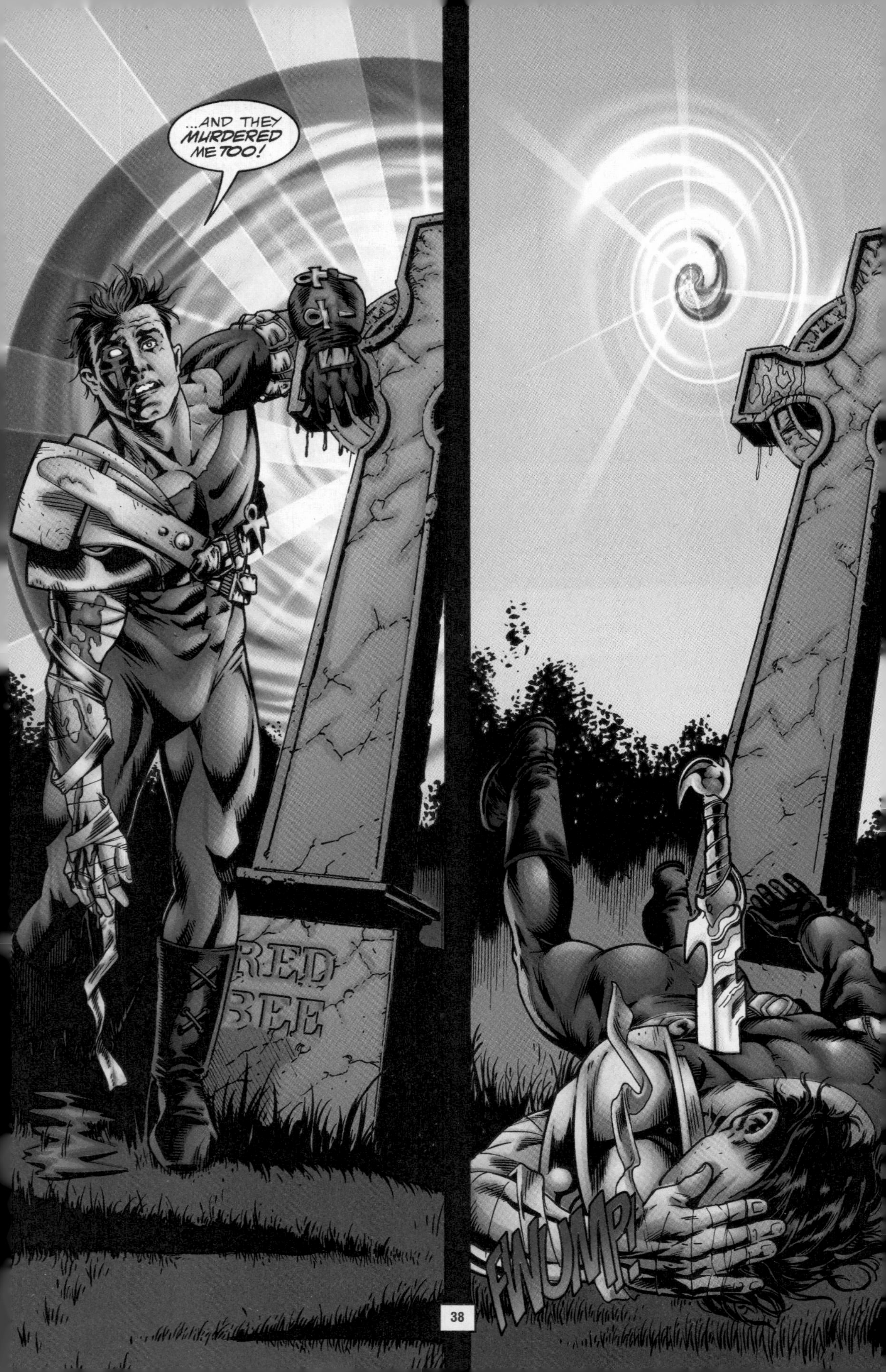
...AND THEY MURDERED ME TOO!
RED
BEE
FWUMP!

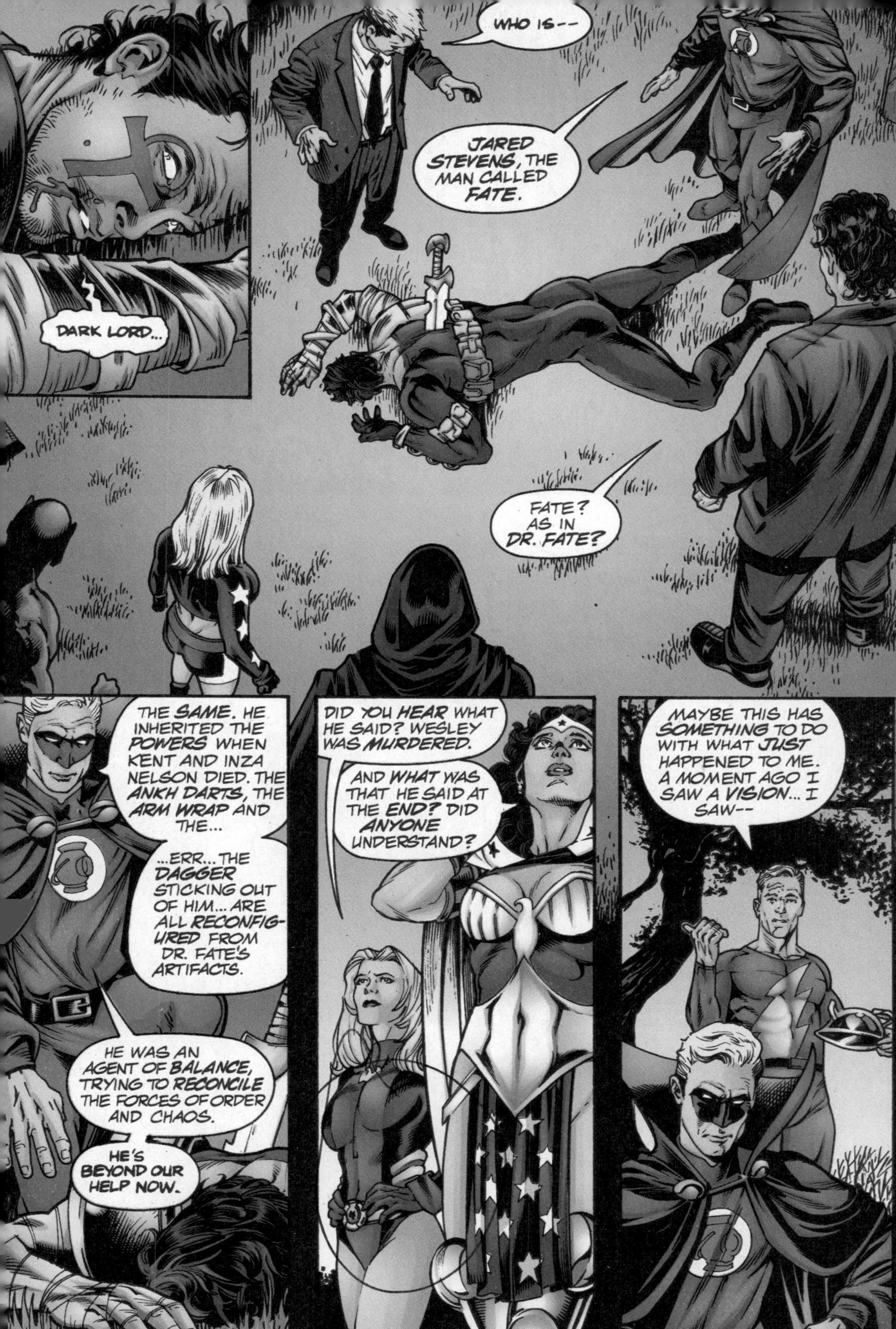
DARK LORD...
WHO IS--
JARED STEVENS, THE MAN CALLED FATE.
FATE? AS IN DR. FATE?
THE SAME. HE INHERITED THE POWERS WHEN KENT AND INZA NELSON DIED. THE ANKH DARTS, THE ARM WRAP AND THE...
...ERR... THE DAGGER STICKING OUT OF HIM... ARE ALL RECONFIGURED FROM DR. FATE'S ARTIFACTS.
HE WAS AN AGENT OF BALANCE, TRYING TO RECONCILE THE FORCES OF ORDER AND CHAOS.
HE'S BEYOND OUR HELP NOW.
DID YOU HEAR WHAT HE SAID? WESLEY WAS MURDERED.
AND WHAT WAS THAT HE SAID AT THE END? DID ANYONE UNDERSTAND?
MAYBE THIS HAS SOMETHING TO DO WITH WHAT JUST HAPPENED TO ME. A MOMENT AGO I SAW A VISION... I SAW--

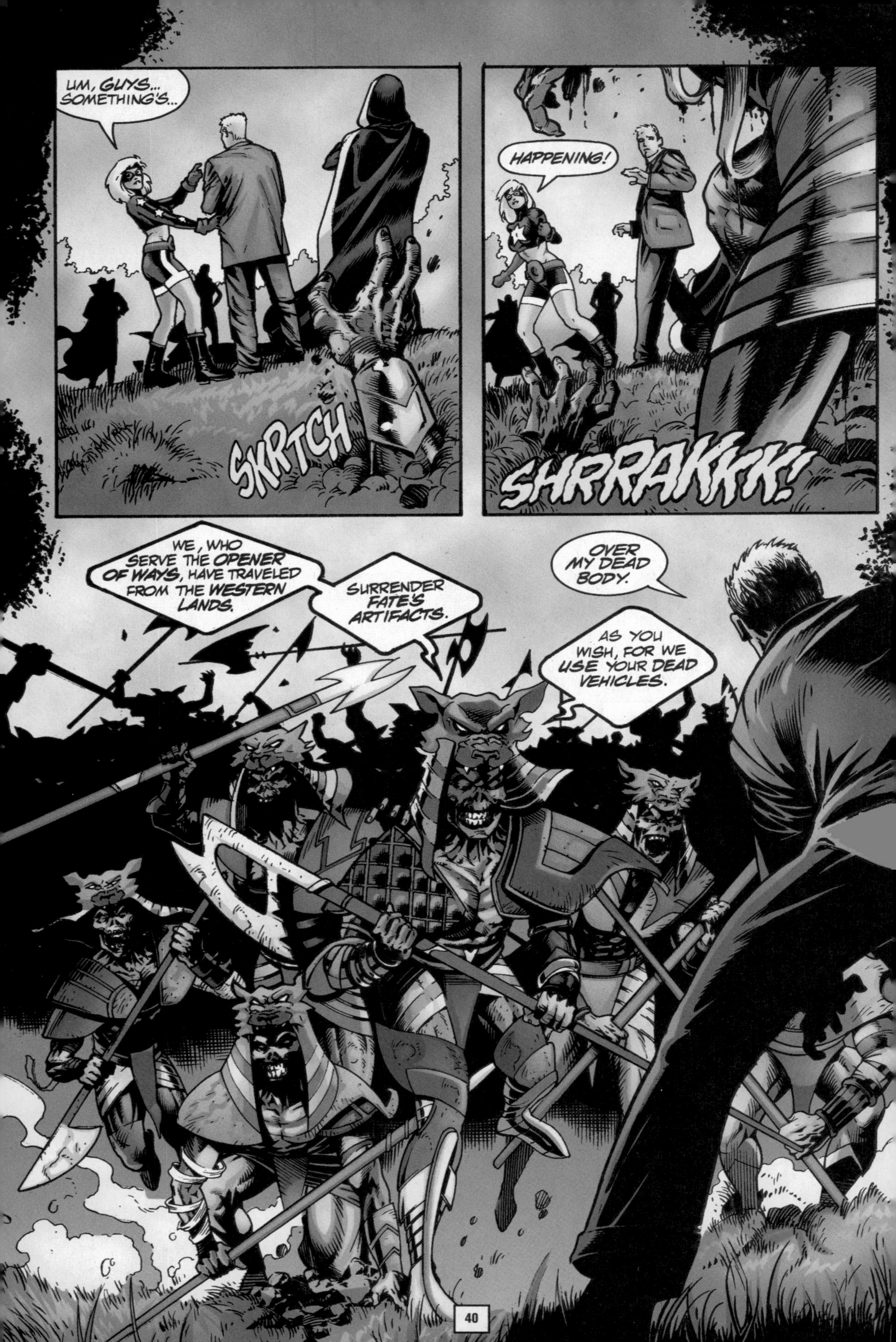
UM, GUYS... SOMETHING'S...
SKRTCH
HAPPENING!
SHRRAKKK!
WE, WHO SERVE THE OPENER OF WAYS, HAVE TRAVELED FROM THE WESTERN LANDS.
SURRENDER FATE'S ARTIFACTS.
OVER MY DEAD BODY.
AS YOU WISH, FOR WE USE YOUR DEAD VEHICLES.

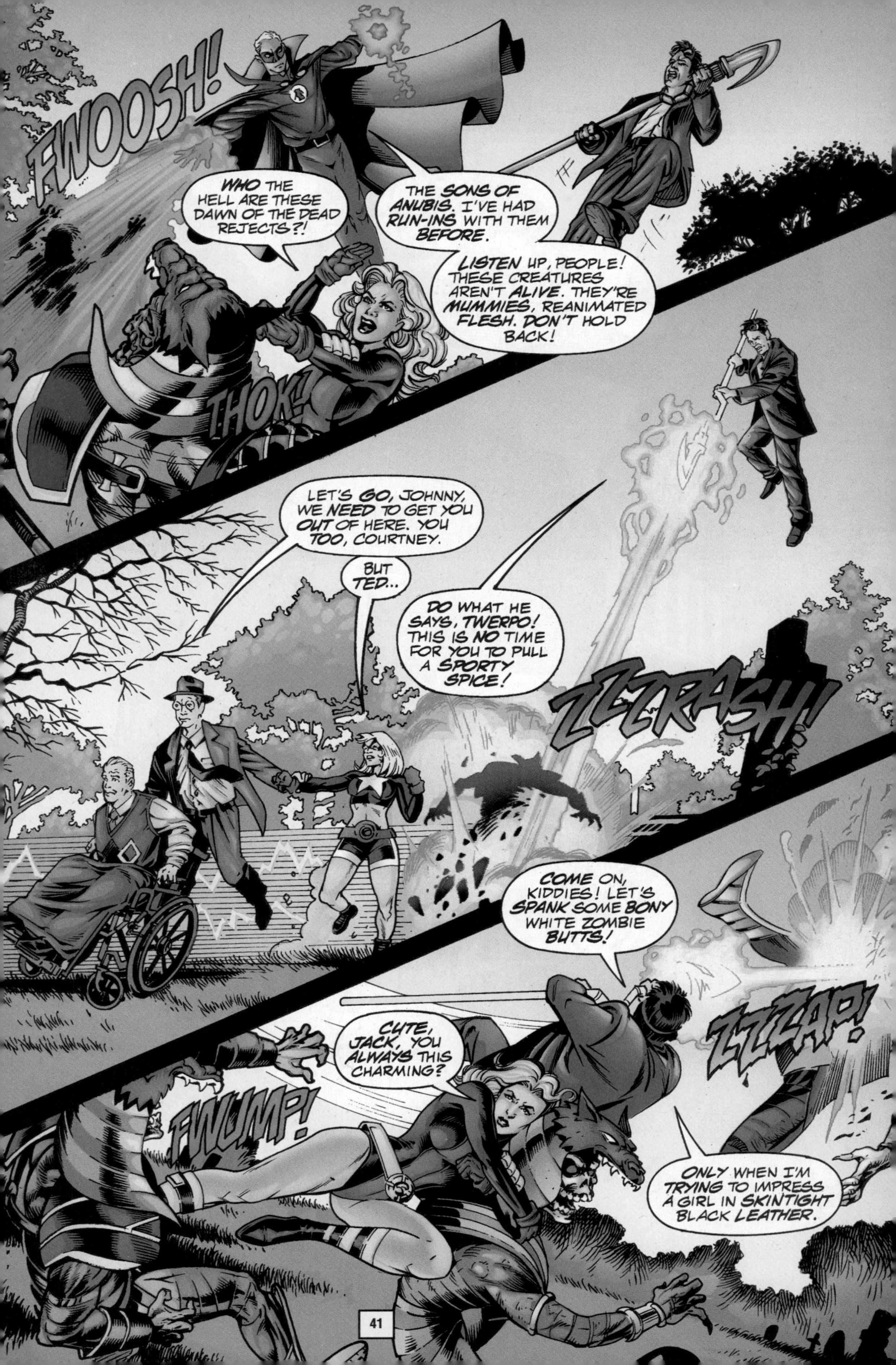
FWOOSH!
WHO THE HELL ARE THESE DAWN OF THE DEAD REJECTS?!
THE SONS OF ANUBIS. I'VE HAD RUN-INS WITH THEM BEFORE.
LISTEN UP, PEOPLE! THESE CREATURES AREN'T ALIVE. THEY'RE MUMMIES, REANIMATED FLESH. DON'T HOLD BACK!
THOK!
LET'S GO, JOHNNY, WE NEED TO GET YOU OUT OF HERE. YOU TOO, COURTNEY.
BUT TED...
DO WHAT HE SAYS, TWERPO! THIS IS NO TIME FOR YOU TO PULL A SPORTY SPICE!
ZZZRASH!
COME ON, KIDDIES! LET'S SPANK SOME BONY WHITE ZOMBIE BUTTS!
ZZZAP!
CUTE, JACK, YOU ALWAYS THIS CHARMING?
FWUMP!
ONLY WHEN I'M TRYING TO IMPRESS A GIRL IN SKINTIGHT BLACK LEATHER.

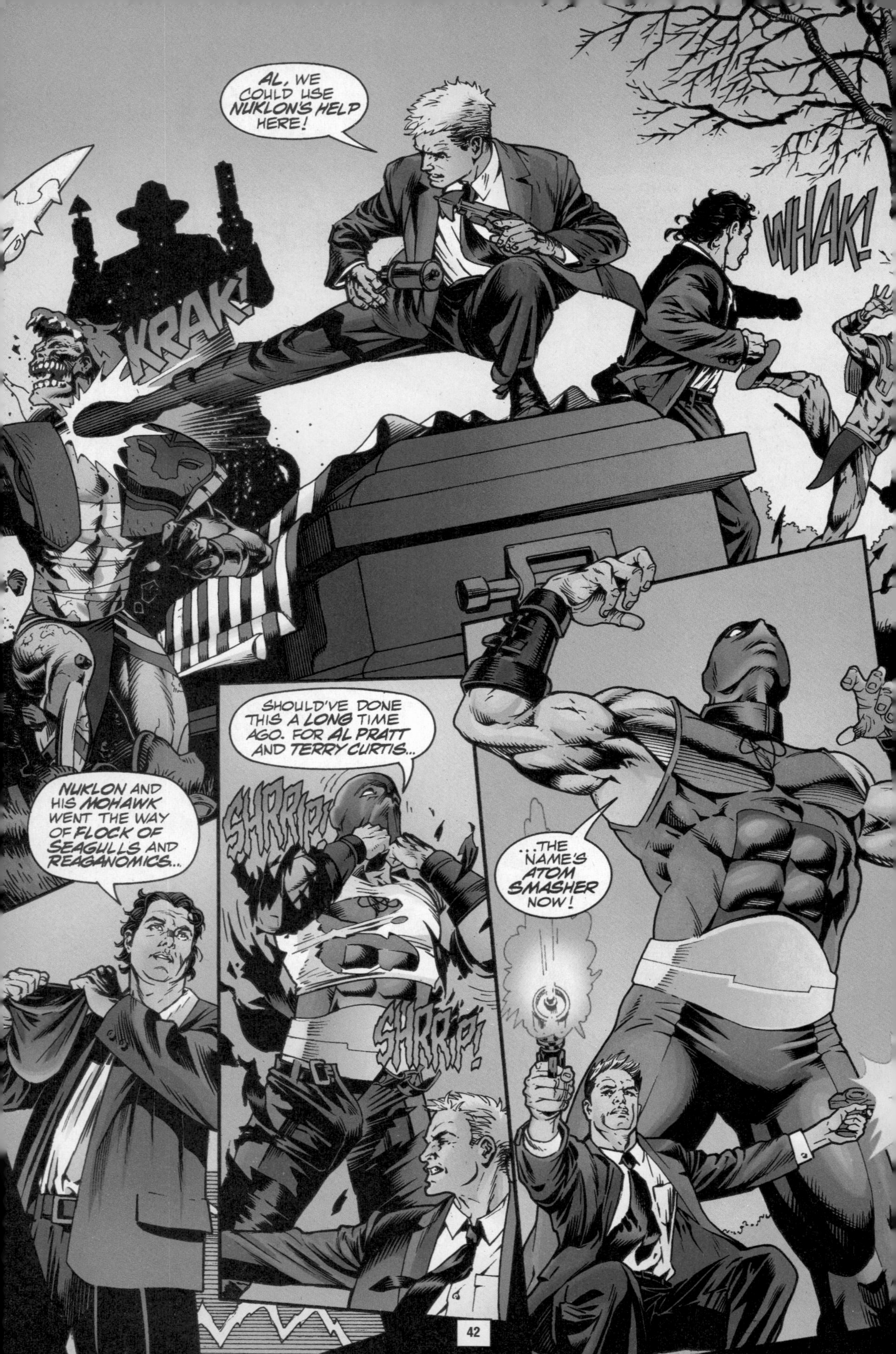
AL, WE COULD USE NUKLON'S HELP HERE!
KRAK!
WHAK!
SHOULD'VE DONE THIS A LONG TIME AGO. FOR AL PRATT AND TERRY CURTIS...
NUKLON AND HIS MOHAWK WENT THE WAY OF FLOCK OF SEAGULLS AND REAGANOMICS...
SHRRIP!
SHRRIP!
...THE NAME'S ATOM SMASHER NOW!

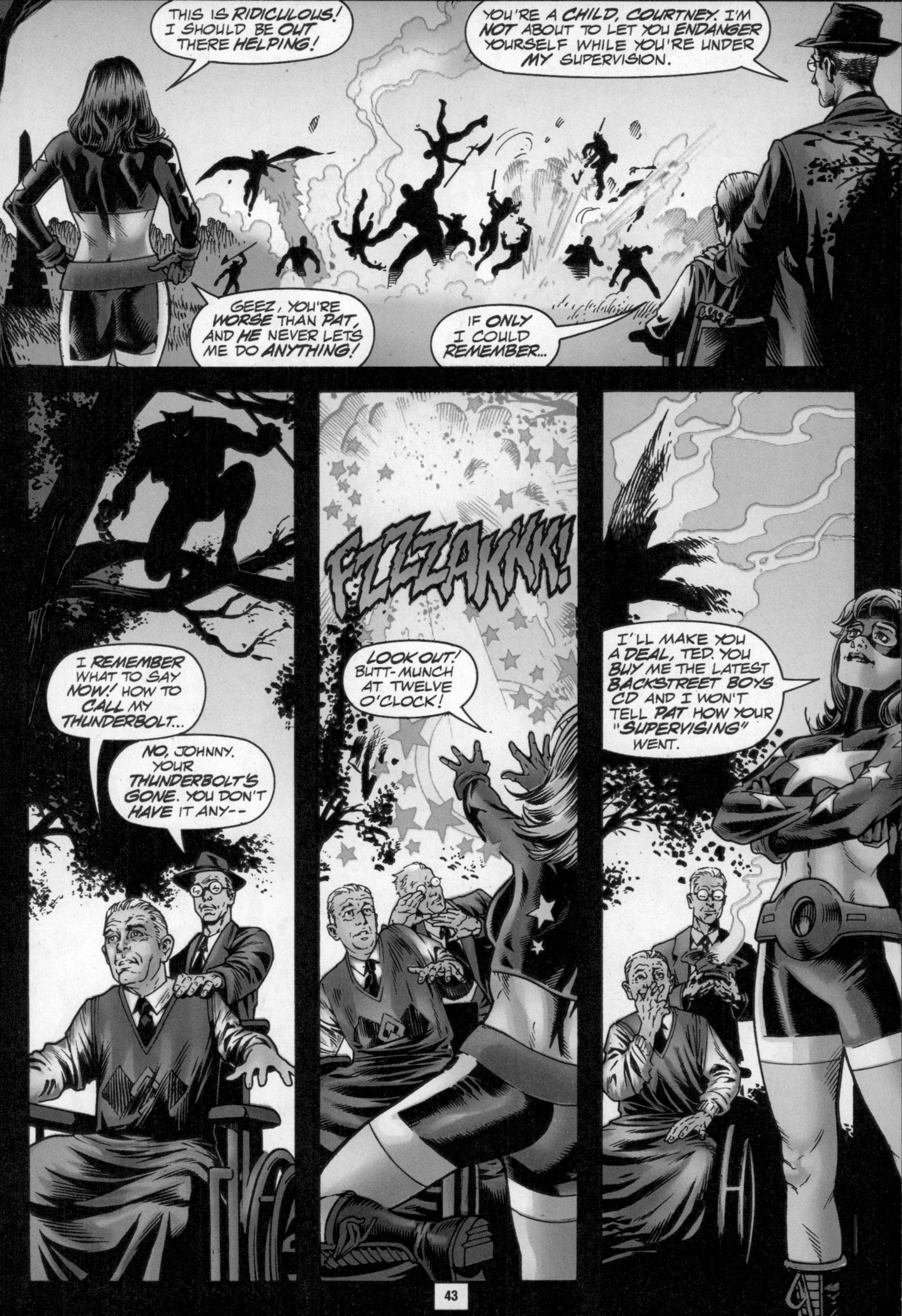
THIS IS RIDICULOUS! I SHOULD BE OUT THERE HELPING!
YOU'RE A CHILD, COURTNEY. I'M NOT ABOUT TO LET YOU ENDANGER YOURSELF WHILE YOU'RE UNDER MY SUPERVISION.
GEEZ, YOU'RE WORSE THAN PAT, AND HE NEVER LETS ME DO ANYTHING!
IF ONLY I COULD REMEMBER...
I REMEMBER WHAT TO SAY NOW! HOW TO CALL MY THUNDERBOLT...
NO, JOHNNY. YOUR THUNDERBOLT'S GONE. YOU DON'T HAVE IT ANY--
FZZZAKKK!
LOOK OUT! BUTT-MUNCH AT TWELVE O'CLOCK!
I'LL MAKE YOU A DEAL, TED. YOU BUY ME THE LATEST BACKSTREET BOYS CD AND I WON'T TELL PAT HOW YOUR "SUPERVISING" WENT.

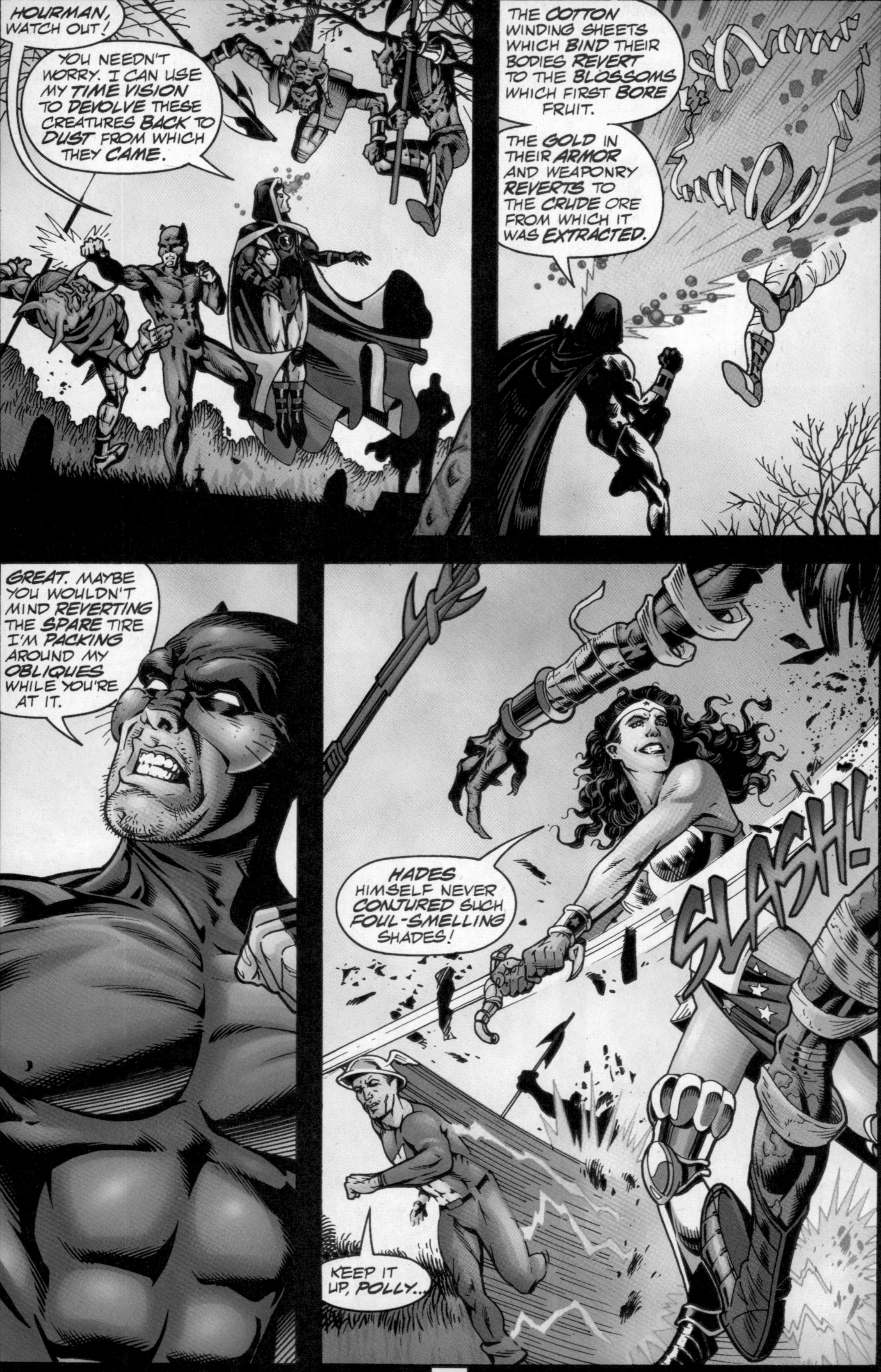
HOURMAN, WATCH OUT!
YOU NEEDN'T WORRY. I CAN USE MY TIME VISION TO DEVOLVE THESE CREATURES BACK TO DUST FROM WHICH THEY CAME.
THE COTTON WINDING SHEETS WHICH BIND THEIR BODIES REVERT TO THE BLOSSOMS WHICH FIRST BORE FRUIT.
THE GOLD IN THEIR ARMOR AND WEAPONRY REVERTS TO THE CRUDE ORE FROM WHICH IT WAS EXTRACTED.
GREAT. MAYBE YOU WOULDN'T MIND REVERTING THE SPARE TIRE I'M PACKING AROUND MY OBLIQUES WHILE YOU'RE AT IT.
HADES HIMSELF NEVER CONJURED SUCH FOUL-SMELLING SHADES!
SLASH!
KEEP IT UP, POLLY...

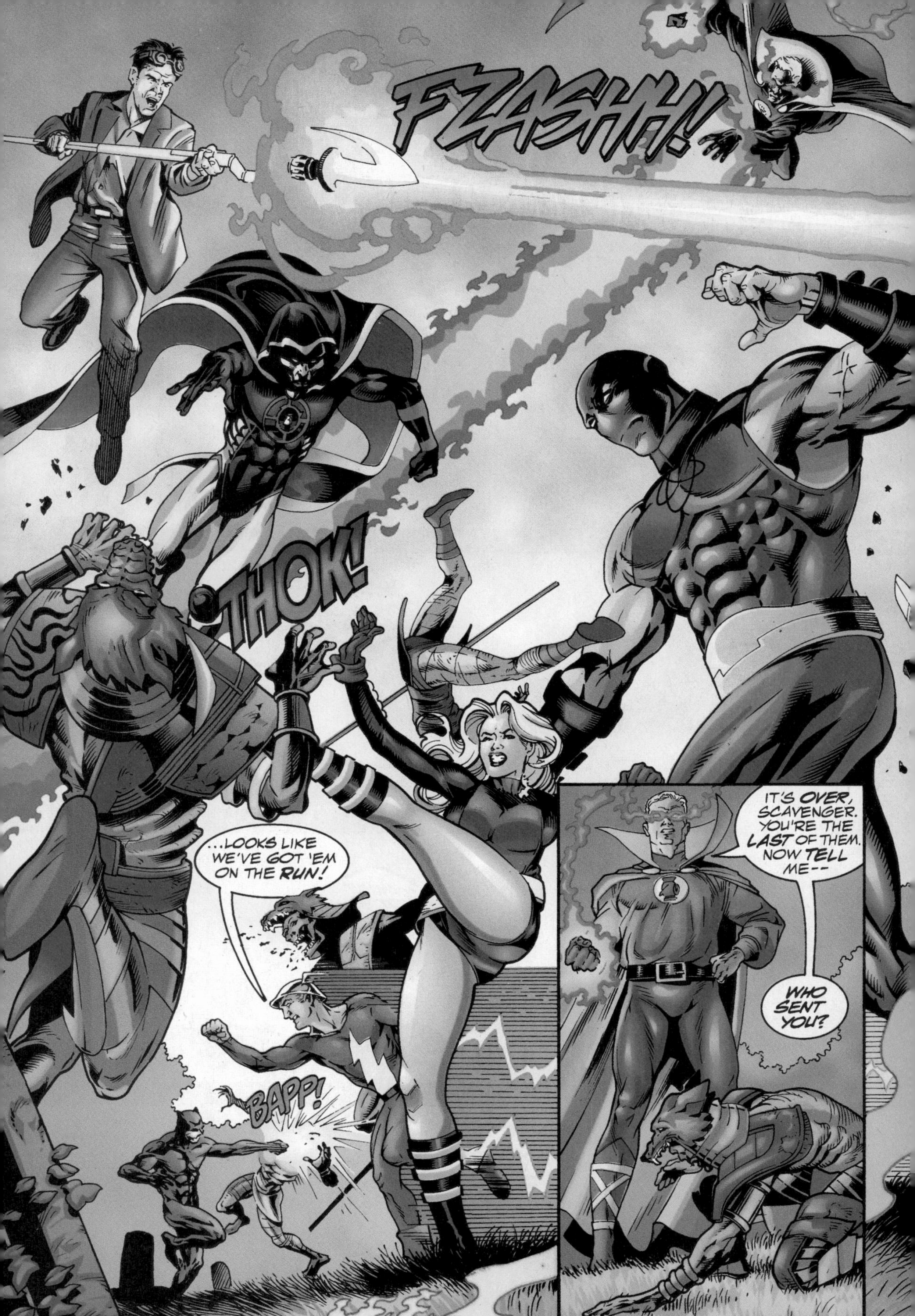
FZASHH!
THOK!
...LOOKS LIKE WE'VE GOT 'EM ON THE RUN!
BAPP!
IT'S OVER, SCAVENGER. YOU'RE THE LAST OF THEM. NOW TELL ME--
WHO SENT YOU?

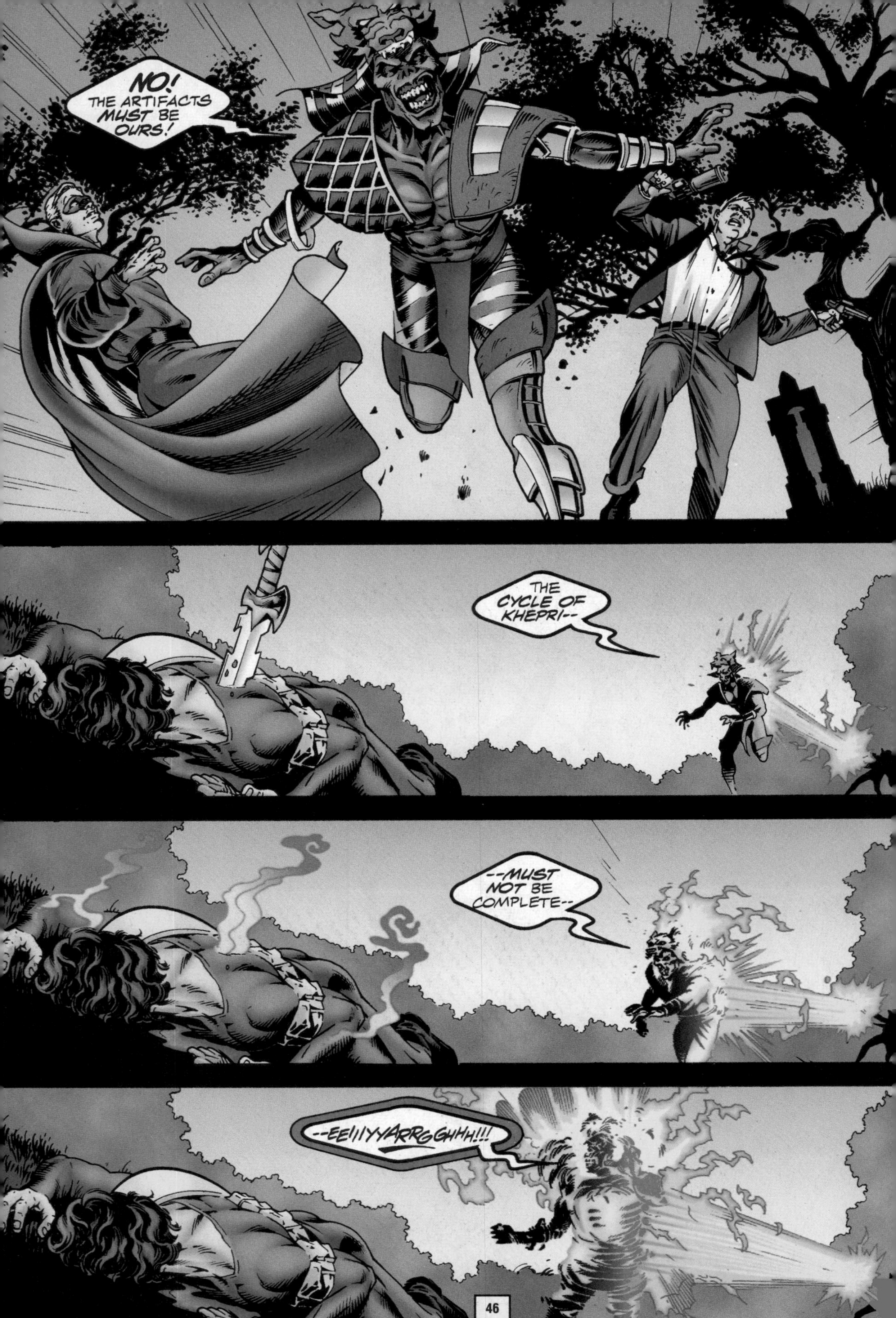
NO! THE ARTIFACTS MUST BE OURS!
THE CYCLE OF KHEPRI--
--MUST NOT BE COMPLETE--
--EEIIIYYARRGGHHH!!!

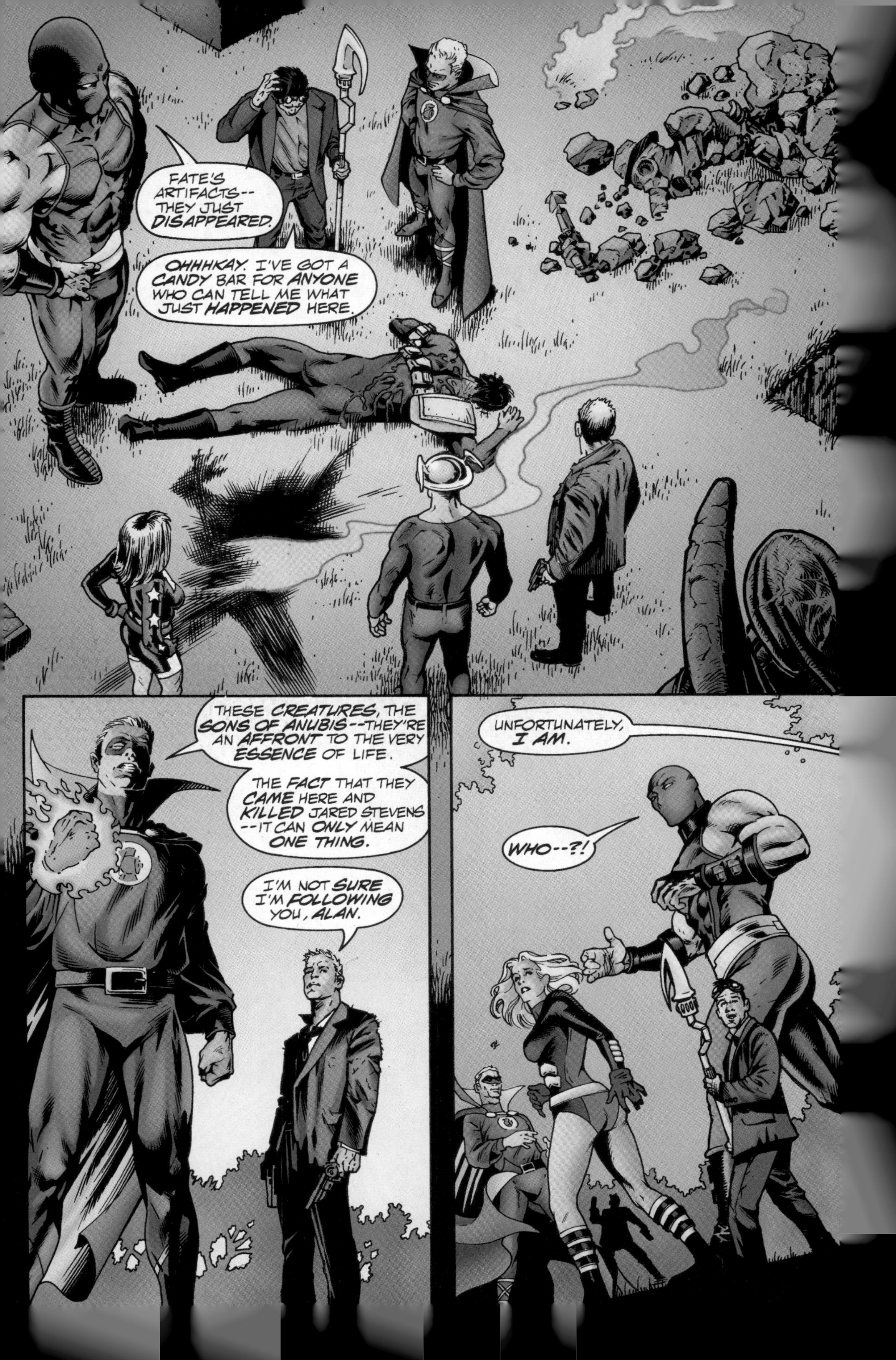
FATE'S ARTIFACTS-- THEY JUST DISAPPEARED.
OHHHKAY. I'VE GOT A CANDY BAR FOR ANYONE WHO CAN TELL ME WHAT JUST HAPPENED HERE.
THESE CREATURES, THE SONS OF ANUBIS--THEY'RE AN AFFRONT TO THE VERY ESSENCE OF LIFE.
THE FACT THAT THEY CAME HERE AND KILLED JARED STEVENS --IT CAN ONLY MEAN ONE THING.
I'M NOT SURE I'M FOLLOWING YOU, ALAN.
UNFORTUNATELY, I AM.
WHO--?!

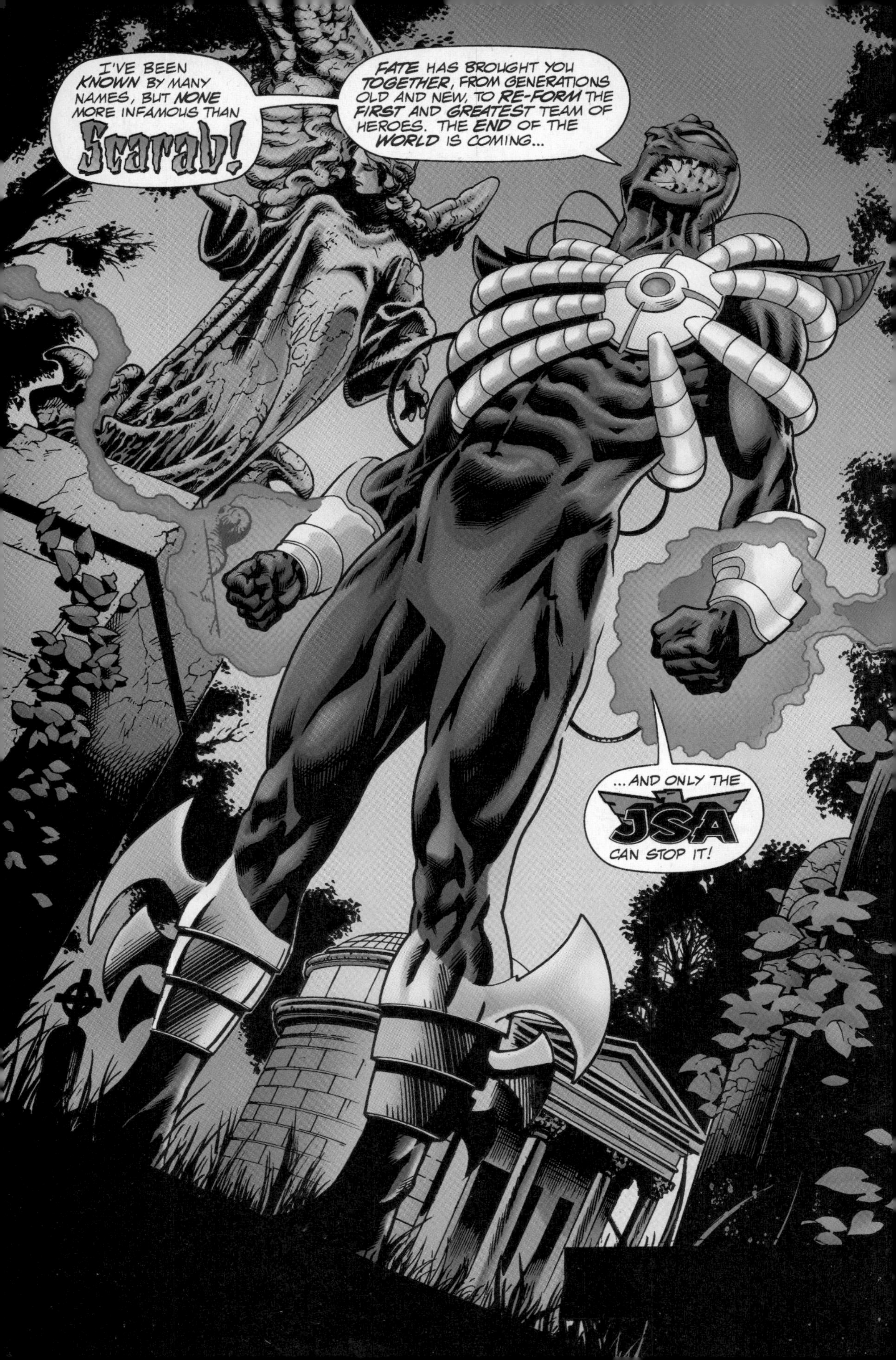
I'VE BEEN KNOWN BY MANY NAMES, BUT NONE MORE INFAMOUS THAN Scarab!
FATE HAS BROUGHT YOU TOGETHER, FROM GENERATIONS OLD AND NEW, TO RE-FORM THE FIRST AND GREATEST TEAM OF HEROES. THE END OF THE WORLD IS COMING...
...AND ONLY THE JSA CAN STOP IT!

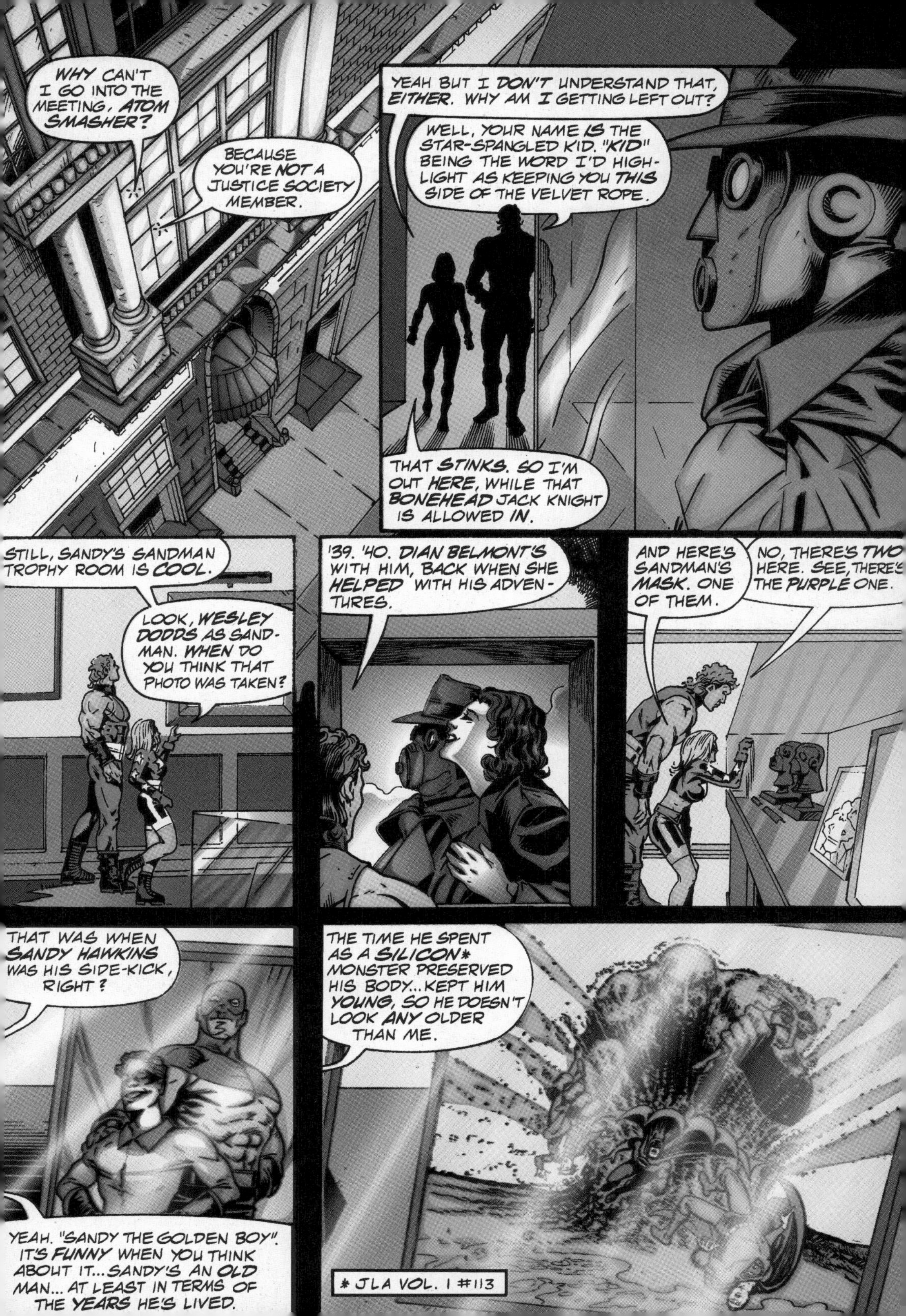
WHY CAN'T I GO INTO THE MEETING, ATOM SMASHER?
BECAUSE YOU'RE NOT A JUSTICE SOCIETY MEMBER.
YEAH BUT I DON'T UNDERSTAND THAT, EITHER. WHY AM I GETTING LEFT OUT?
WELL, YOUR NAME IS THE STAR-SPANGLED KID. "KID" BEING THE WORD I'D HIGH-LIGHT AS KEEPING YOU THIS SIDE OF THE VELVET ROPE.
THAT STINKS. SO I'M OUT HERE, WHILE THAT BONEHEAD JACK KNIGHT IS ALLOWED IN.
STILL, SANDY'S SANDMAN TROPHY ROOM IS COOL.
LOOK, WESLEY DODDS AS SAND-MAN. WHEN DO YOU THINK THAT PHOTO WAS TAKEN?
'39. '40. DIAN BELMONT'S WITH HIM, BACK WHEN SHE HELPED WITH HIS ADVEN-TURES.
AND HERE'S SANDMAN'S MASK. ONE OF THEM.
NO, THERE'S TWO HERE. SEE, THERE'S THE PURPLE ONE.
THAT WAS WHEN SANDY HAWKINS WAS HIS SIDE-KICK, RIGHT?
YEAH. "SANDY THE GOLDEN BOY". IT'S FUNNY WHEN YOU THINK ABOUT IT... SANDY'S AN OLD MAN... AT LEAST IN TERMS OF THE YEARS HE'S LIVED.
THE TIME HE SPENT AS A SILICON* MONSTER PRESERVED HIS BODY... KEPT HIM YOUNG, SO HE DOESN'T LOOK ANY OLDER THAN ME.
* JLA VOL. 1 #113

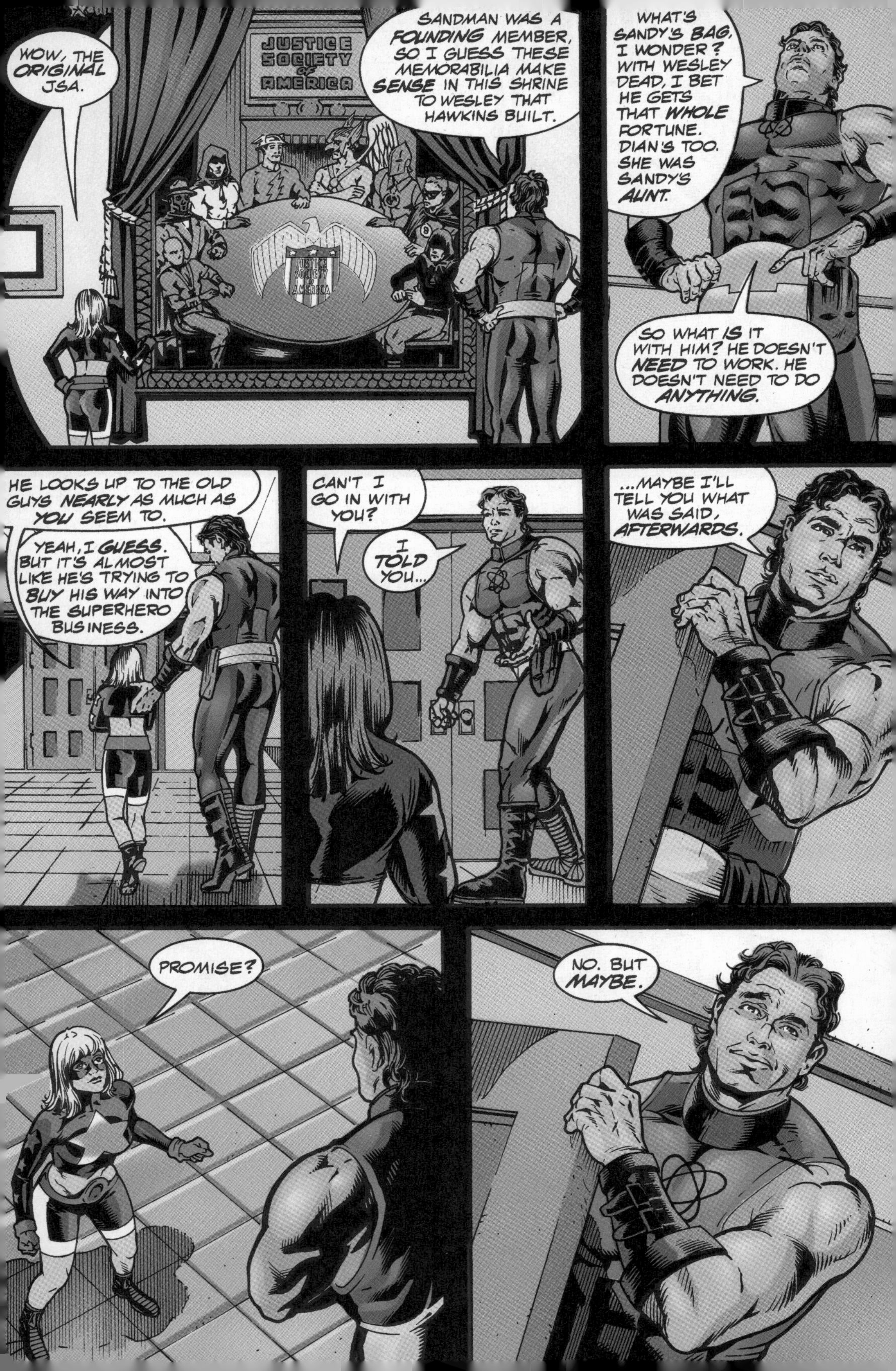
WOW, THE ORIGINAL JSA.
JUSTICE SOCIETY OF AMERICA
SANDMAN WAS A FOUNDING MEMBER, SO I GUESS THESE MEMORABILIA MAKE SENSE IN THIS SHRINE TO WESLEY THAT HAWKINS BUILT.
JUSTICE SOCIETY OF AMERICA
WHAT'S SANDY'S BAG, I WONDER? WITH WESLEY DEAD, I BET HE GETS THAT WHOLE FORTUNE. DIAN'S TOO. SHE WAS SANDY'S AUNT.
SO WHAT IS IT WITH HIM? HE DOESN'T NEED TO WORK. HE DOESN'T NEED TO DO ANYTHING.
HE LOOKS UP TO THE OLD GUYS NEARLY AS MUCH AS YOU SEEM TO.
YEAH, I GUESS. BUT IT'S ALMOST LIKE HE'S TRYING TO BUY HIS WAY INTO THE SUPERHERO BUSINESS.
CAN'T I GO IN WITH YOU?
I TOLD YOU...
...MAYBE I'LL TELL YOU WHAT WAS SAID, AFTERWARDS.
PROMISE?
NO. BUT MAYBE.

ALL RIGHT SCARAB. I THINK YOU OWE US AN EXPLANATION.

MY REAL NAME IS LOUIS SENDAK. DECADES AGO, I FOUGHT ALONGSIDE SOME OF YOUR PEERS--

I REMEMBER. THE KING OF TEARS AFFAIR. YOU DROPPED OUT OF SIGHT AFTER '44.

YES. I RETURNED BRIEFLY, SOME YEARS AGO. AND NOW IT SEEMS MY SERVICES ARE NEEDED ONCE AGAIN.

THAT'S GREAT. BUT WHAT DOES ANY OF THIS HAVE TO DO WITH WESLEY? THAT FATE CHARACTER SAID HE'D BEEN MURDERED.

JUSTICE SOCIETY of AMERICA

"Birth was the death of him".
-Samuel Beckett

THE WHEEL OF LIFE

JAMES ROBINSON & GOYER	DAVID	STEPHEN SADOWSKI	MICHAEL BAIR	KEN LOPEZ	JOHN KALISZ	HEROIC AGE	L.A. WILLIAMS	PETER TOMASI
WRITERS		PENCILLER	INKER	LETTERER	COLORIST	SEPARATOR	ASS'T EDITOR	EDITOR

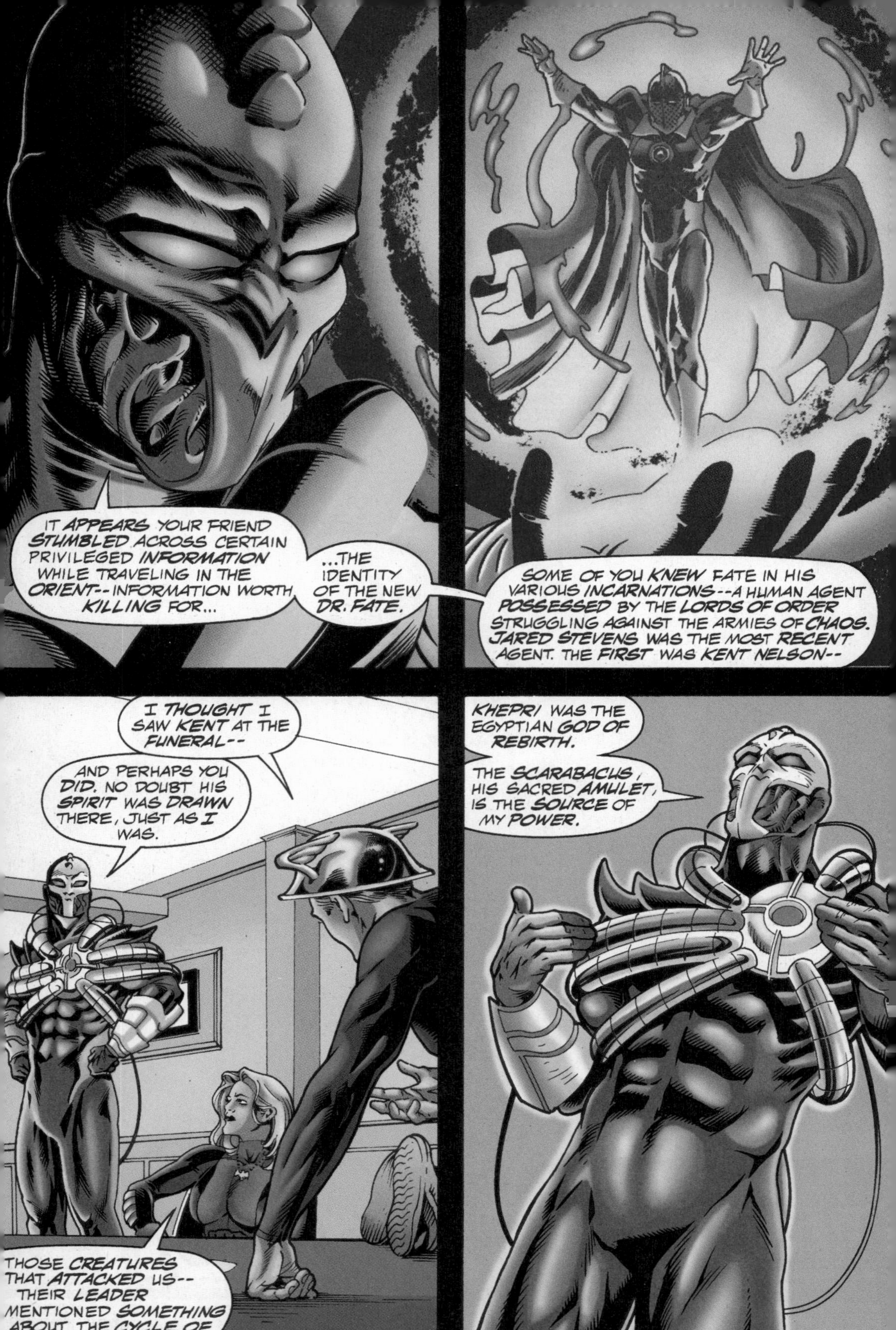

IT APPEARS YOUR FRIEND STUMBLED ACROSS CERTAIN PRIVILEGED INFORMATION WHILE TRAVELING IN THE ORIENT--INFORMATION WORTH KILLING FOR...
...THE IDENTITY OF THE NEW DR. FATE.
SOME OF YOU KNEW FATE IN HIS VARIOUS INCARNATIONS--A HUMAN AGENT POSSESSED BY THE LORDS OF ORDER STRUGGLING AGAINST THE ARMIES OF CHAOS. JARED STEVENS WAS THE MOST RECENT AGENT. THE FIRST WAS KENT NELSON--
I THOUGHT I SAW KENT AT THE FUNERAL--
AND PERHAPS YOU DID. NO DOUBT HIS SPIRIT WAS DRAWN THERE, JUST AS I WAS.
THOSE CREATURES THAT ATTACKED US-- THEIR LEADER MENTIONED SOMETHING ABOUT THE CYCLE OF KHEPRI--
KHEPRI WAS THE EGYPTIAN GOD OF REBIRTH.
THE SCARABACUS, HIS SACRED AMULET, IS THE SOURCE OF MY POWER.

THE *WHEEL OF LIFE* IS *TURNING ONCE AGAIN.* A NEW *DR. FATE* IS *DESTINED* TO BE *BORN.* AND THERE ARE *FORCES* AT WORK WHO WOULD SEEK TO PREVENT THIS.

WHAT CAN WE DO?

YOUR FRIEND *WESLEY SUCCEEDED* IN IDENTIFYING *THREE* INFANTS WITH THE *POTENTIAL* TO ASSUME *FATE'S MANTLE.* THEY ARE *SCATTERED* ABOUT YOUR *WORLD* -- IN *BRITISH COLUMBIA, TIBET, VENICE, ITALY.*

ONE OF THEM IS THE *FATE-CHILD.*

AN *IMMORTAL* CALLING HIMSELF THE *DARK LORD* HAS BEEN *HUNTING* AGENTS OF *ORDER* AND *CHAOS* ALIKE, *STEALING* THEIR POWER --

HE HAS *ALREADY MURDERED KID ETERNITY* AND *KESTREL,* AND PERHAPS EVEN THE *GRAY MAN. NOW* HE SEEKS TO *ADD* THE *FATE-CHILD* TO HIS LIST.

YOU *MUST NOT* LET THIS *HAPPEN.* YOU *MUST* REACH THE CHILDREN *BEFORE* THE *DARK LORD* AND HIS AGENTS DO.

HOW WILL WE KNOW *WHICH* BAMBINO'S THE *LUCKY WINNER?*

ACCORDING TO *PROPHECY,* THE *FATE-CHILD* WILL HAVE A *BIRTHMARK* -- SHAPED LIKE AN *ANKH* -- *SOMEWHERE* ON ITS BODY.

THE *JUSTICE SOCIETY* REPRESENTED THE *GREATEST* THE *GOLDEN AGE OF HEROES* HAD TO OFFER. DR. *FATE* WAS A FOUNDING MEMBER. *SOME* OF YOU HERE WERE HIS *TEAMMATES, SOME* OF YOU ARE THE *SONS* AND *DAUGHTERS* OF THOSE *TEAMMATES* --

-- IN *MEMORY* OF THAT *LEGACY* I *BEG* YOU TO *HELP* ME.

MY DAD RAN INTO THIS *CAT* BACK IN THE '*40S*. HE SAID THE GUY REALLY *CREEPED* HIM OUT.

SAME WITH MY *MOM*. AND HE SMELLS *FUNNY*, TOO.

I THINK I *SPEAK* FOR *EVERYONE* HERE WHEN I SAY WE'LL DO *ANYTHING* WE CAN TO *HELP* YOU.

WE SHOULD *SPLIT* INTO *TEAMS*. I'VE SPENT SOME *TIME* IN TIBET WITH *WESLEY*--

CAN YOU *TRANSPORT* US THERE, *ALAN*?

IN A *HEARTBEAT*.

COUNT ME IN, *TOO*. WESLEY *DODDS* WAS A GOOD FRIEND.

I'LL TAKE *VENICE*. JACK, DINAH, YOU TWO WANT TO *RIDE SHOTGUN* COURTESY OF THE *SPEED FORCE*?

WOULDN'T *MISS* IT FOR THE *WORLD*.

DITTO.

ALWAYS WANTED TO GO THERE SINCE I SAW *SUTHERLAND* CRUISING THE CANALS IN "*DON'T LOOK NOW*." KILLER DWARVES AND *JULIE CHRISTIE*. WHAT *MORE* CAN A GUY ASK FOR?

GUESS THAT LEAVES THE *THREE* OF US.

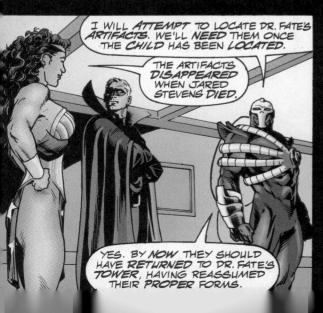

I WILL *ATTEMPT* TO LOCATE DR. FATE'S *ARTIFACTS*. WE'LL *NEED* THEM ONCE THE *CHILD* HAS BEEN *LOCATED*.

THE ARTIFACTS *DISAPPEARED* WHEN JARED STEVENS *DIED*.

YES. BY *NOW* THEY SHOULD HAVE *RETURNED* TO DR. FATE'S *TOWER*, HAVING REASSUMED THEIR *PROPER* FORMS.

THE TOWER'S BEEN *DESTROYED*. I *SAW* IT HAPPEN *MYSELF*.

HOW CAN YOU *DESTROY* SOMETHING THAT *EXISTS* OUTSIDE OF *SPACE* AND *TIME*?

YOU SAW ONLY *ONE* ASPECT OF THE TOWER LAID WASTE. THE FORTRESS *STILL* EXISTS, AND WE MUST *FIND* IT.

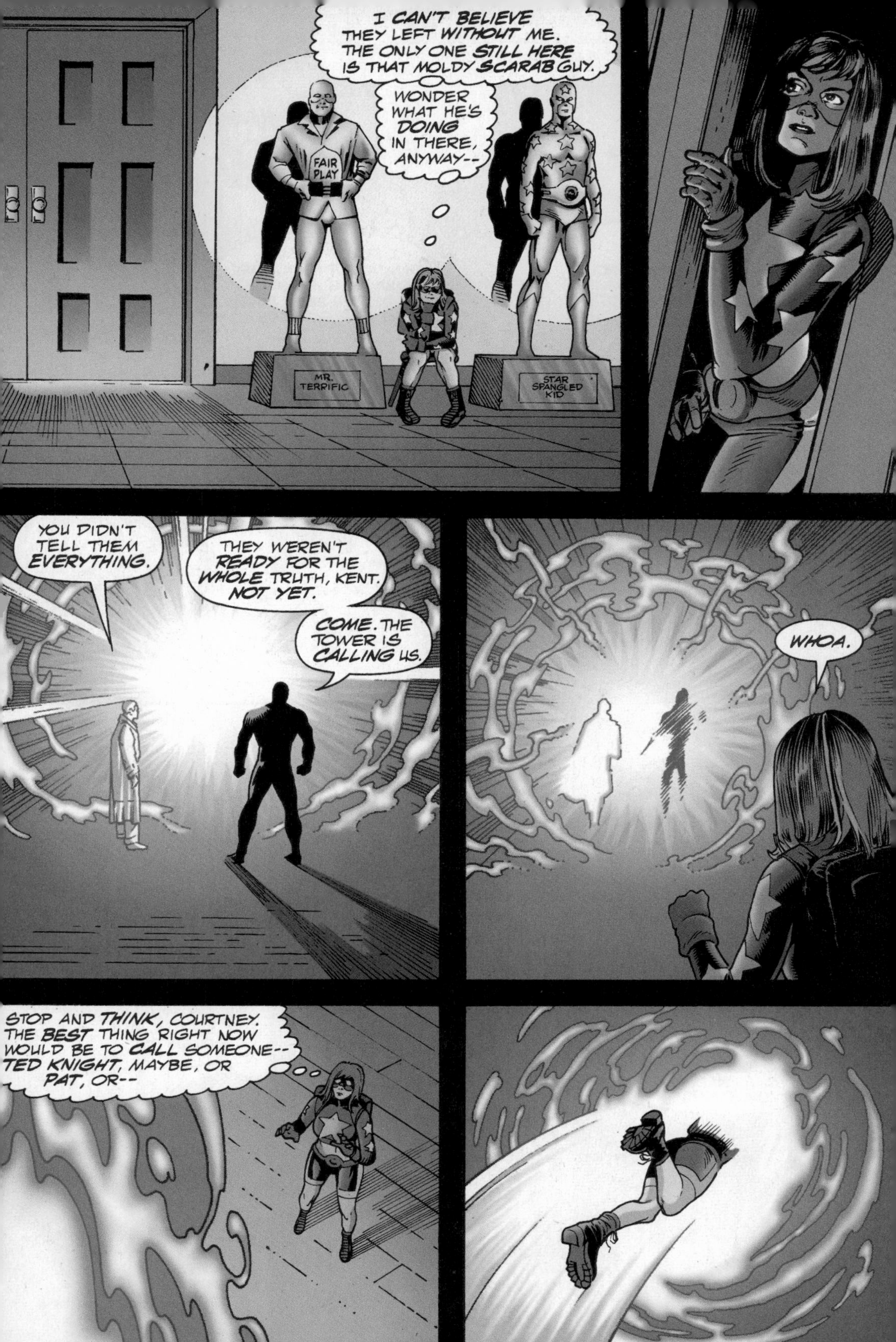

I CAN'T BELIEVE THEY LEFT WITHOUT ME. THE ONLY ONE STILL HERE IS THAT MOLDY SCARAB GUY.
WONDER WHAT HE'S DOING IN THERE, ANYWAY--
FAIR PLAY
MR. TERRIFIC
STAR SPANGLED KID
YOU DIDN'T TELL THEM EVERYTHING.
THEY WEREN'T READY FOR THE WHOLE TRUTH, KENT. NOT YET.
COME. THE TOWER IS CALLING US.
WHOA.
STOP AND THINK, COURTNEY. THE BEST THING RIGHT NOW WOULD BE TO CALL SOMEONE-- TED KNIGHT, MAYBE, OR PAT, OR--

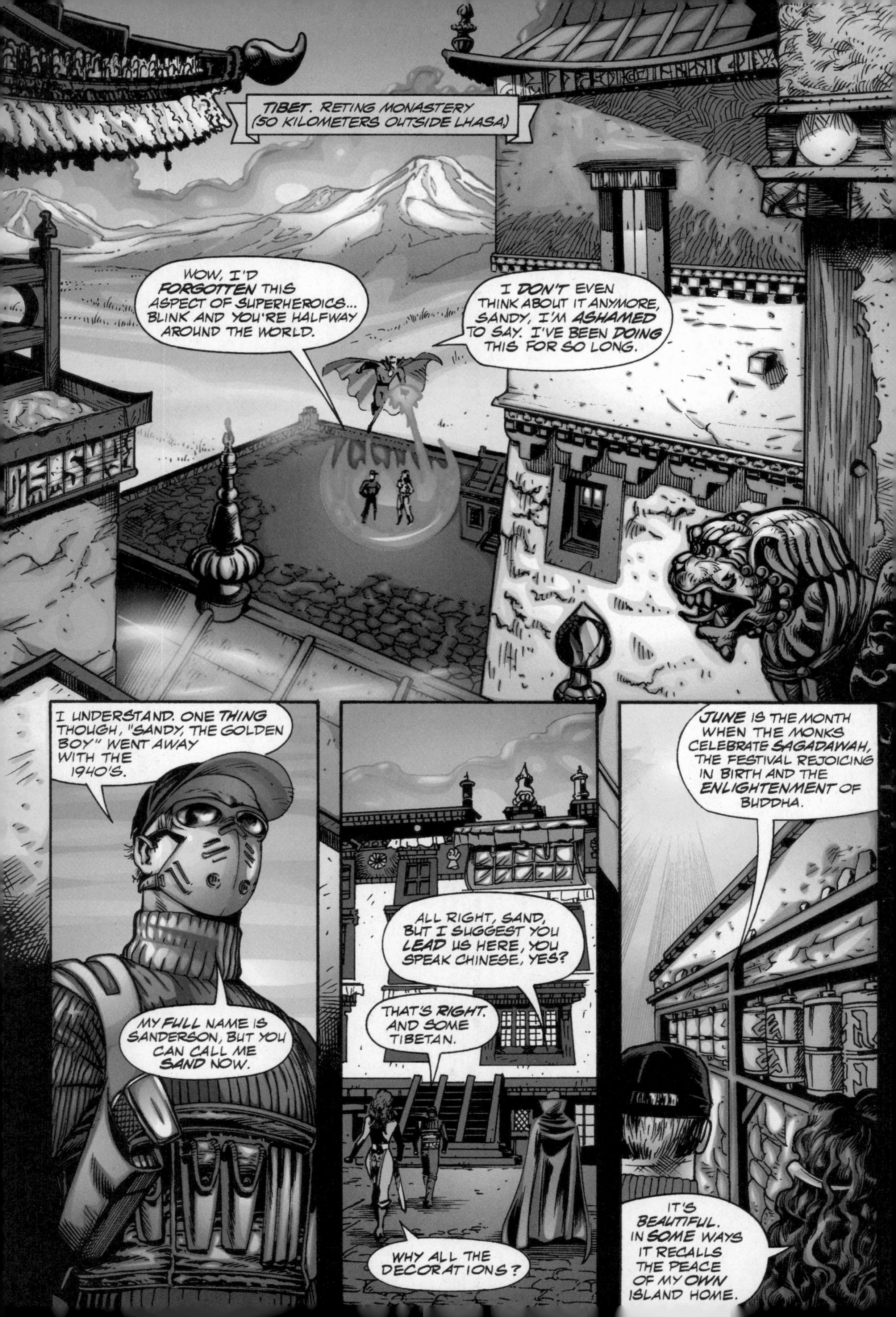
TIBET. RETING MONASTERY (50 KILOMETERS OUTSIDE LHASA)
WOW, I'D FORGOTTEN THIS ASPECT OF SUPERHEROICS... BLINK AND YOU'RE HALFWAY AROUND THE WORLD.
I DON'T EVEN THINK ABOUT IT ANYMORE, SANDY, I'M ASHAMED TO SAY. I'VE BEEN DOING THIS FOR SO LONG.
I UNDERSTAND. ONE THING THOUGH, "SANDY, THE GOLDEN BOY" WENT AWAY WITH THE 1940'S.
MY FULL NAME IS SANDERSON, BUT YOU CAN CALL ME SAND NOW.
ALL RIGHT, SAND, BUT I SUGGEST YOU LEAD US HERE, YOU SPEAK CHINESE, YES?
THAT'S RIGHT. AND SOME TIBETAN.
WHY ALL THE DECORATIONS?
JUNE IS THE MONTH WHEN THE MONKS CELEBRATE SAGADAWAH, THE FESTIVAL REJOICING IN BIRTH AND THE ENLIGHTENMENT OF BUDDHA.
IT'S BEAUTIFUL. IN SOME WAYS IT RECALLS THE PEACE OF MY OWN ISLAND HOME.

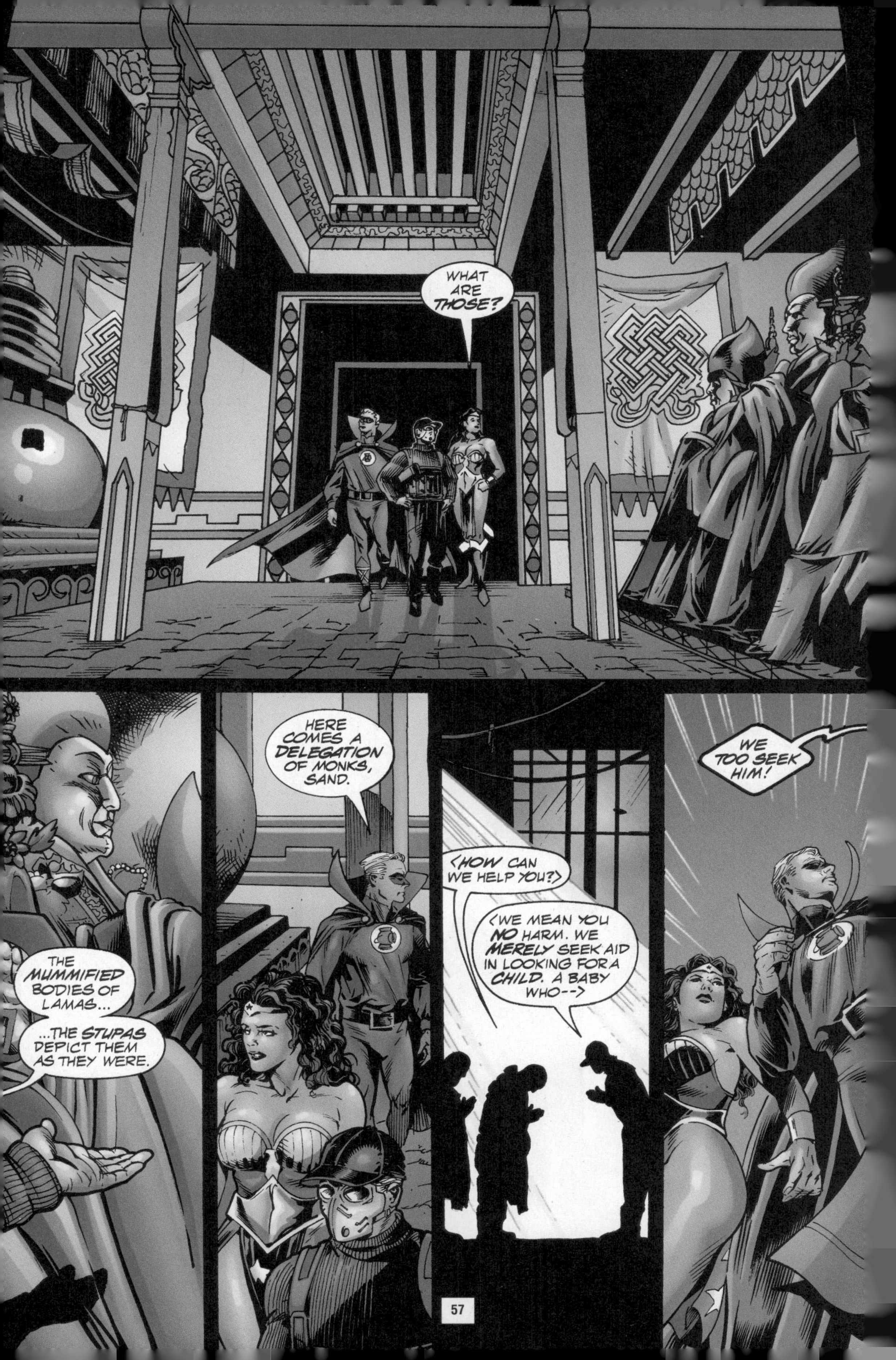
WHAT ARE THOSE?
THE MUMMIFIED BODIES OF LAMAS...
...THE STUPAS DEPICT THEM AS THEY WERE.
HERE COMES A DELEGATION OF MONKS, SAND.
<HOW CAN WE HELP YOU?>
<WE MEAN YOU NO HARM. WE MERELY SEEK AID IN LOOKING FOR A CHILD. A BABY WHO-->
WE TOO SEEK HIM!

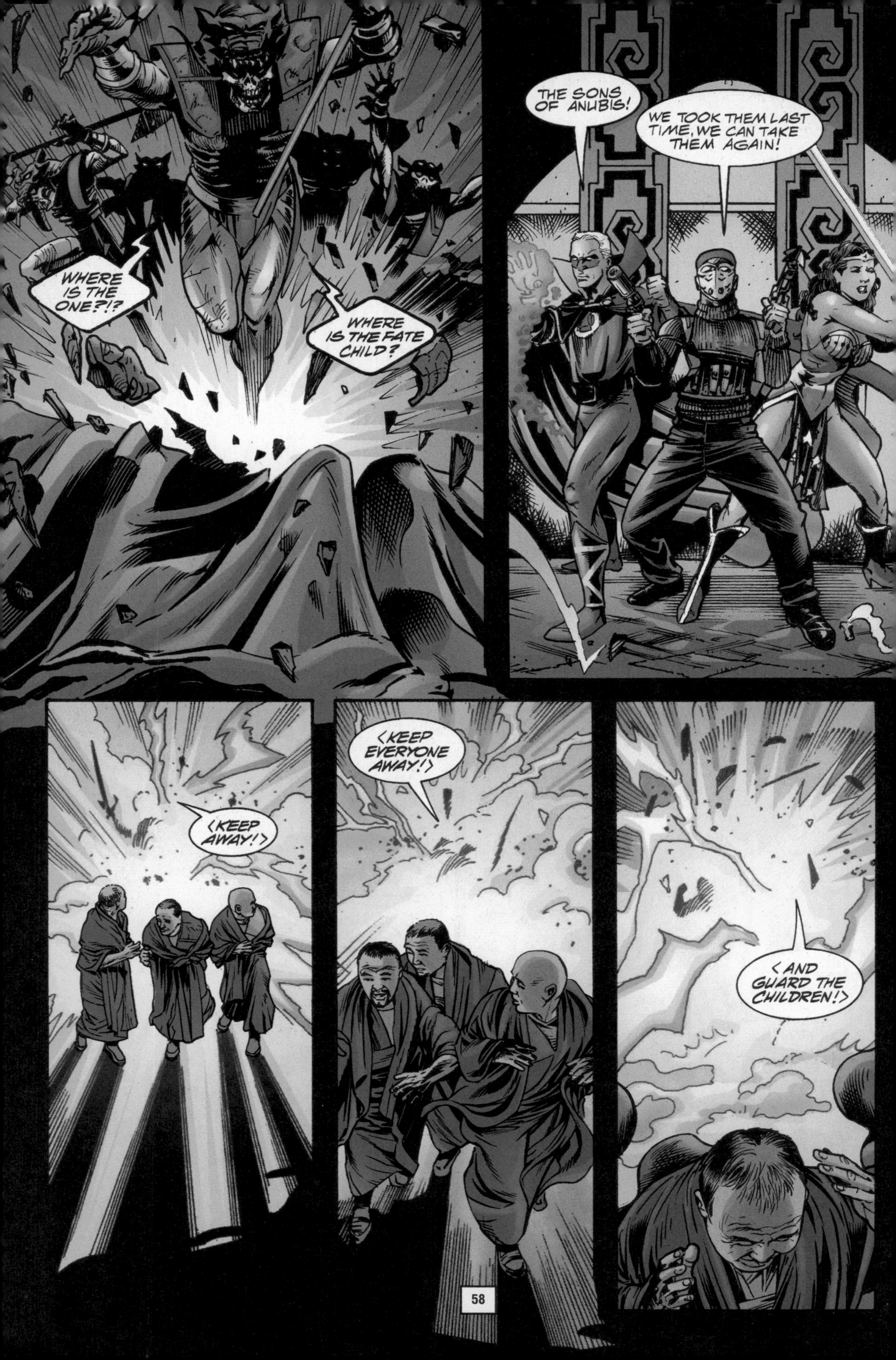
WHERE IS THE ONE?!?
WHERE IS THE FATE CHILD?
THE SONS OF ANUBIS!
WE TOOK THEM LAST TIME, WE CAN TAKE THEM AGAIN!
<KEEP AWAY!>
<KEEP EVERYONE AWAY!>
<AND GUARD THE CHILDREN!>

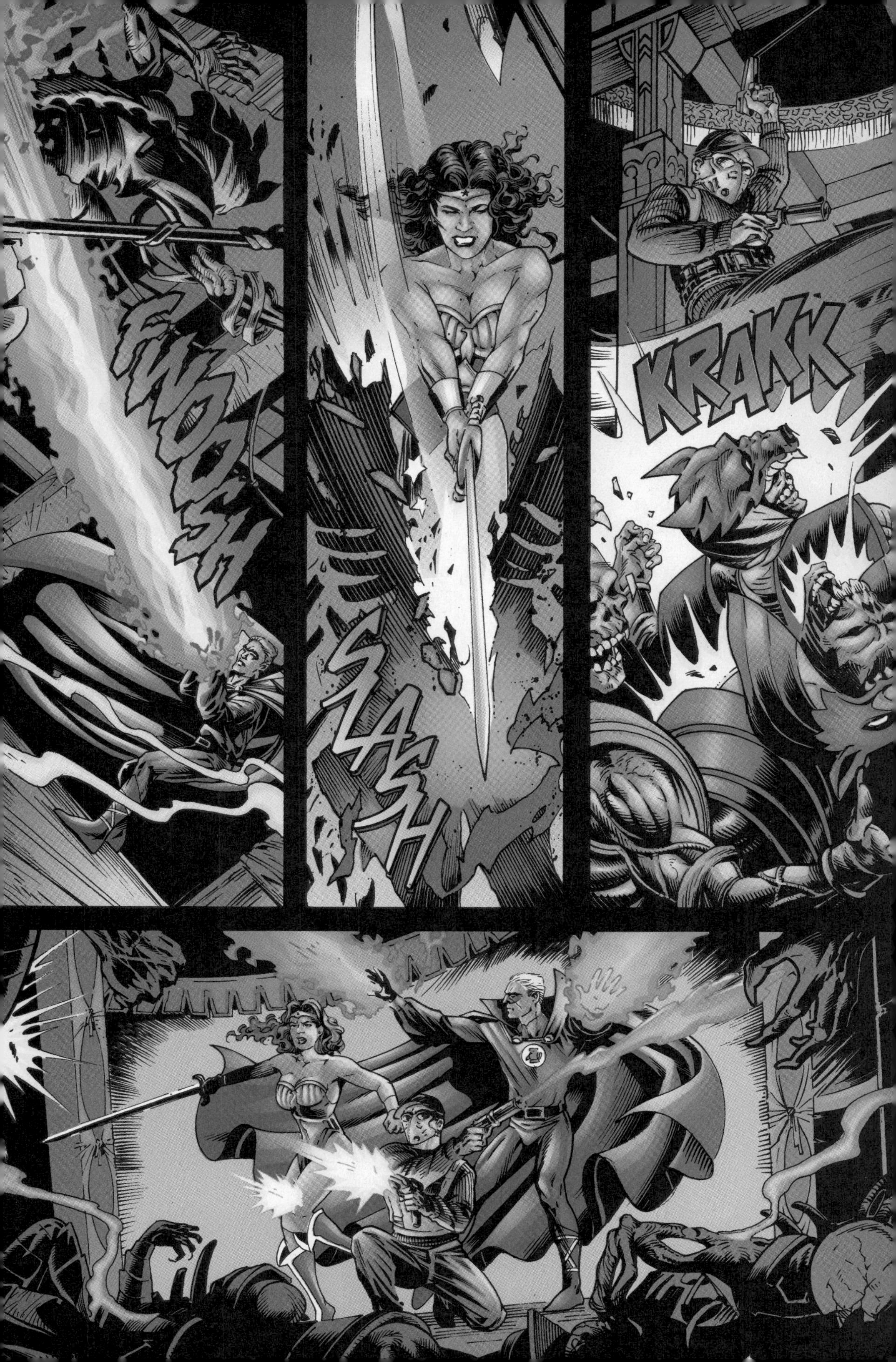
FWOOSH
SLASH
KRAKK

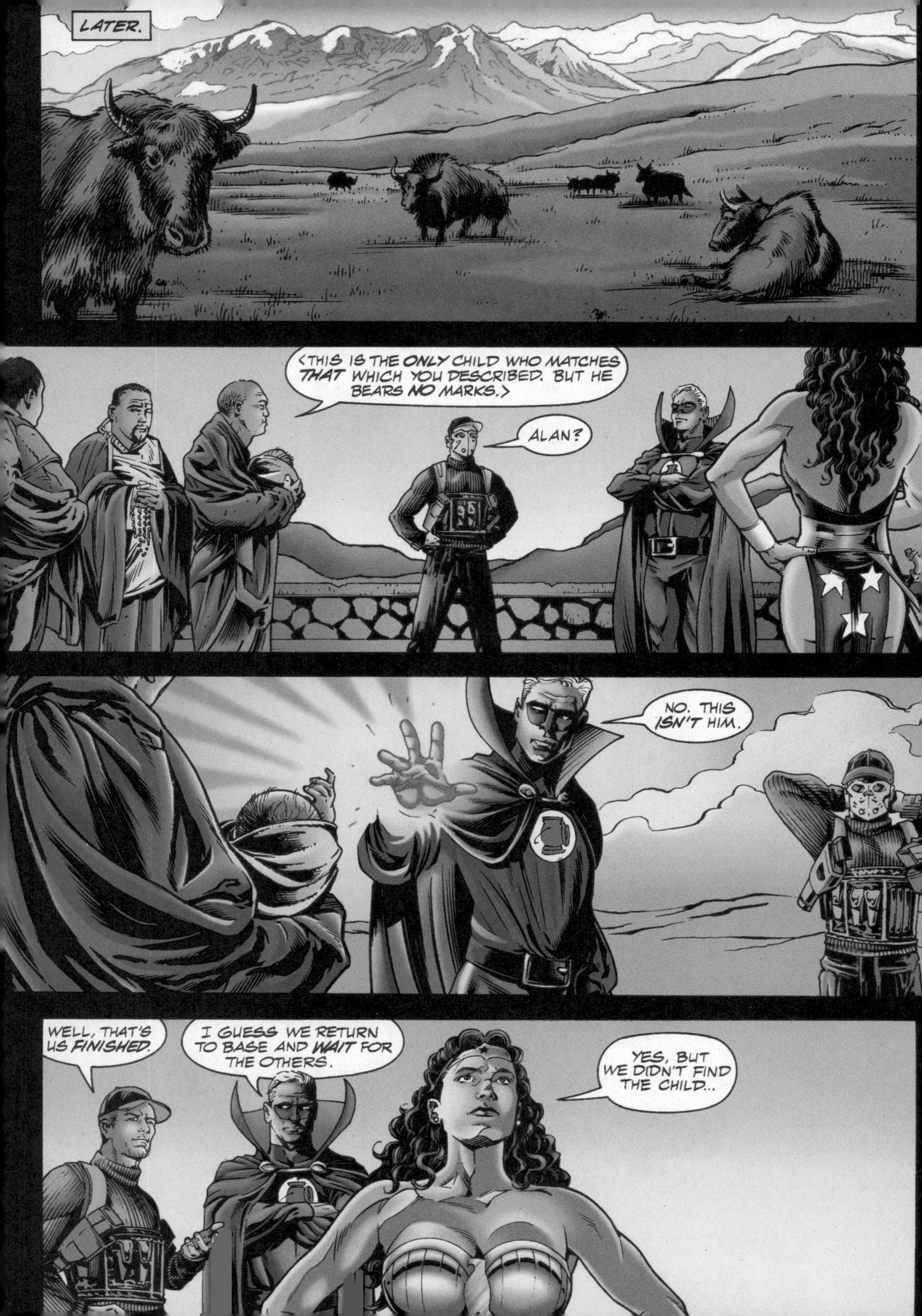
LATER.
<THIS IS THE ONLY CHILD WHO MATCHES THAT WHICH YOU DESCRIBED. BUT HE BEARS NO MARKS.>
ALAN?
NO. THIS ISN'T HIM.
WELL, THAT'S US FINISHED.
I GUESS WE RETURN TO BASE AND WAIT FOR THE OTHERS.
YES, BUT WE DIDN'T FIND THE CHILD...

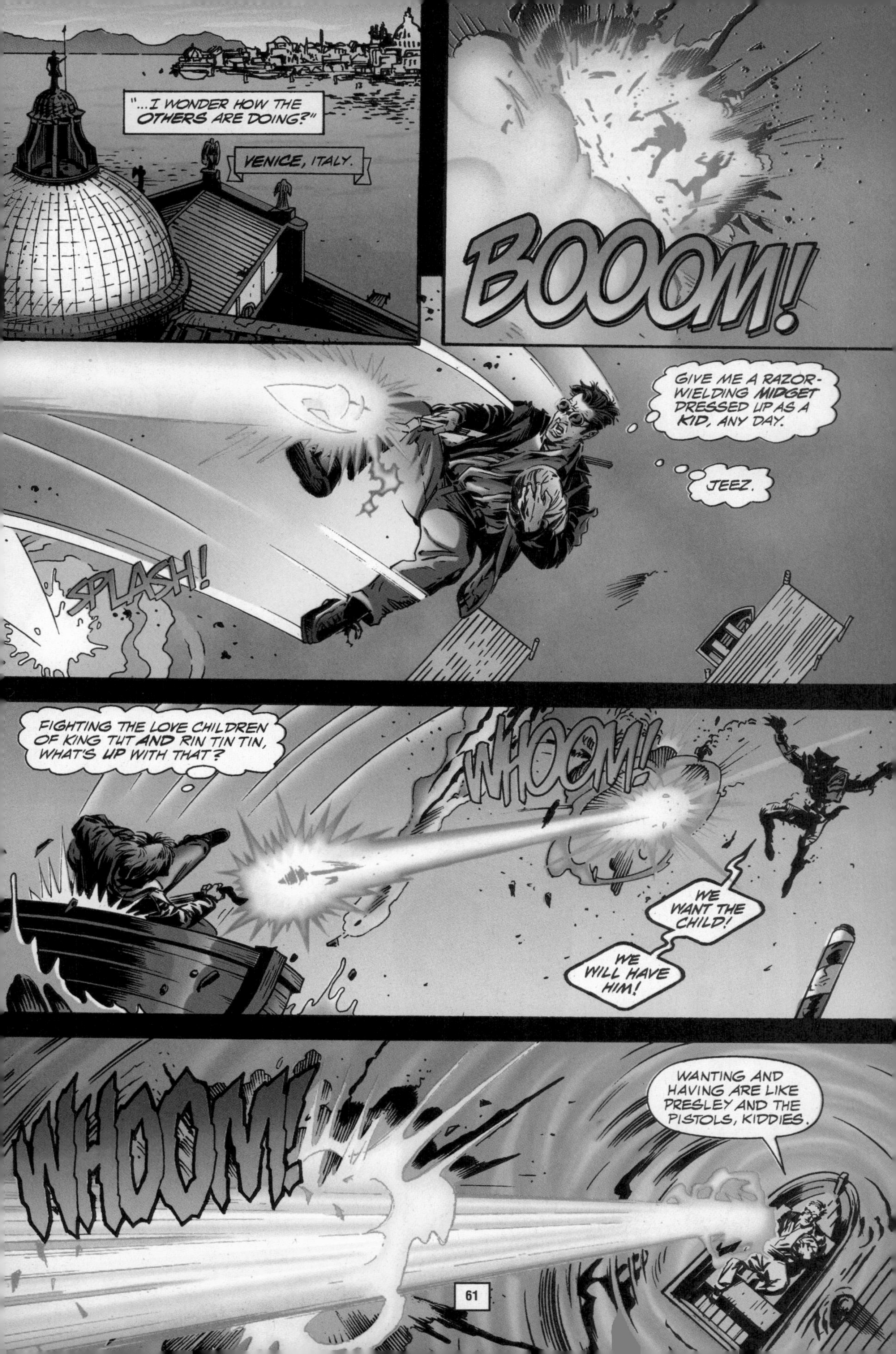
"...I WONDER HOW THE OTHERS ARE DOING?"
VENICE, ITALY.
BOOOM!
GIVE ME A RAZOR-WIELDING MIDGET DRESSED UP AS A KID, ANY DAY.
JEEZ.
SPLASH!
FIGHTING THE LOVE CHILDREN OF KING TUT AND RIN TIN TIN, WHAT'S UP WITH THAT?
WHOOM!
WE WANT THE CHILD!
WE WILL HAVE HIM!
WHOOM!
WANTING AND HAVING ARE LIKE PRESLEY AND THE PISTOLS, KIDDIES.

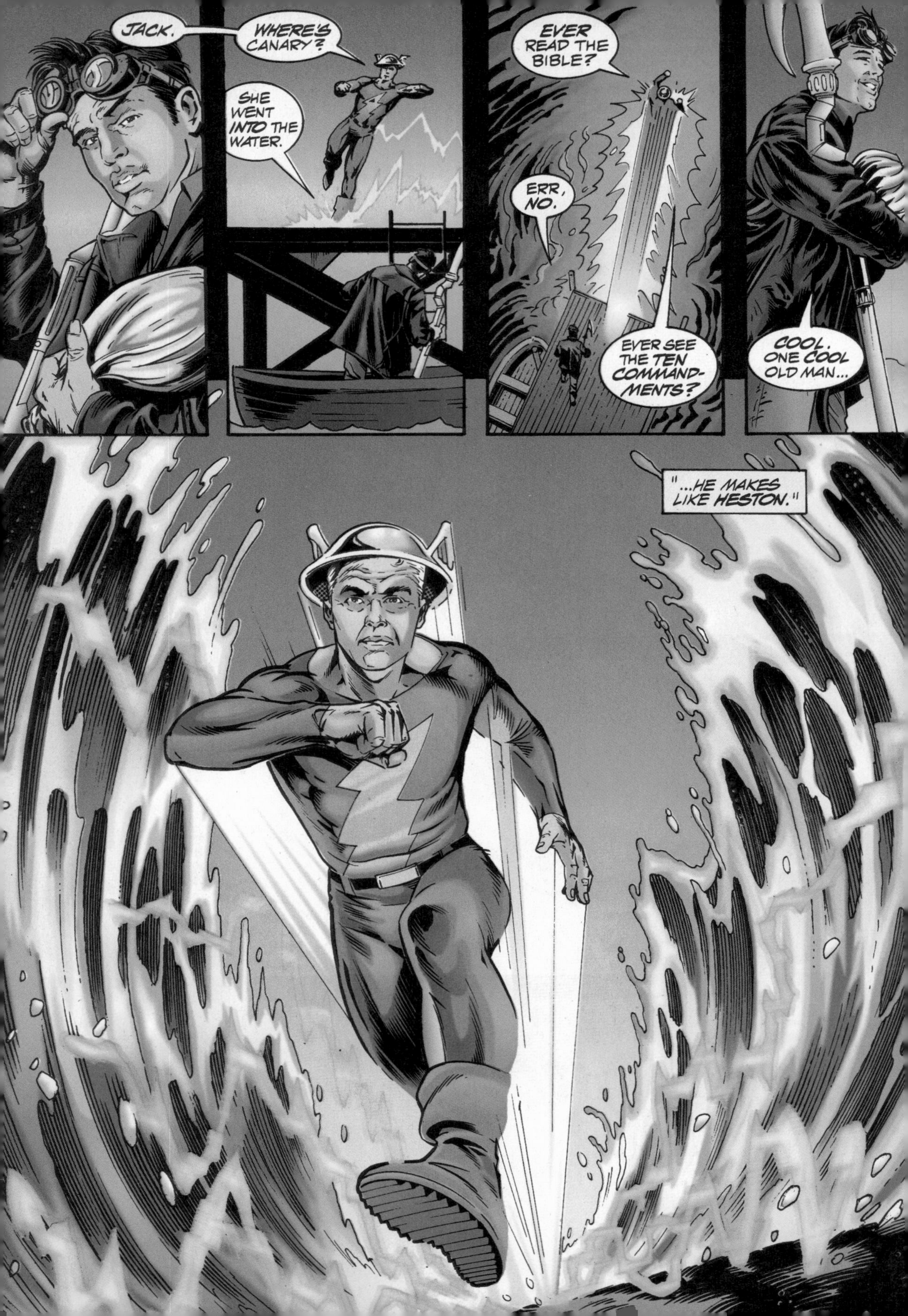
JACK.
WHERE'S CANARY?
SHE WENT INTO THE WATER.
EVER READ THE BIBLE?
ERR, NO.
EVER SEE THE TEN COMMAND-MENTS?
COOL. ONE COOL OLD MAN...
"...HE MAKES LIKE HESTON."

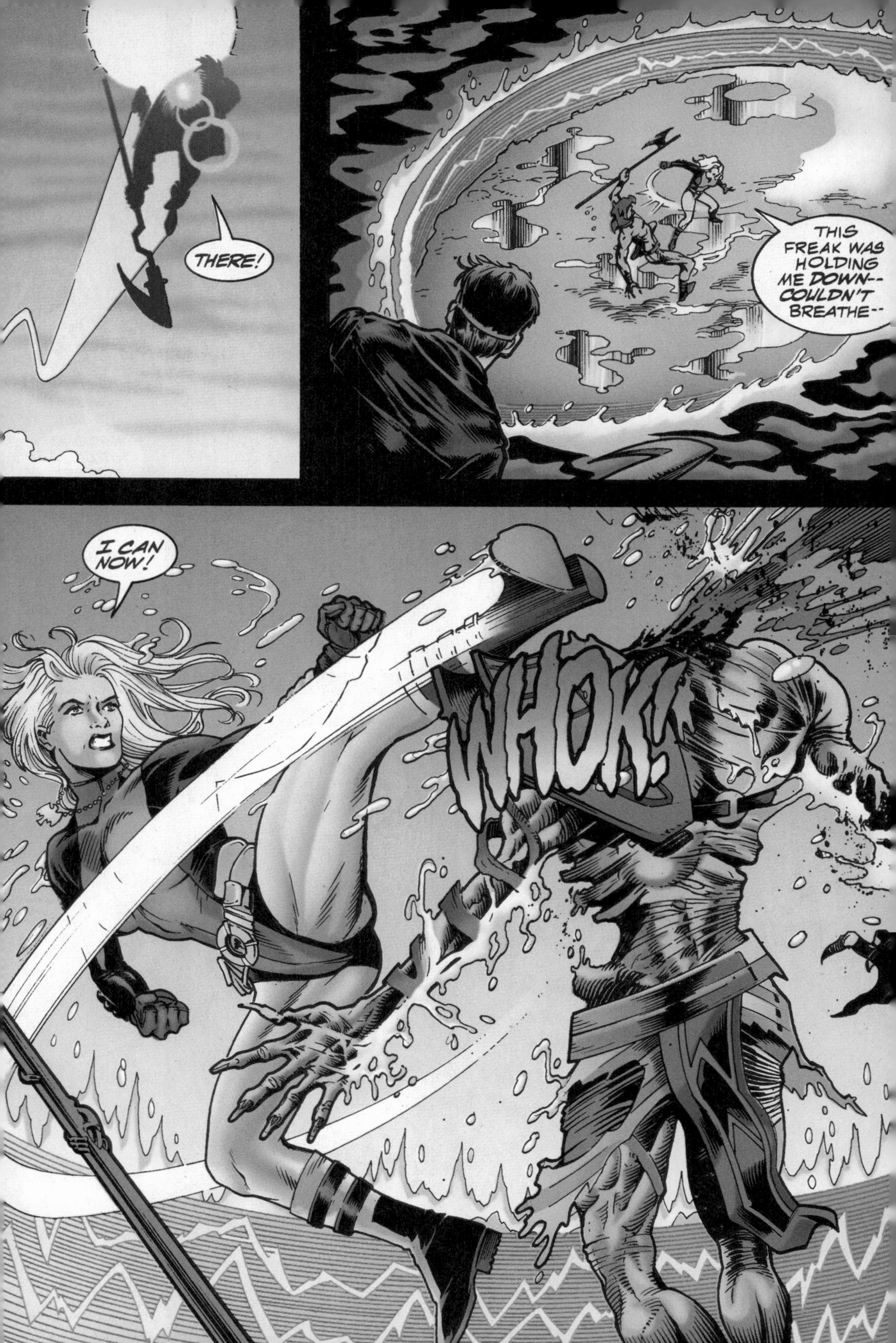
THERE!
THIS FREAK WAS HOLDING ME DOWN-- COULDN'T BREATHE--
I CAN NOW!
WHOK!

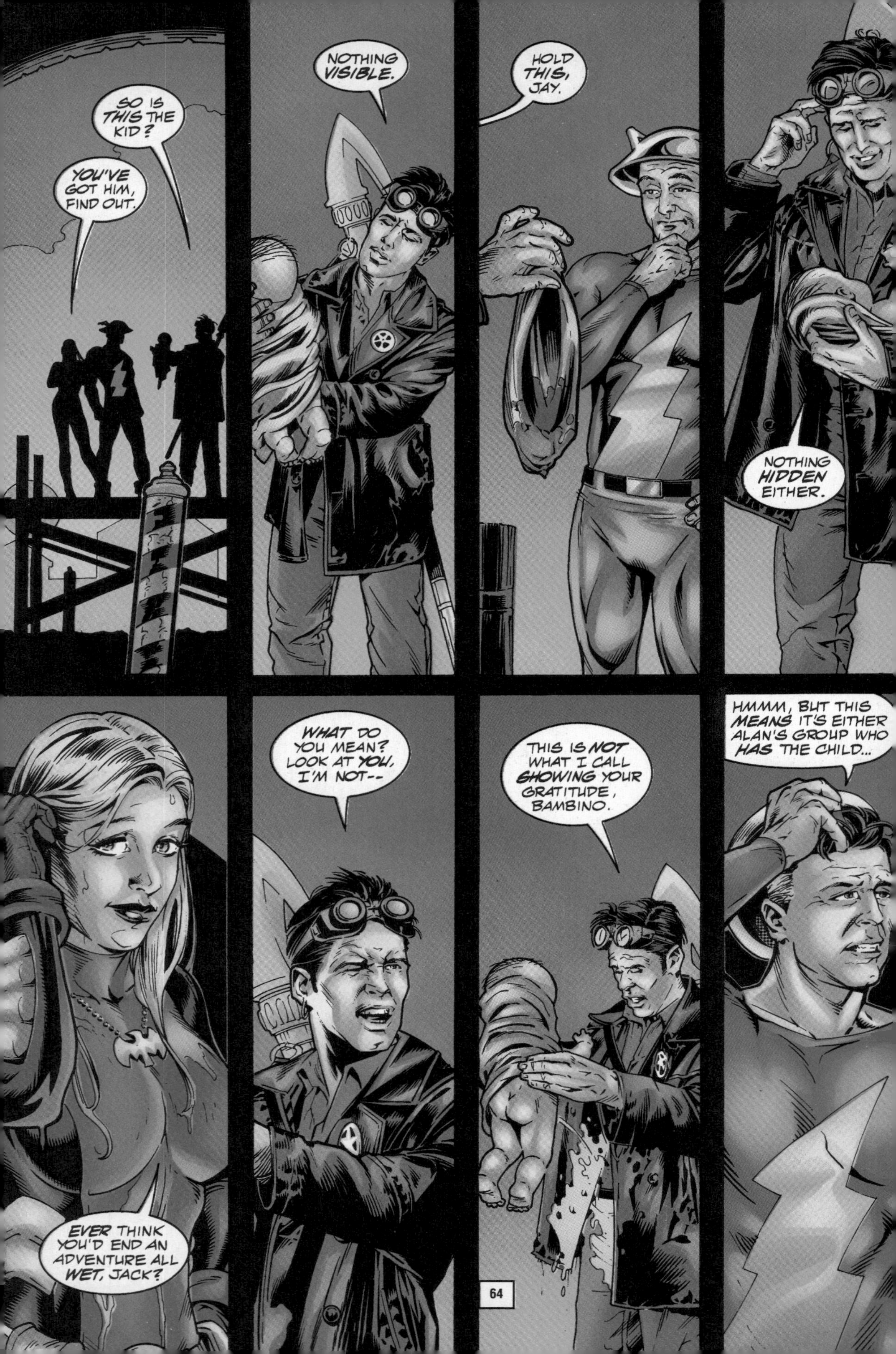
SO IS THIS THE KID?
YOU'VE GOT HIM, FIND OUT.
NOTHING VISIBLE.
HOLD THIS, JAY.
NOTHING HIDDEN EITHER.
EVER THINK YOU'D END AN ADVENTURE ALL WET, JACK?
WHAT DO YOU MEAN? LOOK AT YOU, I'M NOT--
THIS IS NOT WHAT I CALL SHOWING YOUR GRATITUDE, BAMBINO.
HMMM, BUT THIS MEANS IT'S EITHER ALAN'S GROUP WHO HAS THE CHILD...

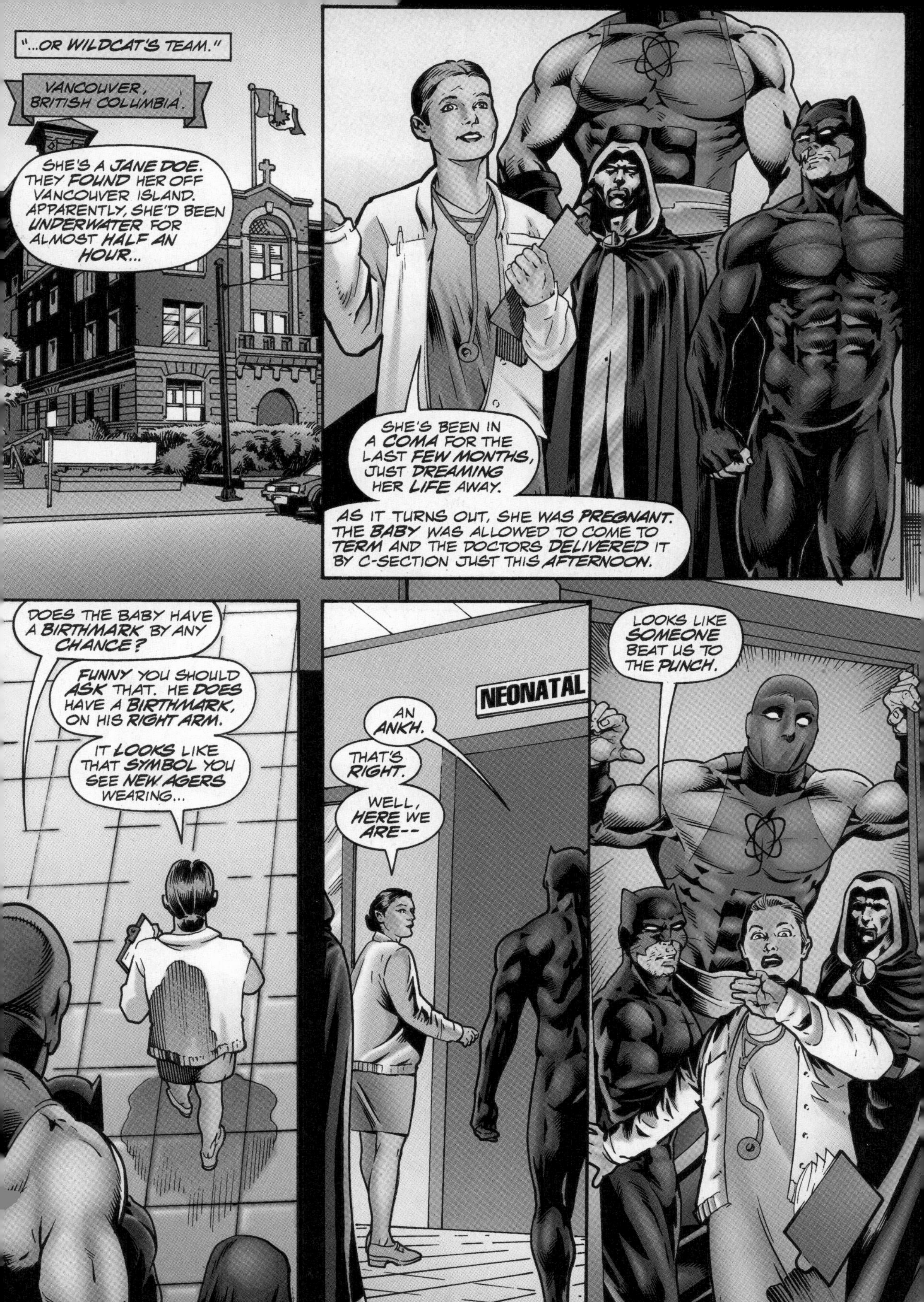

"...OR WILDCAT'S TEAM."
VANCOUVER, BRITISH COLUMBIA.
SHE'S A JANE DOE. THEY FOUND HER OFF VANCOUVER ISLAND. APPARENTLY, SHE'D BEEN UNDERWATER FOR ALMOST HALF AN HOUR...
SHE'S BEEN IN A COMA FOR THE LAST FEW MONTHS, JUST DREAMING HER LIFE AWAY.
AS IT TURNS OUT, SHE WAS PREGNANT. THE BABY WAS ALLOWED TO COME TO TERM AND THE DOCTORS DELIVERED IT BY C-SECTION JUST THIS AFTERNOON.
DOES THE BABY HAVE A BIRTHMARK BY ANY CHANCE?
FUNNY YOU SHOULD ASK THAT. HE DOES HAVE A BIRTHMARK, ON HIS RIGHT ARM.
IT LOOKS LIKE THAT SYMBOL YOU SEE NEW AGERS WEARING...
NEONATAL
AN ANKH.
THAT'S RIGHT.
WELL, HERE WE ARE--
LOOKS LIKE SOMEONE BEAT US TO THE PUNCH.

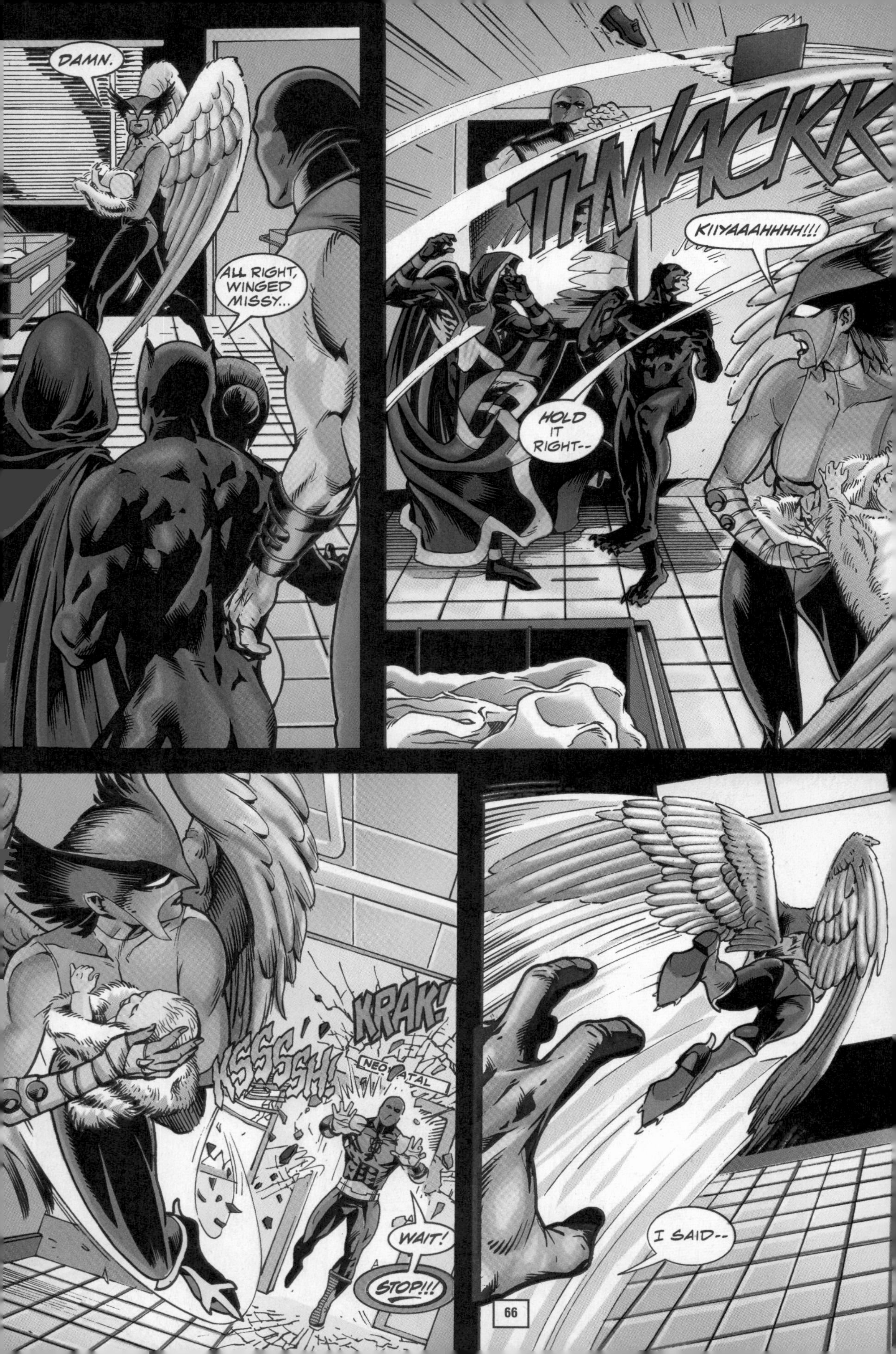
DAMN.
ALL RIGHT, WINGED MISSY...
THWACKK
KIIYAAAHHHH!!!
HOLD IT RIGHT--
KSSSSH!
KRAK!
NEONATAL
WAIT!
STOP!!!
I SAID--

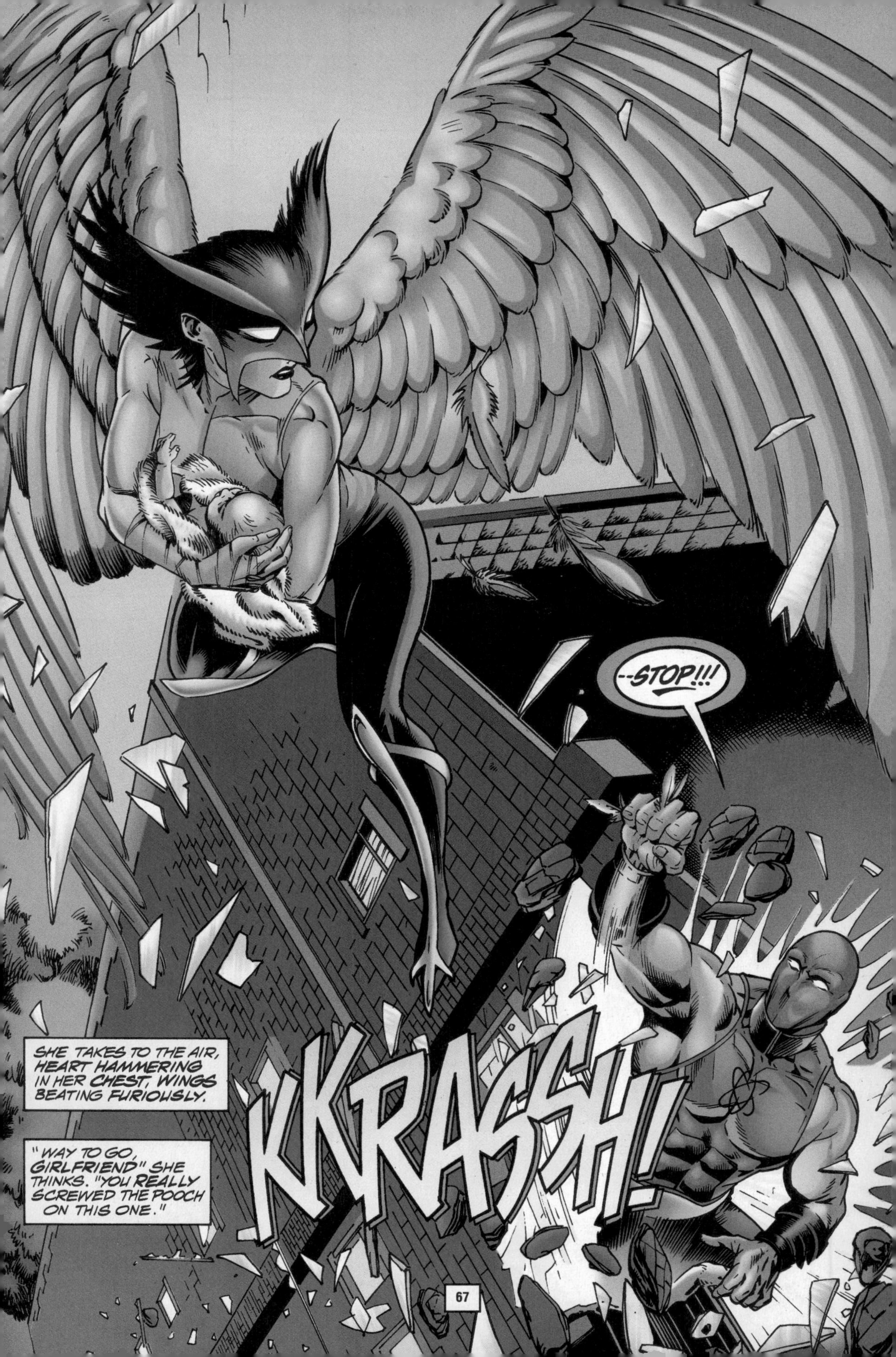
--STOP!!!
SHE TAKES TO THE AIR, HEART HAMMERING IN HER CHEST, WINGS BEATING FURIOUSLY.
"WAY TO GO, GIRLFRIEND" SHE THINKS. "YOU REALLY SCREWED THE POOCH ON THIS ONE."
KKRASSH!

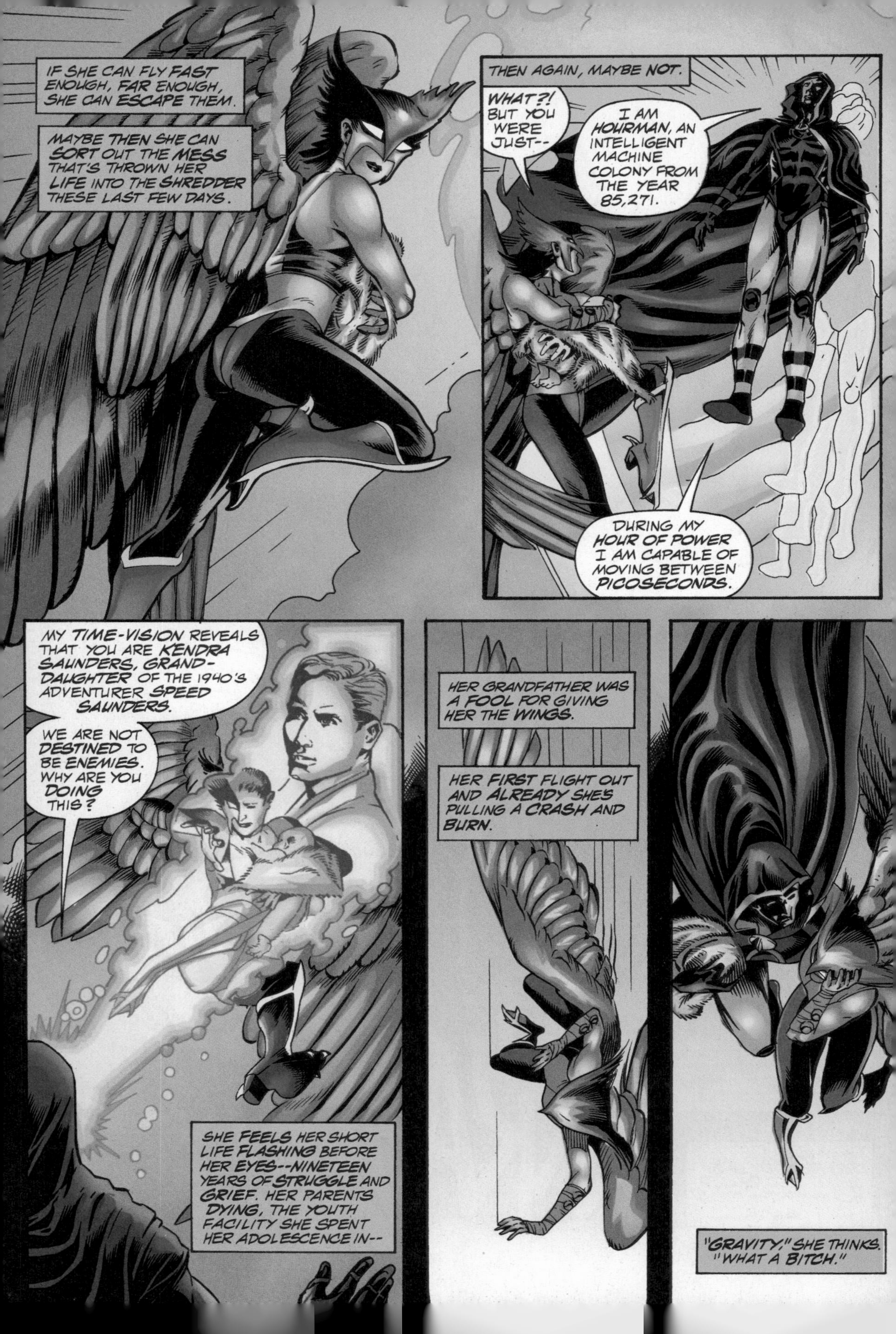
IF SHE CAN FLY FAST ENOUGH, FAR ENOUGH, SHE CAN ESCAPE THEM.
MAYBE THEN SHE CAN SORT OUT THE MESS THAT'S THROWN HER LIFE INTO THE SHREDDER THESE LAST FEW DAYS.
THEN AGAIN, MAYBE NOT.
WHAT?! BUT YOU WERE JUST--
I AM HOURMAN, AN INTELLIGENT MACHINE COLONY FROM THE YEAR 85,271.
DURING MY HOUR OF POWER I AM CAPABLE OF MOVING BETWEEN PICOSECONDS.
MY TIME-VISION REVEALS THAT YOU ARE KENDRA SAUNDERS, GRAND-DAUGHTER OF THE 1940'S ADVENTURER SPEED SAUNDERS.
WE ARE NOT DESTINED TO BE ENEMIES. WHY ARE YOU DOING THIS?
SHE FEELS HER SHORT LIFE FLASHING BEFORE HER EYES--NINETEEN YEARS OF STRUGGLE AND GRIEF. HER PARENTS DYING, THE YOUTH FACILITY SHE SPENT HER ADOLESCENCE IN--
HER GRANDFATHER WAS A FOOL FOR GIVING HER THE WINGS.
HER FIRST FLIGHT OUT AND ALREADY SHE'S PULLING A CRASH AND BURN.
"GRAVITY," SHE THINKS. "WHAT A BITCH."

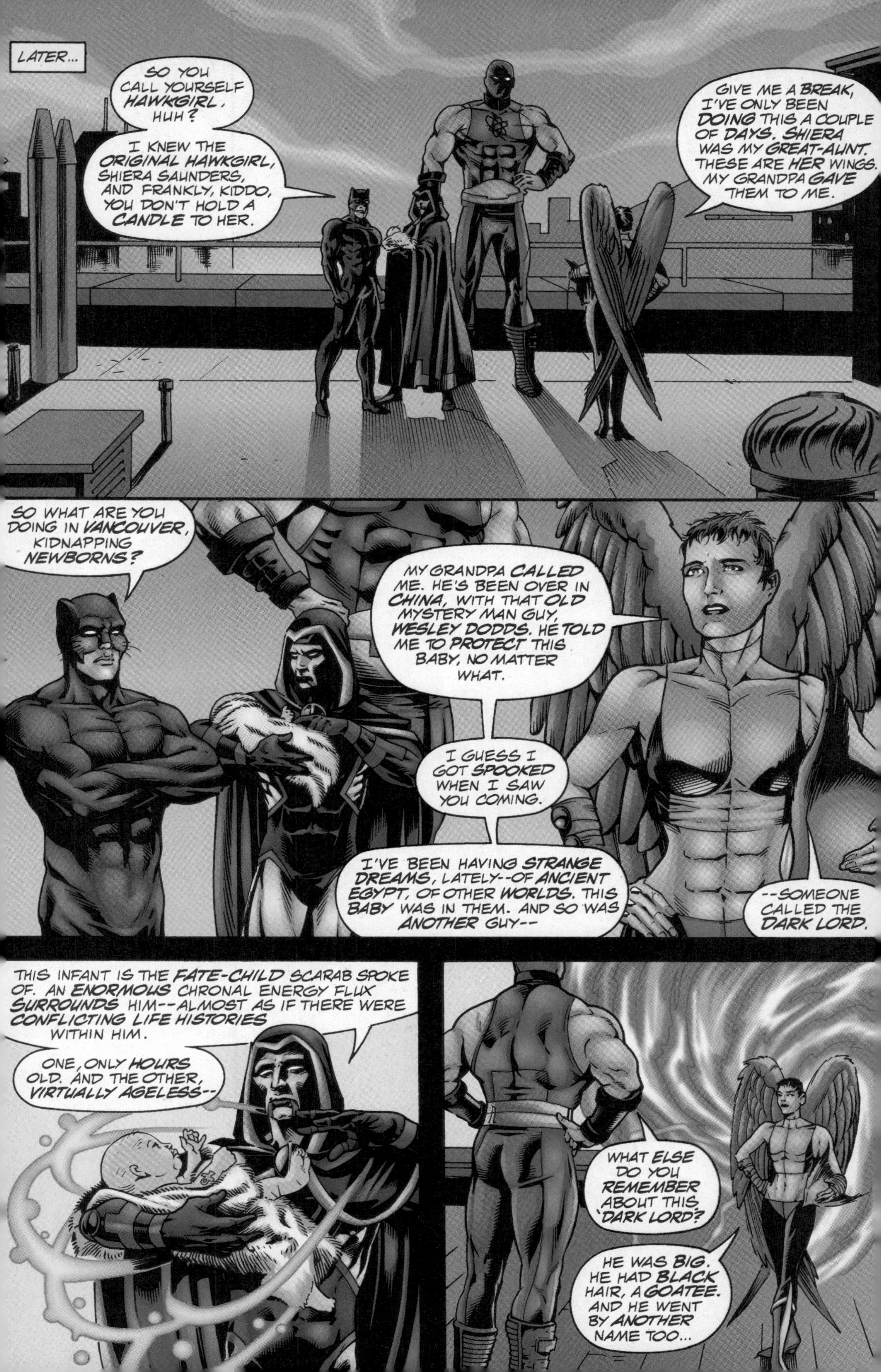
LATER...
SO YOU CALL YOURSELF HAWKGIRL, HUH?
I KNEW THE ORIGINAL HAWKGIRL, SHIERA SAUNDERS, AND FRANKLY, KIDDO, YOU DON'T HOLD A CANDLE TO HER.
GIVE ME A BREAK, I'VE ONLY BEEN DOING THIS A COUPLE OF DAYS. SHIERA WAS MY GREAT-AUNT. THESE ARE HER WINGS. MY GRANDPA GAVE THEM TO ME.
SO WHAT ARE YOU DOING IN VANCOUVER, KIDNAPPING NEWBORNS?
MY GRANDPA CALLED ME. HE'S BEEN OVER IN CHINA, WITH THAT OLD MYSTERY MAN GUY, WESLEY DODDS. HE TOLD ME TO PROTECT THIS BABY, NO MATTER WHAT.
I GUESS I GOT SPOOKED WHEN I SAW YOU COMING.
I'VE BEEN HAVING STRANGE DREAMS, LATELY--OF ANCIENT EGYPT, OF OTHER WORLDS. THIS BABY WAS IN THEM. AND SO WAS ANOTHER GUY--
--SOMEONE CALLED THE DARK LORD.
THIS INFANT IS THE FATE-CHILD SCARAB SPOKE OF. AN ENORMOUS CHRONAL ENERGY FLUX SURROUNDS HIM--ALMOST AS IF THERE WERE CONFLICTING LIFE HISTORIES WITHIN HIM.
ONE, ONLY HOURS OLD. AND THE OTHER, VIRTUALLY AGELESS--
WHAT ELSE DO YOU REMEMBER ABOUT THIS 'DARK LORD'?
HE WAS BIG. HE HAD BLACK HAIR, A GOATEE. AND HE WENT BY ANOTHER NAME TOO...

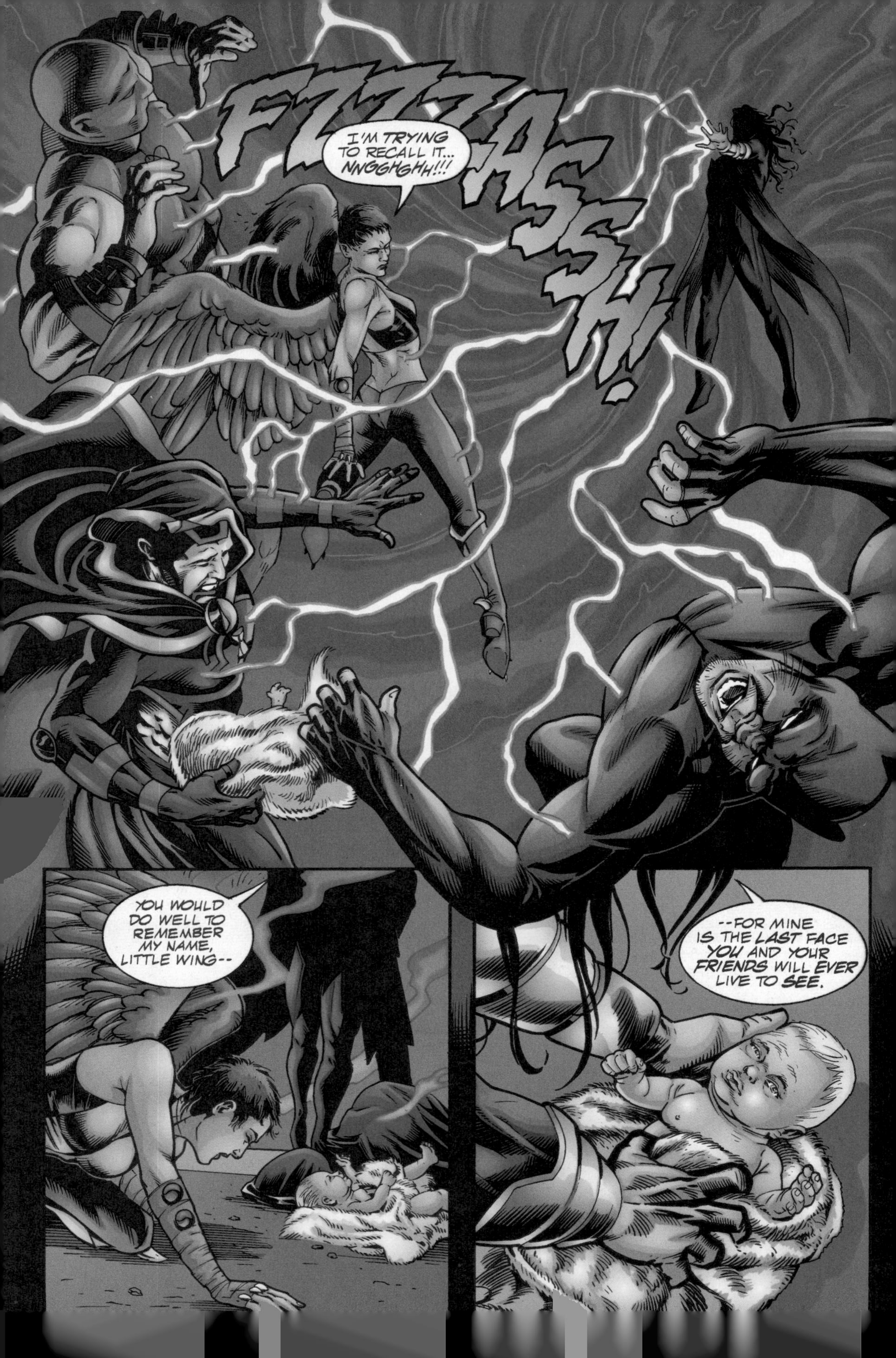
FZZZAASSH!
I'M TRYING TO RECALL IT... NNGGHGHH!!!
YOU WOULD DO WELL TO REMEMBER MY NAME, LITTLE WING--
--FOR MINE IS THE LAST FACE YOU AND YOUR FRIENDS WILL EVER LIVE TO SEE.

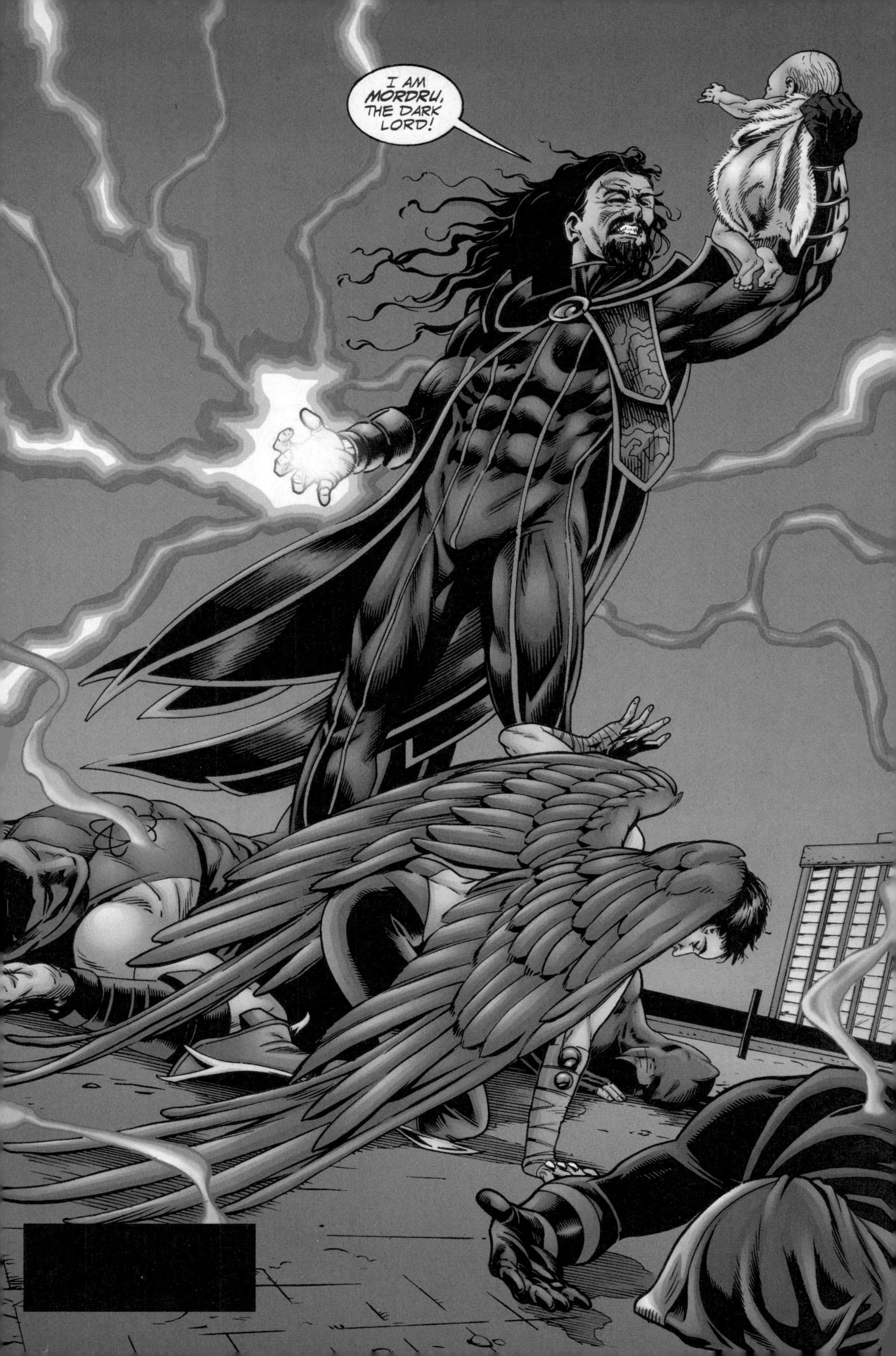
I AM MORDRU, THE DARK LORD!
[redacted]

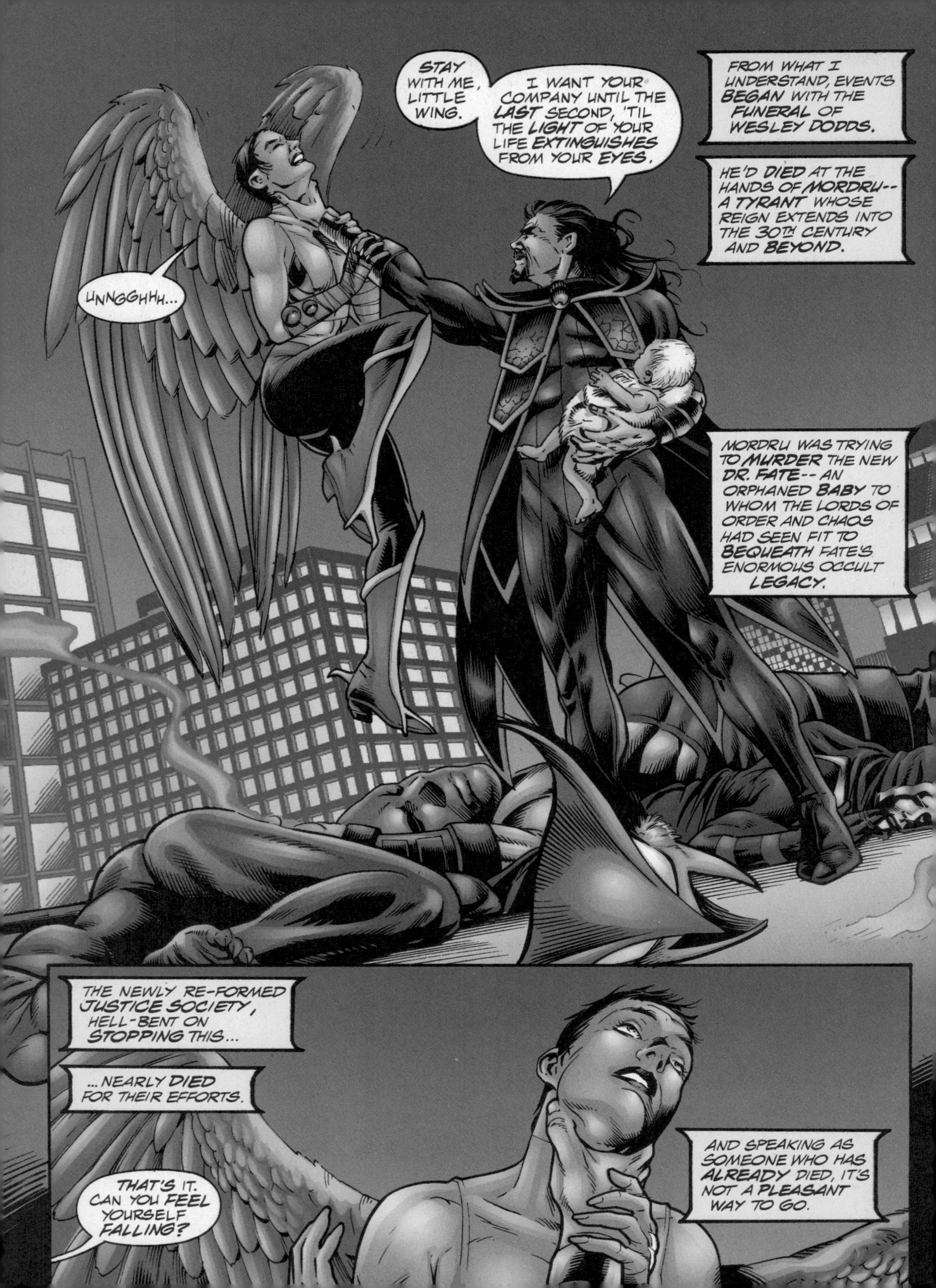
STAY WITH ME, LITTLE WING.
I WANT YOUR COMPANY UNTIL THE LAST SECOND, 'TIL THE LIGHT OF YOUR LIFE EXTINGUISHES FROM YOUR EYES.
FROM WHAT I UNDERSTAND, EVENTS BEGAN WITH THE FUNERAL OF WESLEY DODDS.
HE'D DIED AT THE HANDS OF MORDRU-- A TYRANT WHOSE REIGN EXTENDS INTO THE 30TH CENTURY AND BEYOND.
UNNGGHHH...
MORDRU WAS TRYING TO MURDER THE NEW DR. FATE-- AN ORPHANED BABY TO WHOM THE LORDS OF ORDER AND CHAOS HAD SEEN FIT TO BEQUEATH FATE'S ENORMOUS OCCULT LEGACY.
THE NEWLY RE-FORMED JUSTICE SOCIETY, HELL-BENT ON STOPPING THIS...
...NEARLY DIED FOR THEIR EFFORTS.
THAT'S IT. CAN YOU FEEL YOURSELF FALLING?
AND SPEAKING AS SOMEONE WHO HAS ALREADY DIED, IT'S NOT A PLEASANT WAY TO GO.

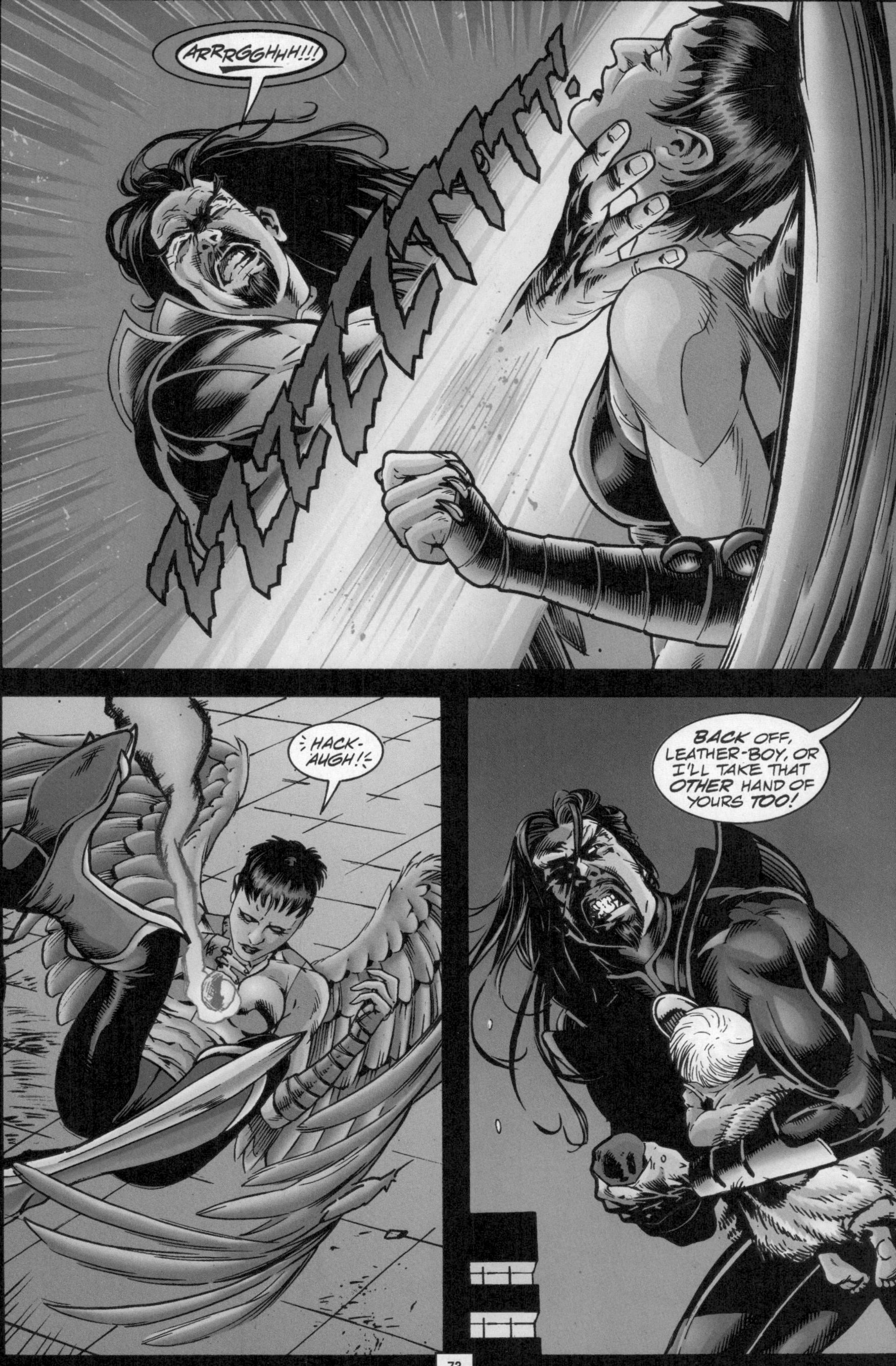
ARRRGGHHH!!!
HACK-AUGH!
BACK OFF, LEATHER-BOY, OR I'LL TAKE THAT OTHER HAND OF YOURS TOO!

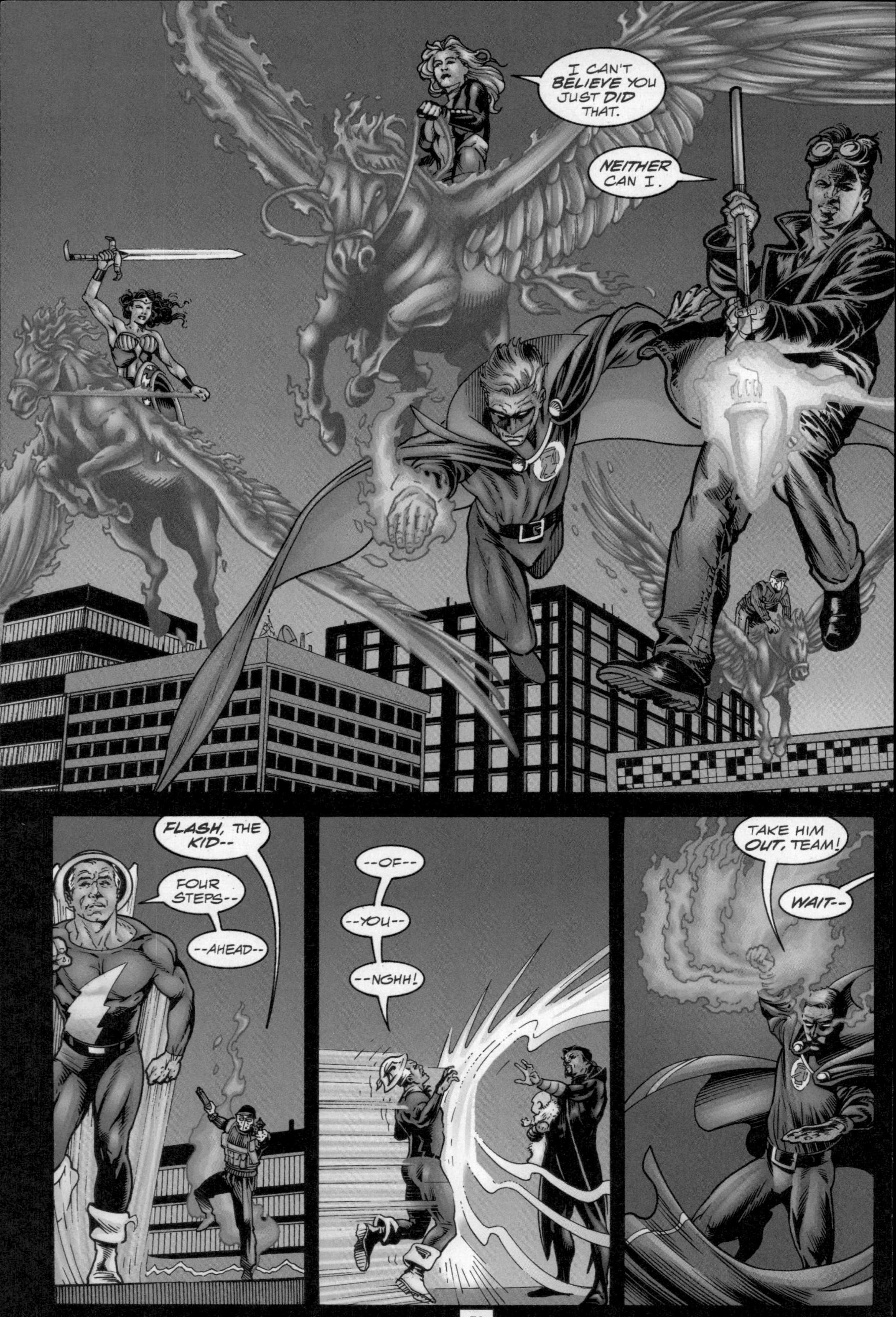
I CAN'T BELIEVE YOU JUST DID THAT.
NEITHER CAN I.
FLASH, THE KID--
FOUR STEPS--
--AHEAD--
--OF--
--YOU--
--NGHH!
TAKE HIM OUT, TEAM!
WAIT--

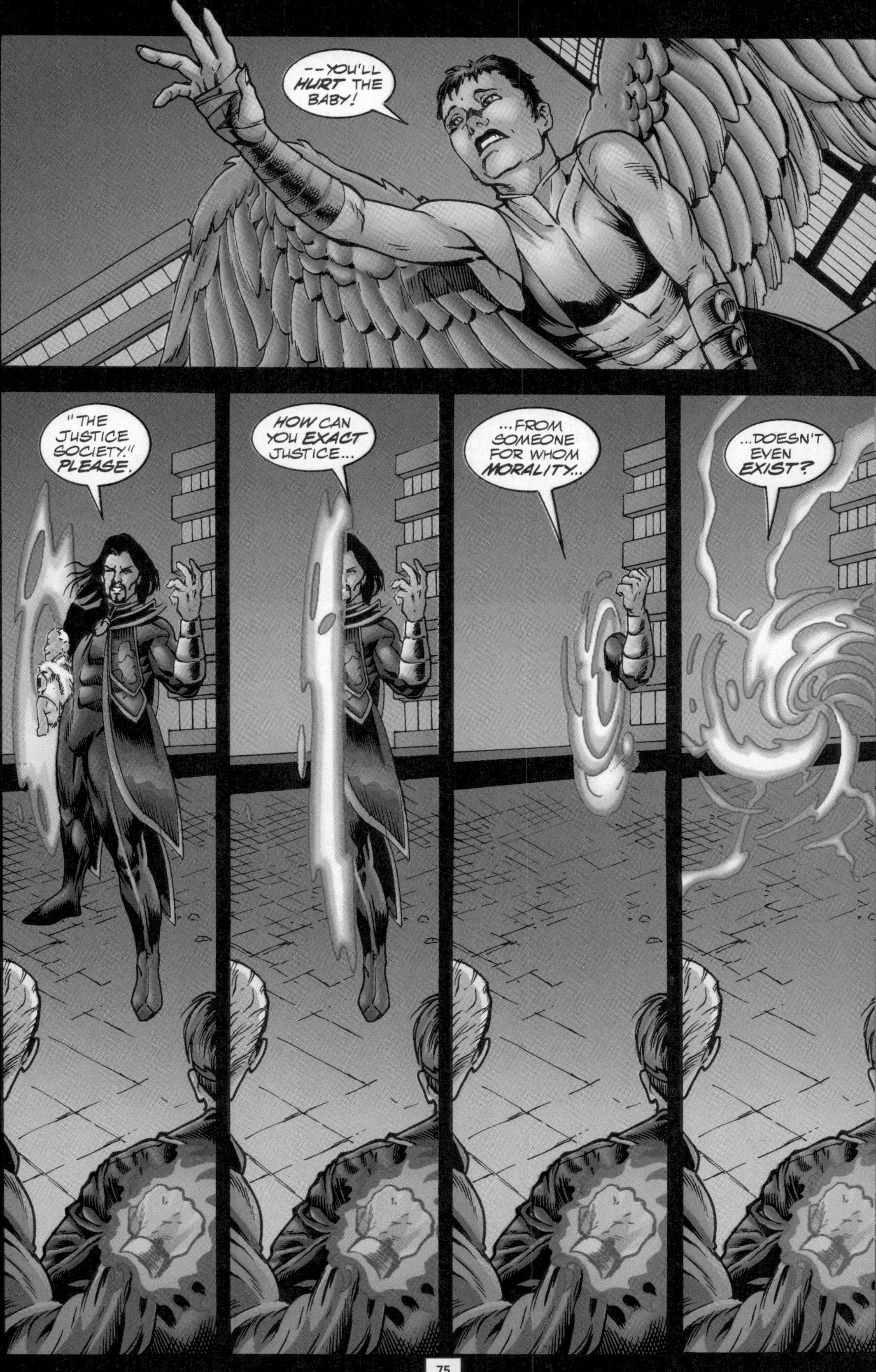
--YOU'LL HURT THE BABY!
"THE JUSTICE SOCIETY." PLEASE.
HOW CAN YOU EXACT JUSTICE...
...FROM SOMEONE FOR WHOM MORALITY...
...DOESN'T EVEN EXIST?

SO WHO ARE YOU *SUPPOSED* TO BE?

HAWKGIRL. MY *REAL* NAME'S *KENDRA SAUNDERS.* IT'S KIND OF A *LONG* STORY.

WE'VE GOT *TIME* TO PLAY CATCH-UP *LATER.* OUR *IMMEDIATE* CONCERN IS THE *DARK LORD.*

HE SAID HIS NAME WAS *MORDRU*--

I'VE *HEARD* OF HIM, ATOM-SMASHER. I'VE SPENT *TIME* IN THE 30TH CENTURY. THIS CAT *STOMPED* THE LEGION OF SUPER HEROES BUT GOOD.

THEN WHAT IS HE *DOING* IN *OUR* TIME, *STARMAN?*

THE MORDRU WE ENCOUNTERED IS *NOT* FROM THE FUTURE, HIPPOLYTA. HE EXISTS *NOW,* IN OUR *PRESENT.* HE'S NOT *DESTINED* TO MENACE THE LEGION FOR ANOTHER *THOUSAND* YEARS.

MEANING *WHAT,* HOURMAN? THE GUY'S *IMMORTAL* OR SOMETHING?

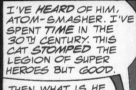

BEFORE I LOST CONSCIOUSNESS, I *ATTEMPTED* TO USE MY TIME-VISION TO *DEVOLVE* HIM BACK ALONG HIS PERSONAL TIME-LINE TO AN AGE WHERE HE WAS NOT SO POWERFUL.

BUT HIS TIME-LINE HAS NO *BEGINNING* OR *END.* AS NEAR AS I CAN TELL, MORDRU WAS NEVER *BOR[N]* NOR WILL HE EVER *DIE.*

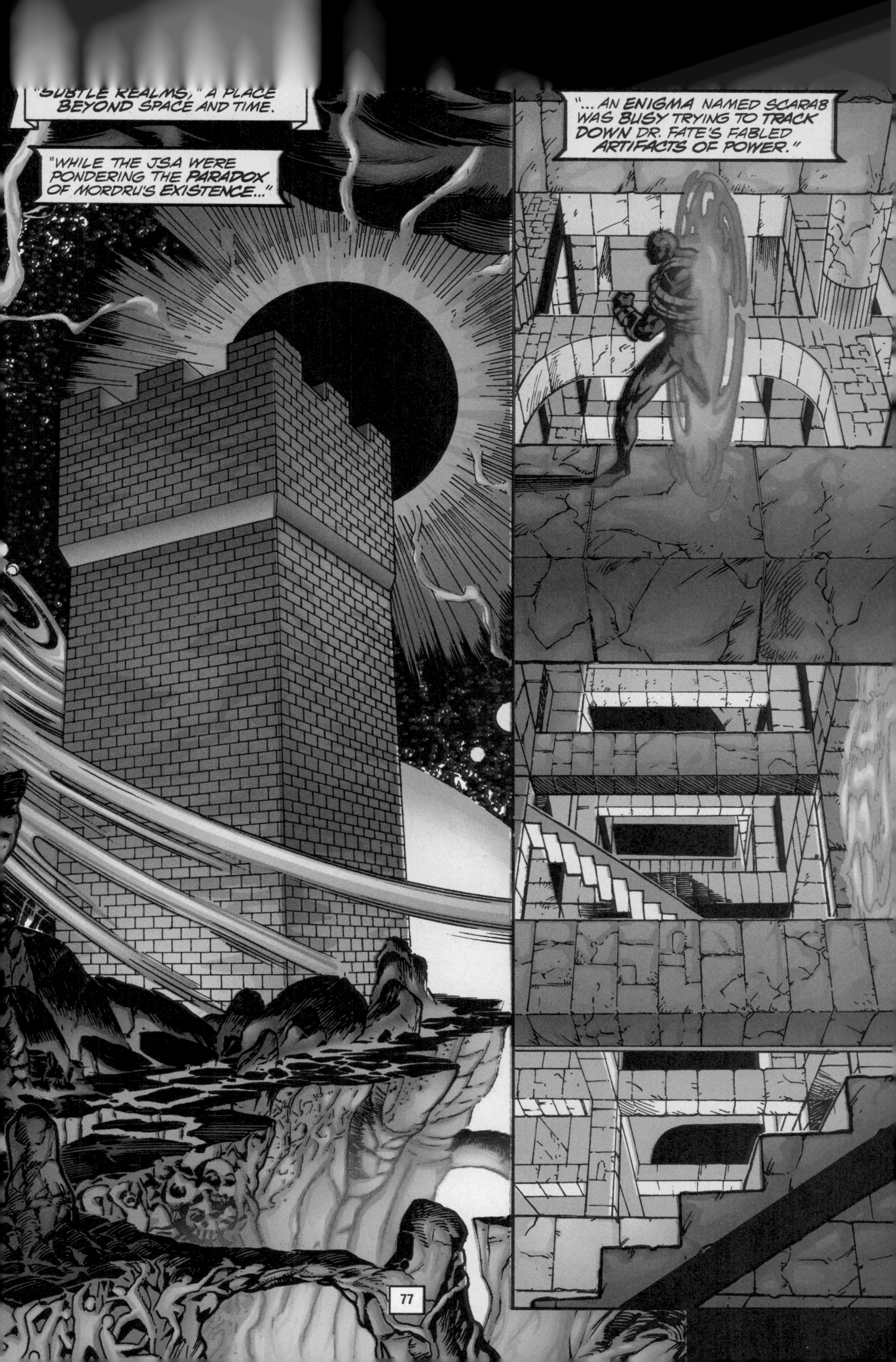
"SUBTLE REALMS," A PLACE BEYOND SPACE AND TIME.
"WHILE THE JSA WERE PONDERING THE PARADOX OF MORDRU'S EXISTENCE..."
"...AN ENIGMA NAMED SCARAB WAS BUSY TRYING TO TRACK DOWN DR. FATE'S FABLED ARTIFACTS OF POWER."

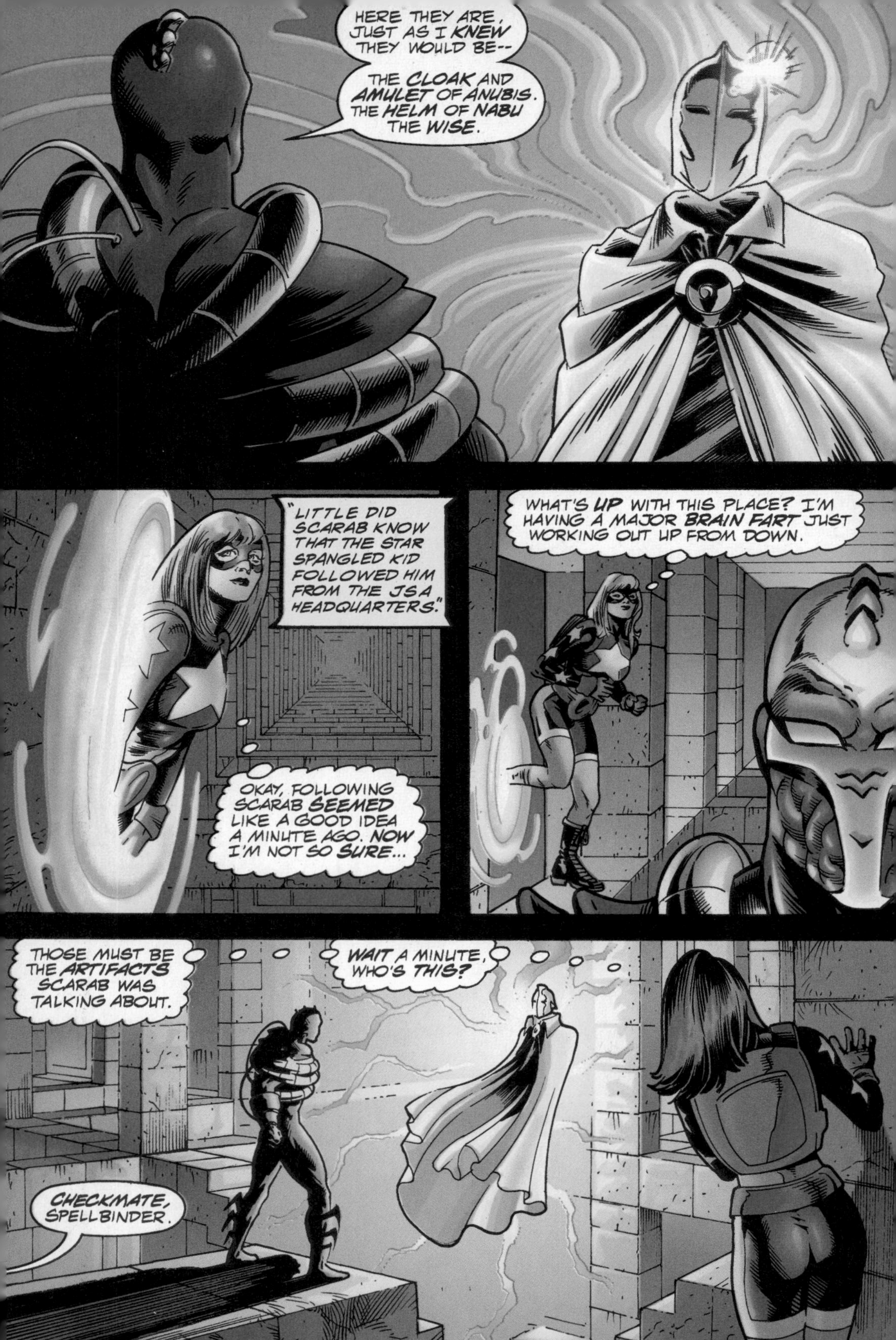
HERE THEY ARE, JUST AS I KNEW THEY WOULD BE--
THE CLOAK AND AMULET OF ANUBIS. THE HELM OF NABU THE WISE.
"LITTLE DID SCARAB KNOW THAT THE STAR SPANGLED KID FOLLOWED HIM FROM THE JSA HEADQUARTERS."
OKAY, FOLLOWING SCARAB SEEMED LIKE A GOOD IDEA A MINUTE AGO. NOW I'M NOT SO SURE...
WHAT'S UP WITH THIS PLACE? I'M HAVING A MAJOR BRAIN FART JUST WORKING OUT UP FROM DOWN.
THOSE MUST BE THE ARTIFACTS SCARAB WAS TALKING ABOUT.
WAIT A MINUTE, WHO'S THIS?
CHECKMATE, SPELLBINDER.

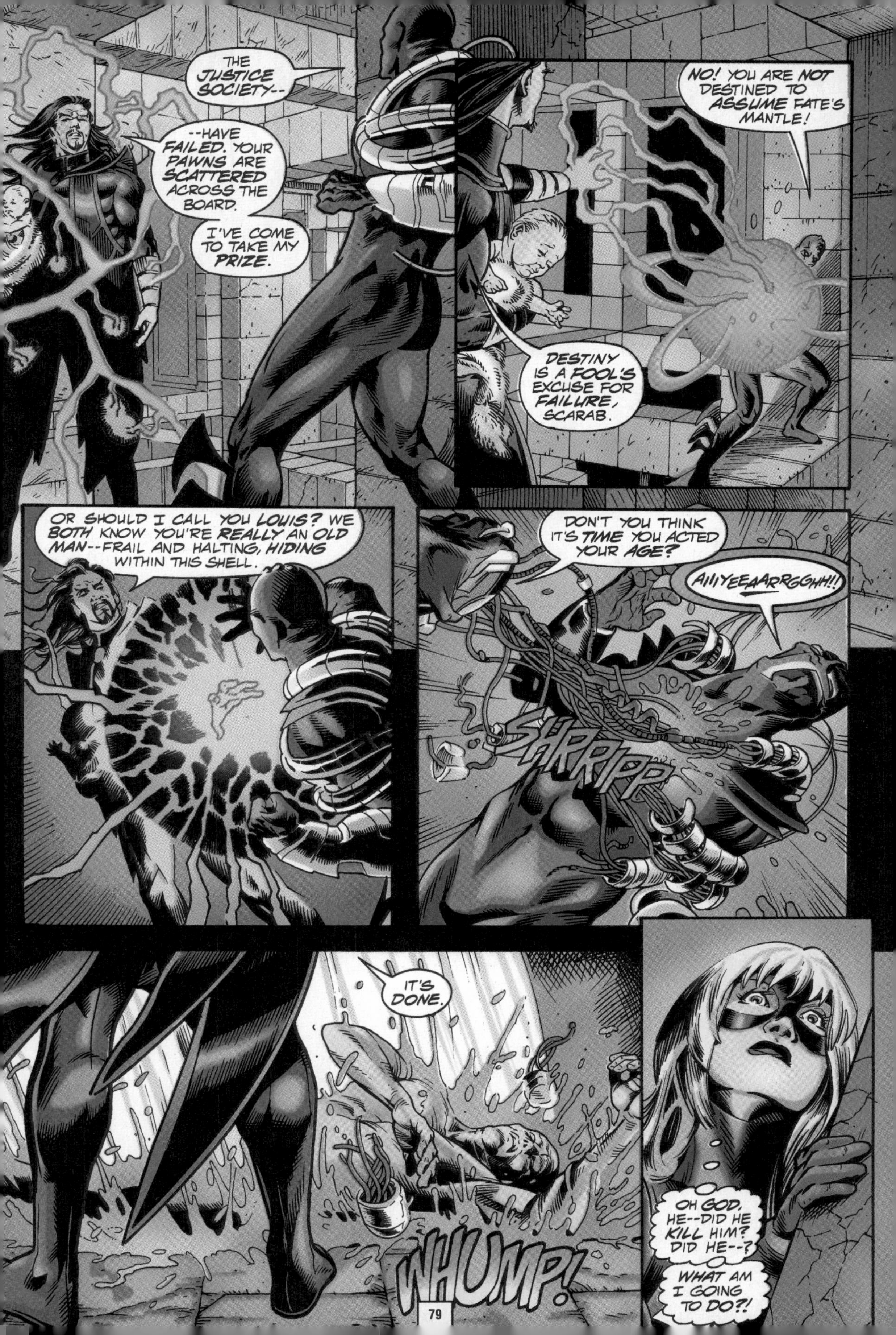
THE JUSTICE SOCIETY--
--HAVE FAILED. YOUR PAWNS ARE SCATTERED ACROSS THE BOARD.
I'VE COME TO TAKE MY PRIZE.
NO! YOU ARE NOT DESTINED TO ASSUME FATE'S MANTLE!
DESTINY IS A FOOL'S EXCUSE FOR FAILURE, SCARAB.
OR SHOULD I CALL YOU LOUIS? WE BOTH KNOW YOU'RE REALLY AN OLD MAN--FRAIL AND HALTING, HIDING WITHIN THIS SHELL.
DON'T YOU THINK IT'S TIME YOU ACTED YOUR AGE?
AIIIYEEAARRGGHH!!
SHRRIPP
IT'S DONE.
WHUMP!
OH GOD, HE--DID HE KILL HIM? DID HE--?
WHAT AM I GOING TO DO?!

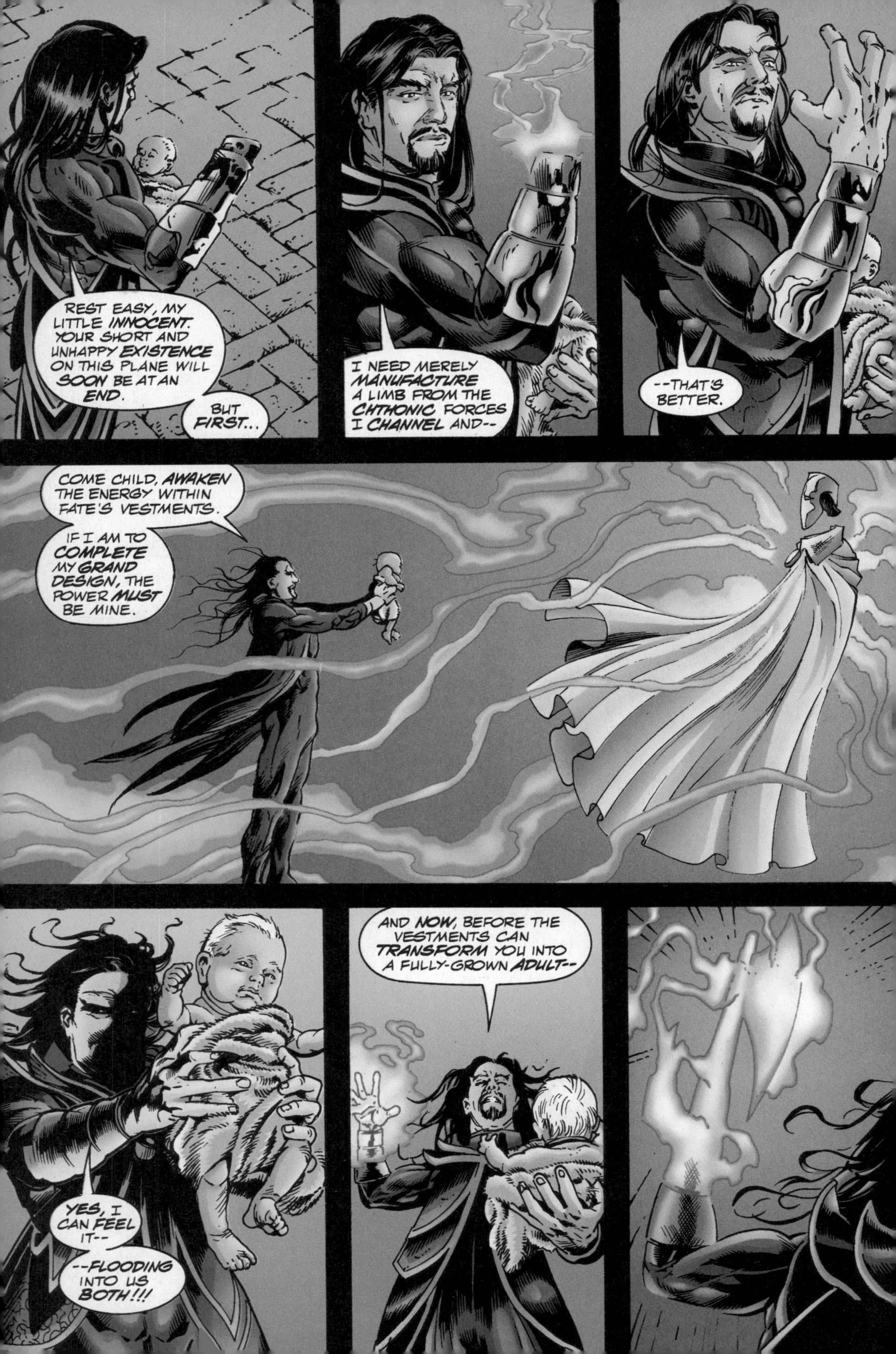

REST EASY, MY LITTLE INNOCENT. YOUR SHORT AND UNHAPPY EXISTENCE ON THIS PLANE WILL SOON BE AT AN END.
BUT FIRST...
I NEED MERELY MANUFACTURE A LIMB FROM THE CHTHONIC FORCES I CHANNEL AND--
--THAT'S BETTER.
COME CHILD, AWAKEN THE ENERGY WITHIN FATE'S VESTMENTS.
IF I AM TO COMPLETE MY GRAND DESIGN, THE POWER MUST BE MINE.
YES, I CAN FEEL IT--
--FLOODING INTO US BOTH!!!
AND NOW, BEFORE THE VESTMENTS CAN TRANSFORM YOU INTO A FULLY-GROWN ADULT--

HEY!!!

TOUCH THAT BABY AND I'LL KILL YOU, I SWEAR!

THOK!

HAHAHA HAHAHAHA HAHAHA!

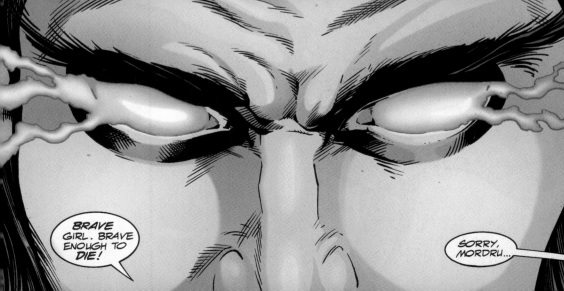

BRAVE GIRL. BRAVE ENOUGH TO DIE!

SORRY, MORDRU...

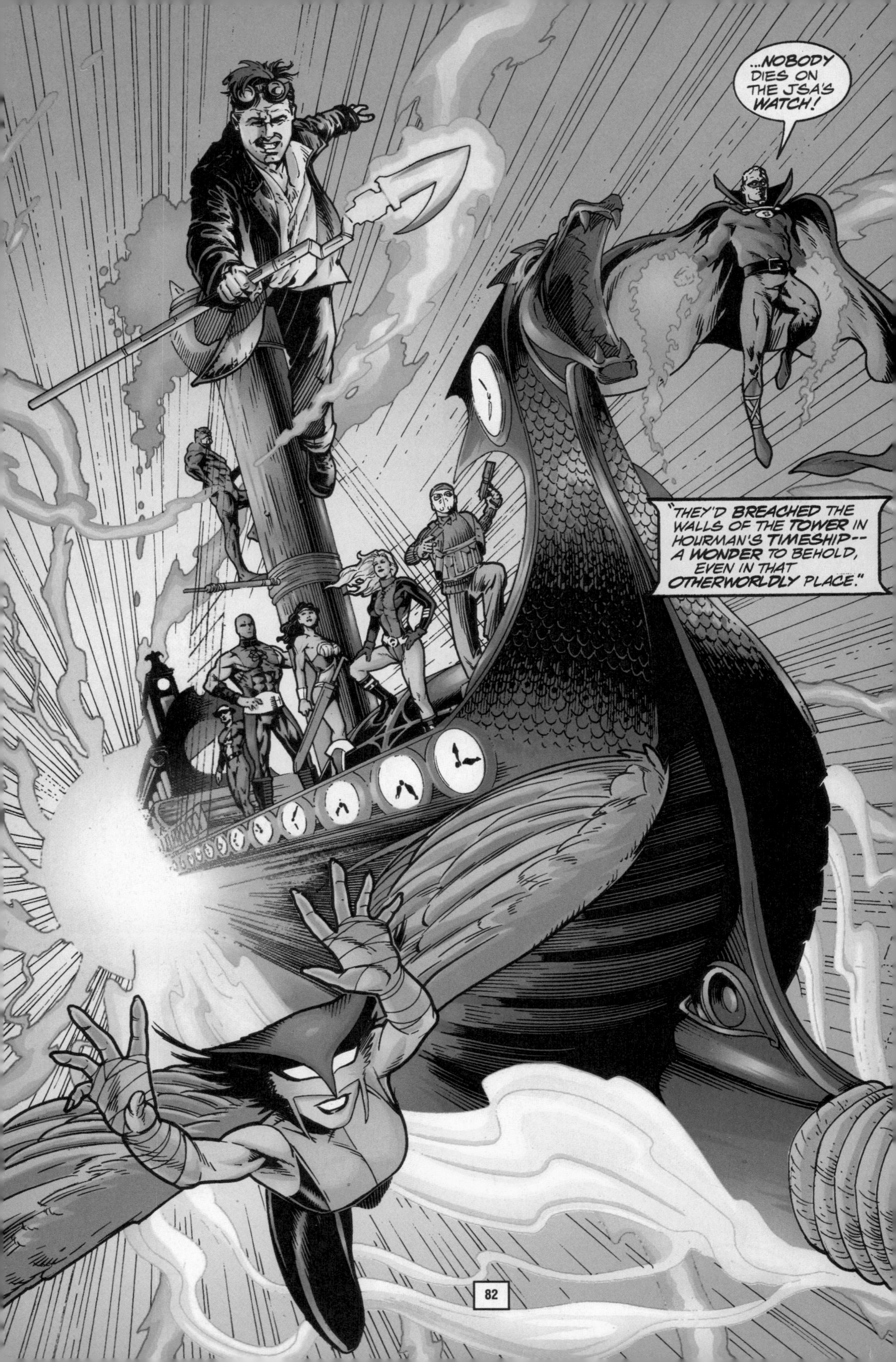
...NOBODY DIES ON THE JSA'S WATCH!
"THEY'D BREACHED THE WALLS OF THE TOWER IN HOURMAN'S TIMESHIP-- A WONDER TO BEHOLD, EVEN IN THAT OTHERWORLDLY PLACE."

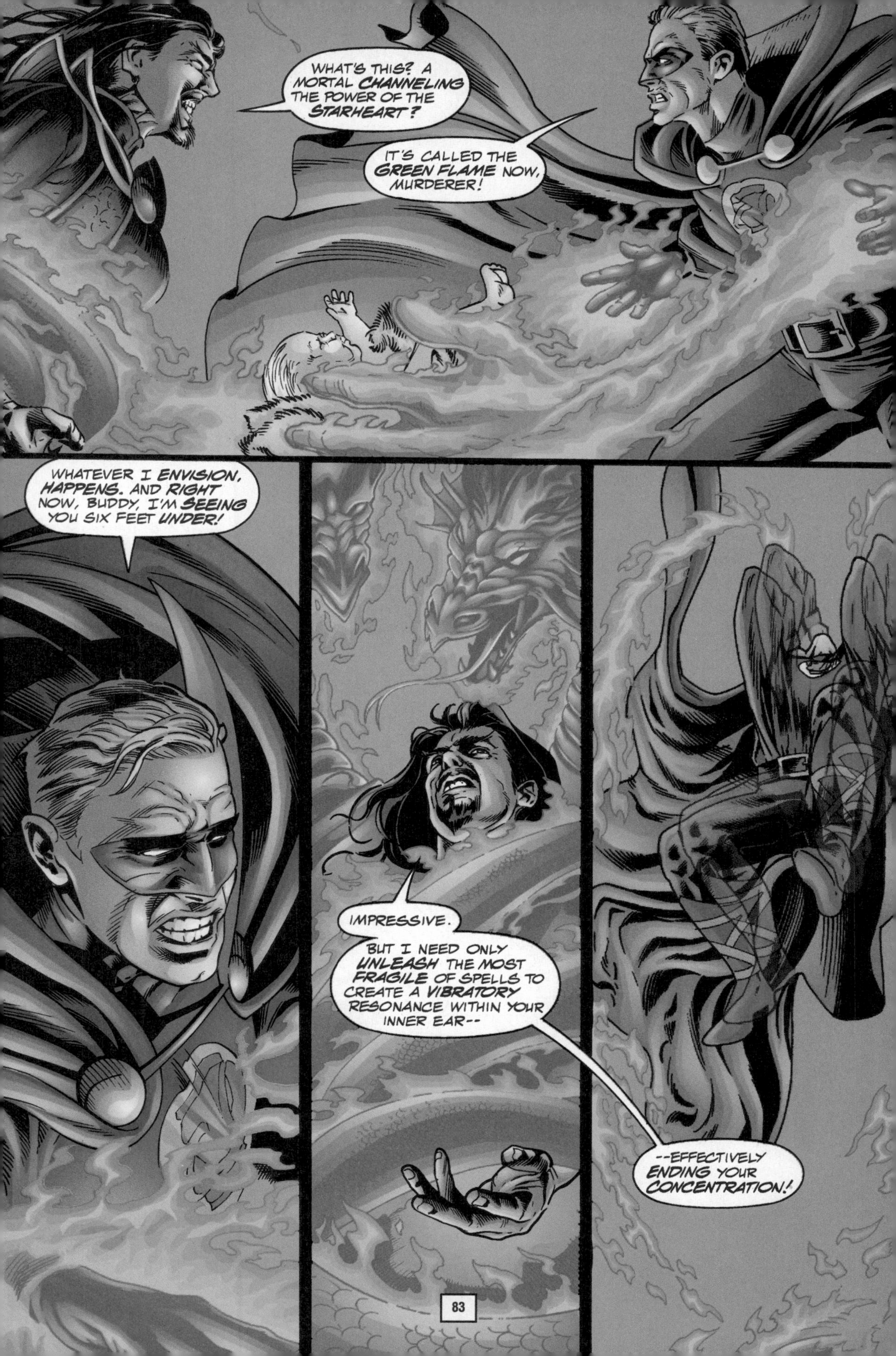
WHAT'S THIS? A MORTAL CHANNELING THE POWER OF THE STARHEART?
IT'S CALLED THE GREEN FLAME NOW, MURDERER!
WHATEVER I ENVISION, HAPPENS. AND RIGHT NOW, BUDDY, I'M SEEING YOU SIX FEET UNDER!
IMPRESSIVE.
BUT I NEED ONLY UNLEASH THE MOST FRAGILE OF SPELLS TO CREATE A VIBRATORY RESONANCE WITHIN YOUR INNER EAR--
--EFFECTIVELY ENDING YOUR CONCENTRATION!

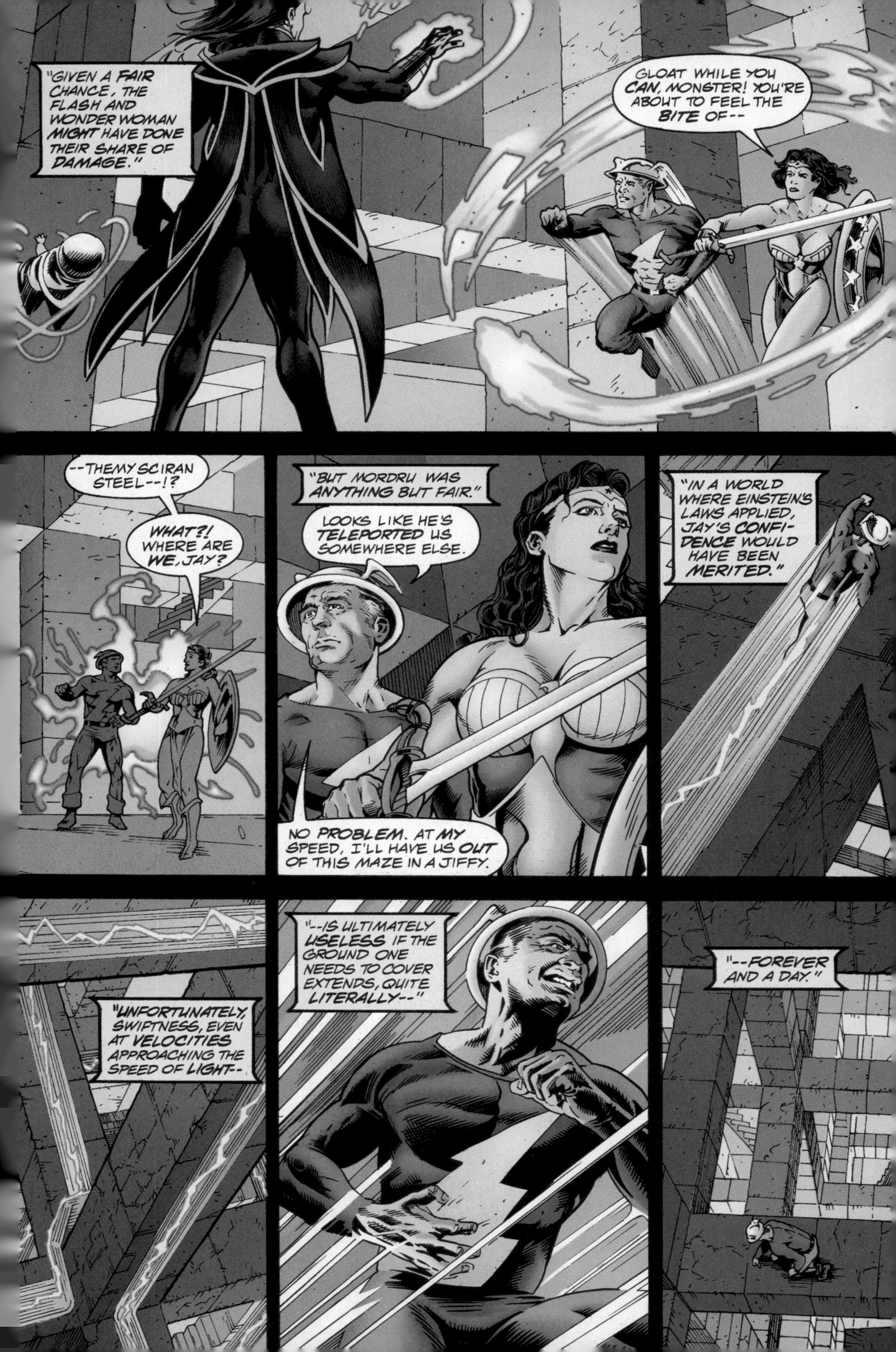
"GIVEN A FAIR CHANCE, THE FLASH AND WONDER WOMAN MIGHT HAVE DONE THEIR SHARE OF DAMAGE."
GLOAT WHILE YOU CAN, MONSTER! YOU'RE ABOUT TO FEEL THE BITE OF--
--THEMYSCIRAN STEEL--!?
WHAT?! WHERE ARE WE, JAY?
"BUT MORDRU WAS ANYTHING BUT FAIR."
LOOKS LIKE HE'S TELEPORTED US SOMEWHERE ELSE.
NO PROBLEM. AT MY SPEED, I'LL HAVE US OUT OF THIS MAZE IN A JIFFY.
"IN A WORLD WHERE EINSTEIN'S LAWS APPLIED, JAY'S CONFI-DENCE WOULD HAVE BEEN MERITED."
"UNFORTUNATELY, SWIFTNESS, EVEN AT VELOCITIES APPROACHING THE SPEED OF LIGHT--
"--IS ULTIMATELY USELESS IF THE GROUND ONE NEEDS TO COVER EXTENDS, QUITE LITERALLY--"
"--FOREVER AND A DAY."

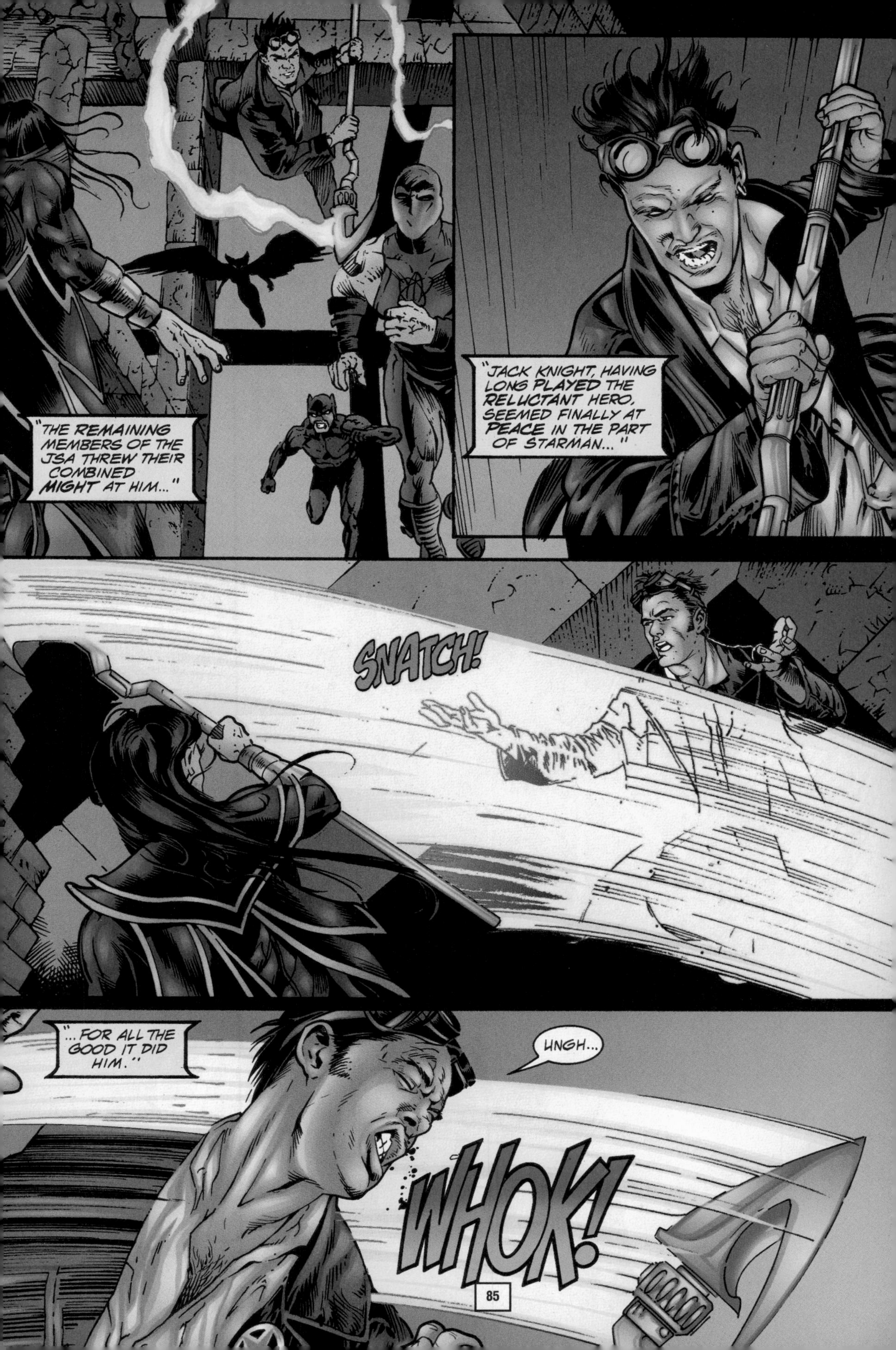
"THE REMAINING MEMBERS OF THE JSA THREW THEIR COMBINED MIGHT AT HIM..."
"JACK KNIGHT, HAVING LONG PLAYED THE RELUCTANT HERO, SEEMED FINALLY AT PEACE IN THE PART OF STARMAN..."
SNATCH!
"...FOR ALL THE GOOD IT DID HIM."
UNGH...
WHOK!

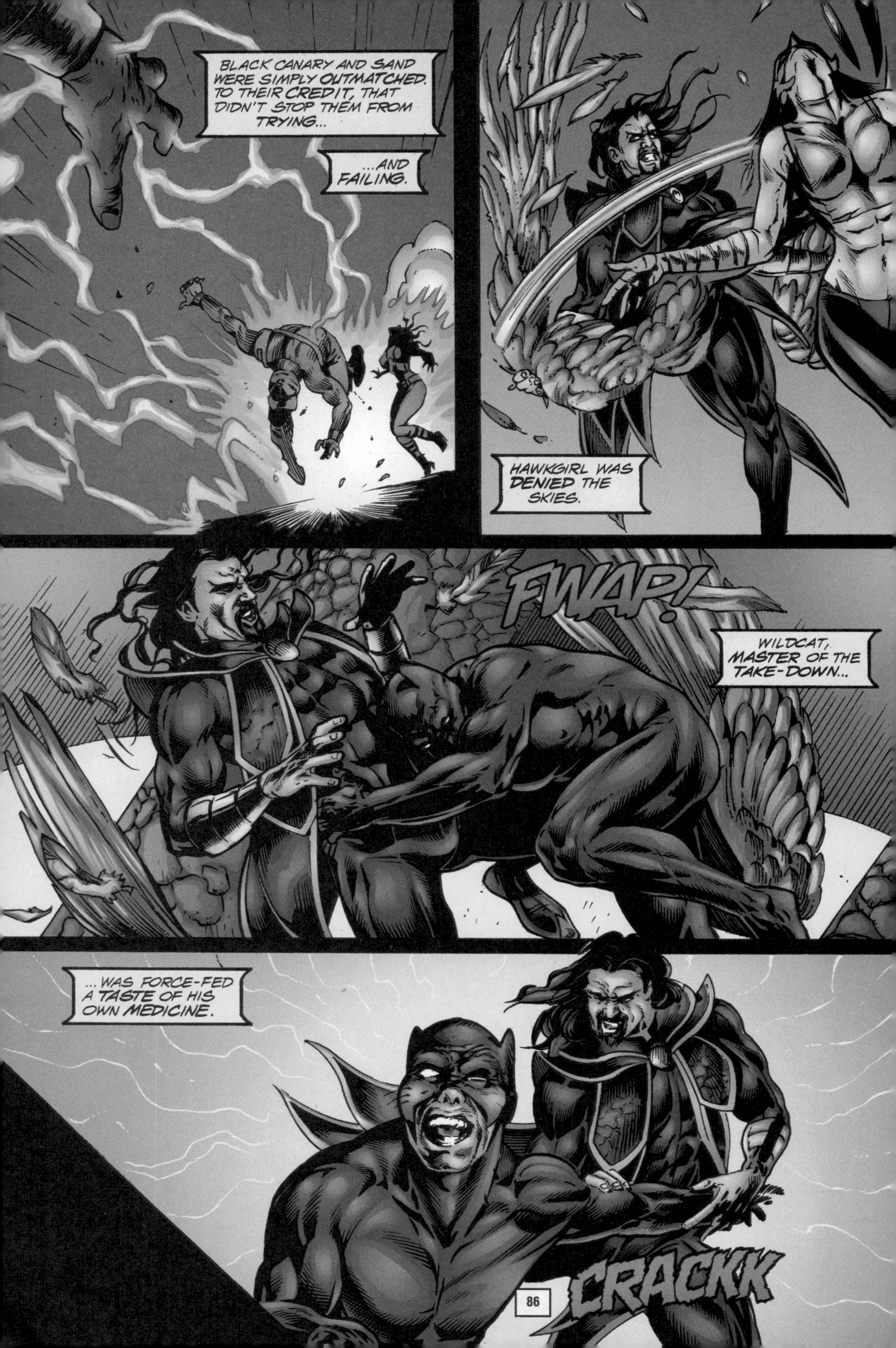
BLACK CANARY AND SAND WERE SIMPLY OUTMATCHED. TO THEIR CREDIT, THAT DIDN'T STOP THEM FROM TRYING...
...AND FAILING.
HAWKGIRL WAS DENIED THE SKIES.
FWAP!
WILDCAT, MASTER OF THE TAKE-DOWN...
...WAS FORCE-FED A TASTE OF HIS OWN MEDICINE.
CRACKK

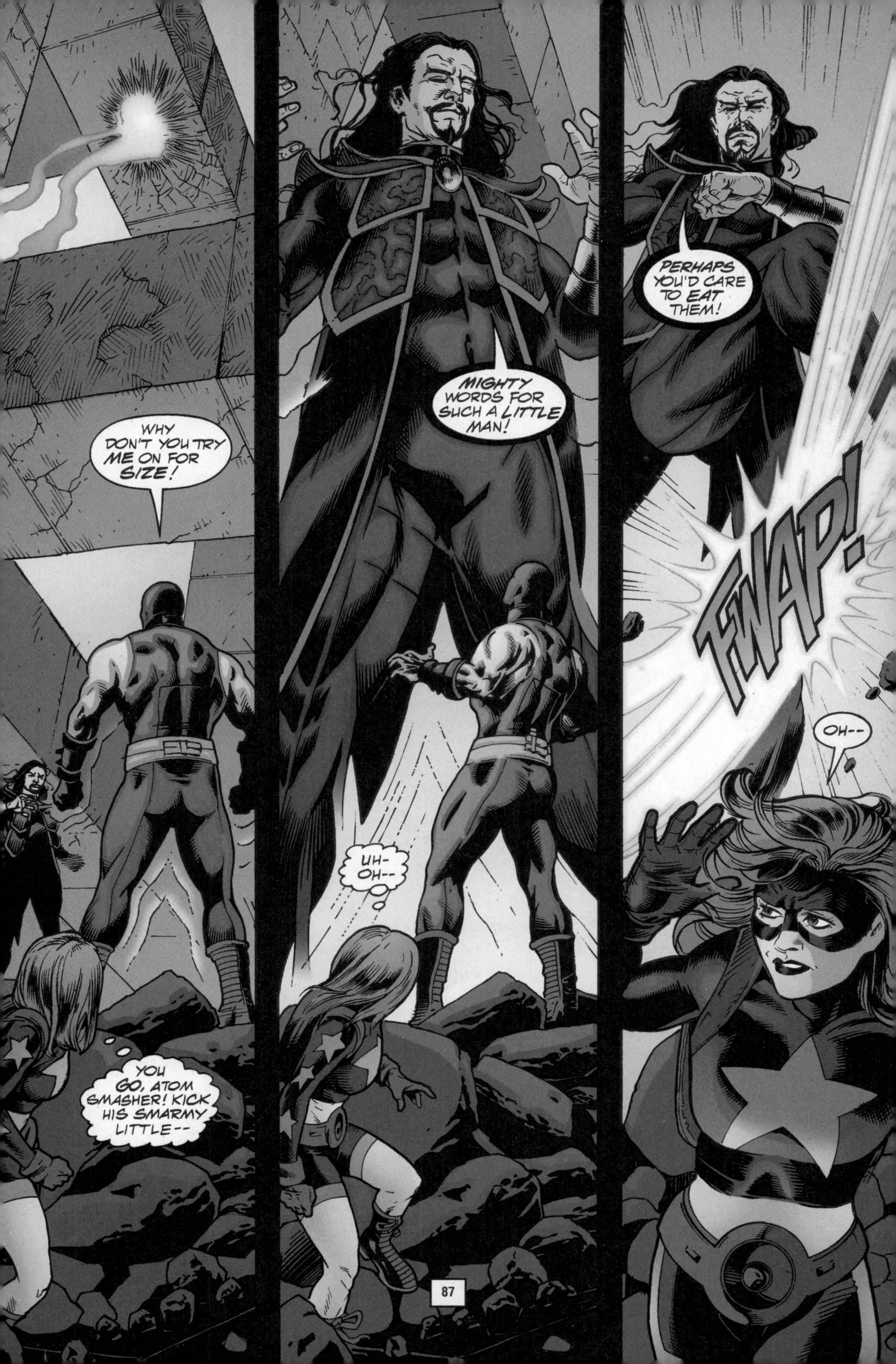
WHY DON'T YOU TRY ME ON FOR SIZE!
YOU GO, ATOM SMASHER! KICK HIS SMARMY LITTLE--
MIGHTY WORDS FOR SUCH A LITTLE MAN!
UH-OH--
PERHAPS YOU'D CARE TO EAT THEM!
FWAP!
OH--

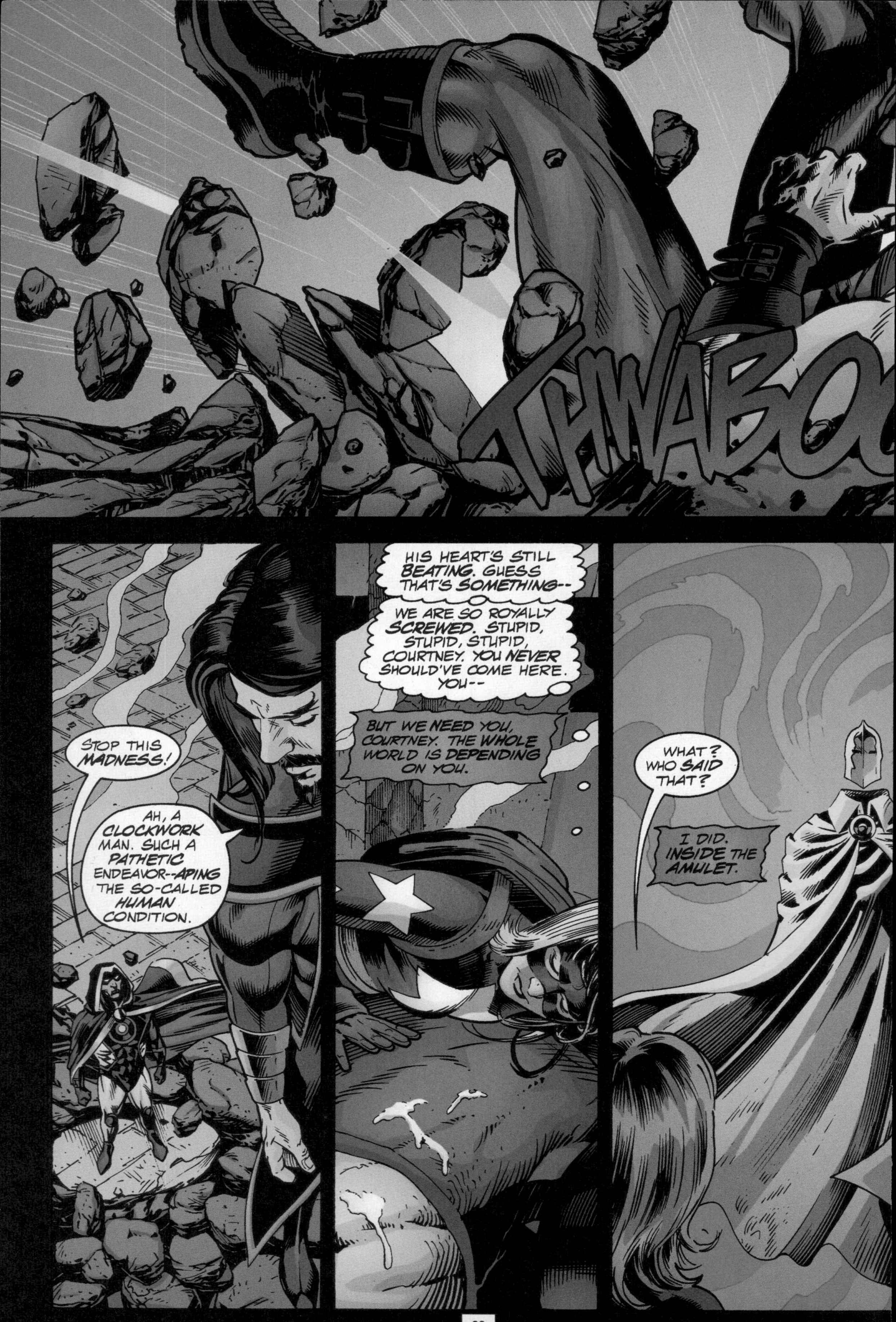
THWABOO
HIS HEART'S STILL BEATING. GUESS THAT'S SOMETHING--
WE ARE SO ROYALLY SCREWED. STUPID, STUPID, STUPID, COURTNEY. YOU NEVER SHOULD'VE COME HERE. YOU--
BUT WE NEED YOU, COURTNEY. THE WHOLE WORLD IS DEPENDING ON YOU.
STOP THIS MADNESS!
AH, A CLOCKWORK MAN. SUCH A PATHETIC ENDEAVOR--APING THE SO-CALLED HUMAN CONDITION.
WHAT? WHO SAID THAT?
I DID. INSIDE THE AMULET.

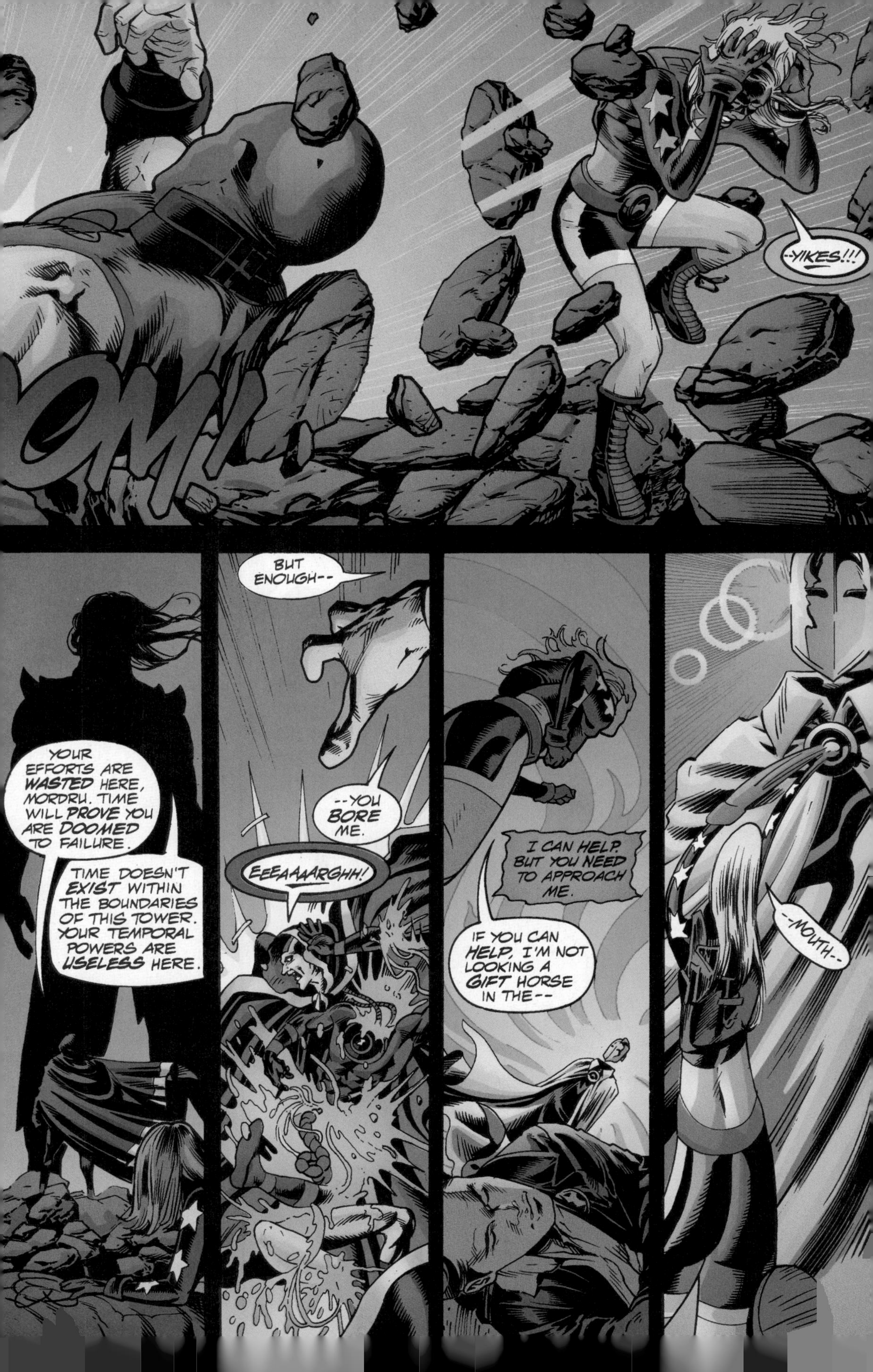
OM!
--YIKES!!!
BUT ENOUGH--
YOUR EFFORTS ARE WASTED HERE, MORDRU. TIME WILL PROVE YOU ARE DOOMED TO FAILURE.
TIME DOESN'T EXIST WITHIN THE BOUNDARIES OF THIS TOWER. YOUR TEMPORAL POWERS ARE USELESS HERE.
--YOU BORE ME.
EEEAAAARGHH!
I CAN HELP. BUT YOU NEED TO APPROACH ME.
IF YOU CAN HELP, I'M NOT LOOKING A GIFT HORSE IN THE--
--MOUTH--

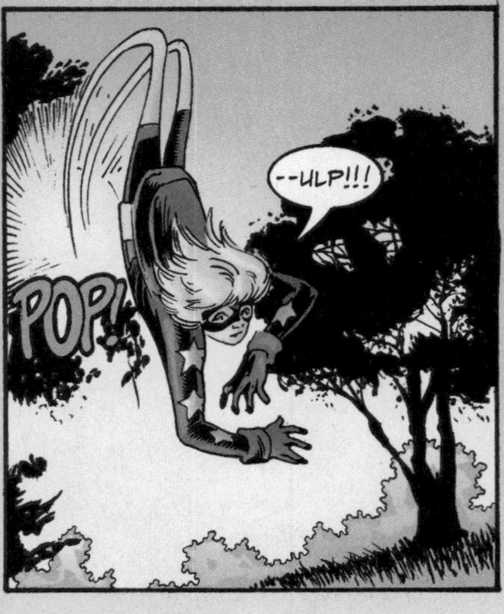
POP!
--ULP!!!

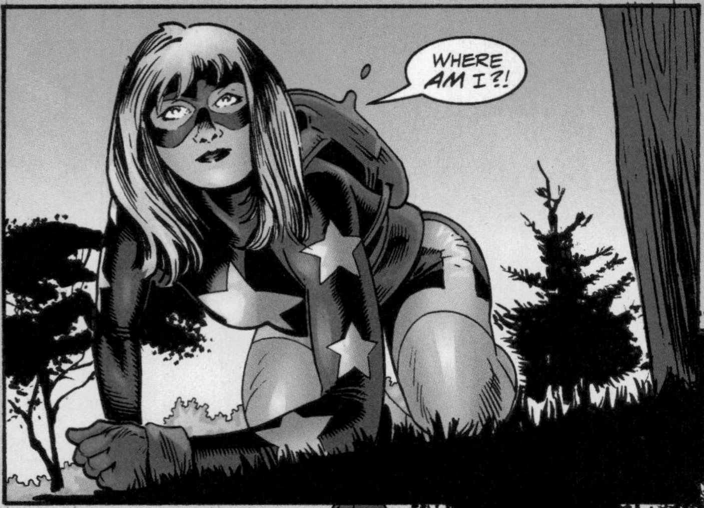
WHERE AM I?!

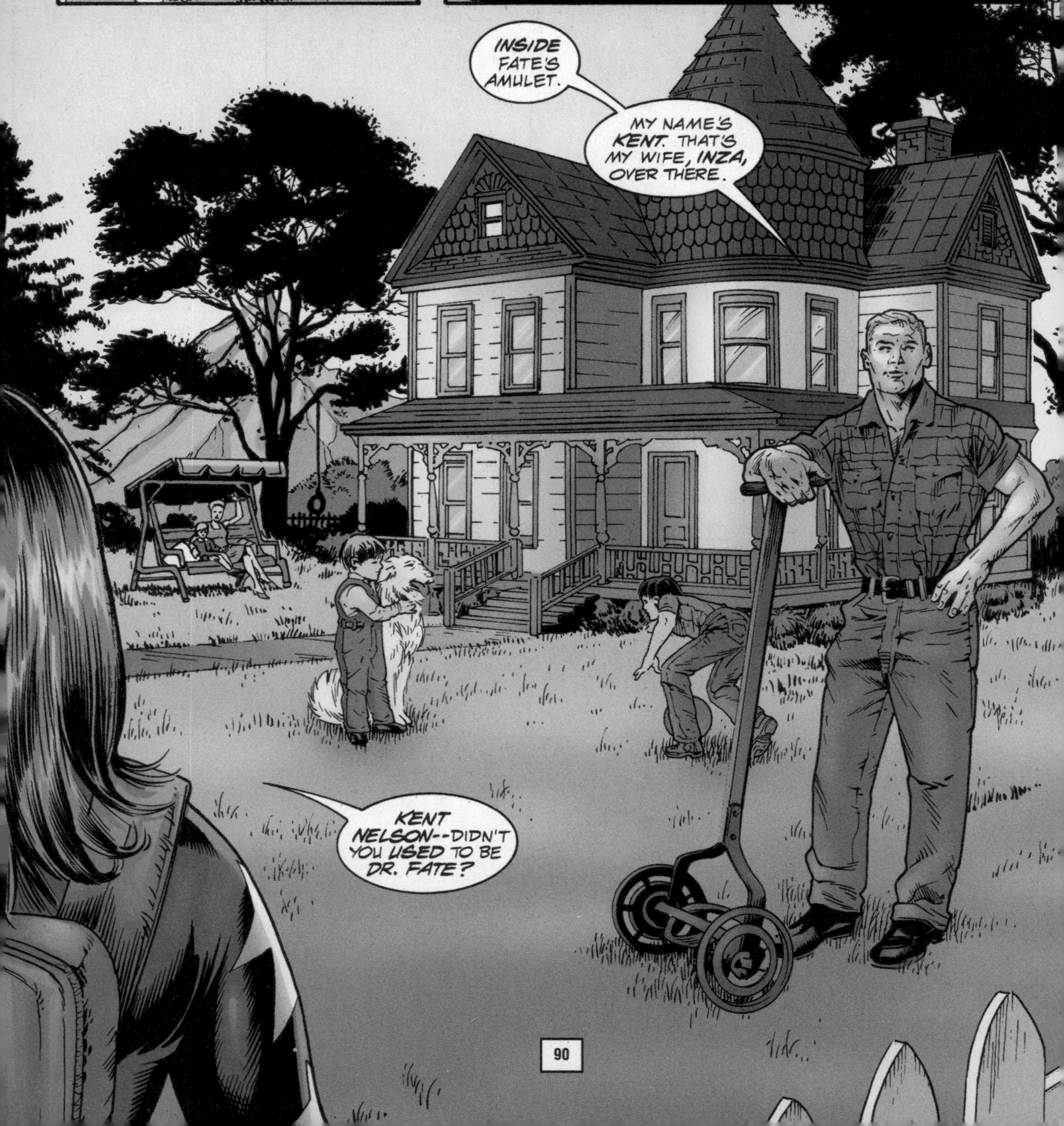
INSIDE FATE'S AMULET.
MY NAME'S KENT. THAT'S MY WIFE, INZA, OVER THERE.
KENT NELSON--DIDN'T YOU USED TO BE DR. FATE?

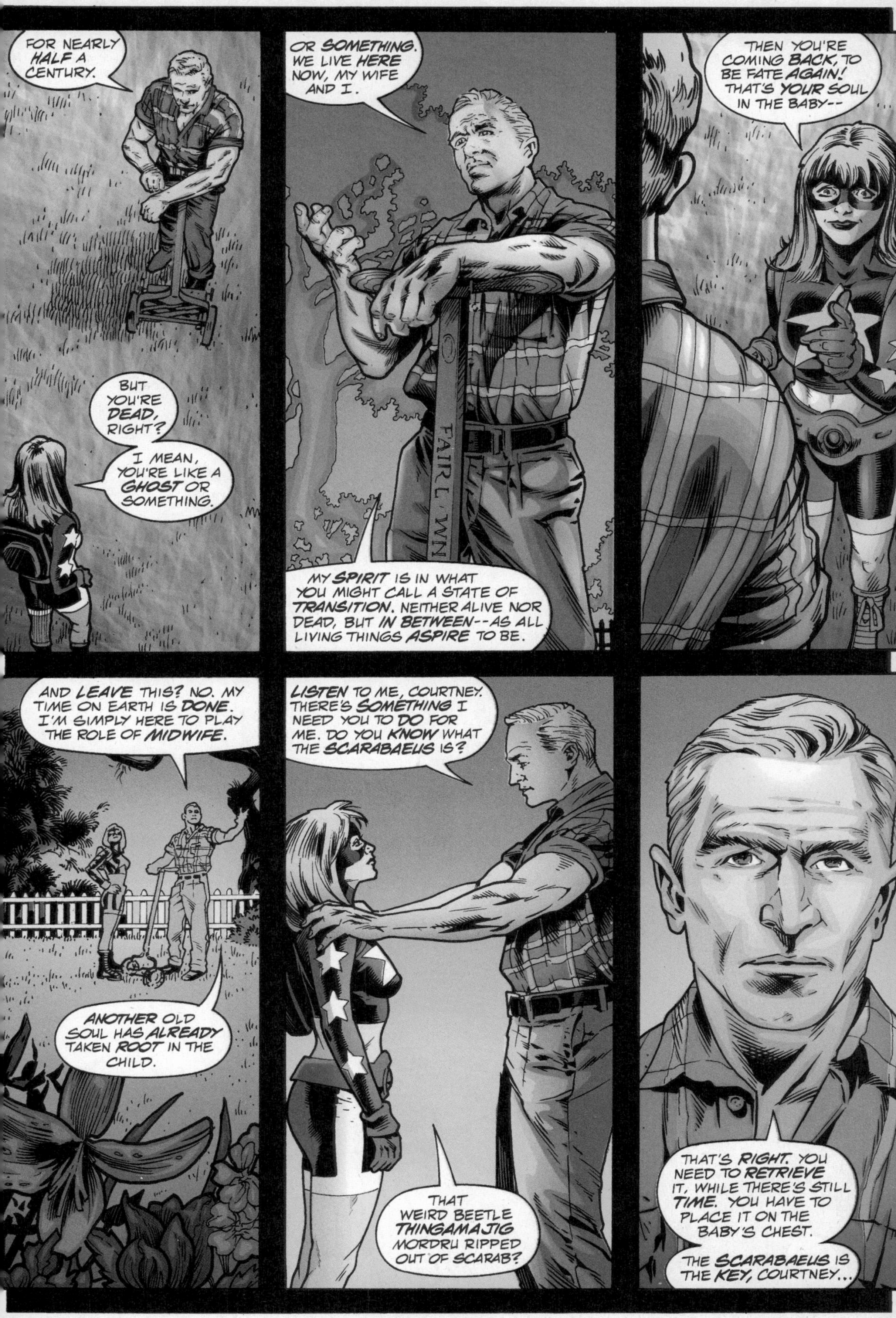
FOR NEARLY HALF A CENTURY.
BUT YOU'RE DEAD, RIGHT?
I MEAN, YOU'RE LIKE A GHOST OR SOMETHING.
OR SOMETHING. WE LIVE HERE NOW, MY WIFE AND I.
FAIRL WN
MY SPIRIT IS IN WHAT YOU MIGHT CALL A STATE OF TRANSITION. NEITHER ALIVE NOR DEAD, BUT IN BETWEEN--AS ALL LIVING THINGS ASPIRE TO BE.
THEN YOU'RE COMING BACK, TO BE FATE AGAIN! THAT'S YOUR SOUL IN THE BABY--
AND LEAVE THIS? NO. MY TIME ON EARTH IS DONE. I'M SIMPLY HERE TO PLAY THE ROLE OF MIDWIFE.
ANOTHER OLD SOUL HAS ALREADY TAKEN ROOT IN THE CHILD.
LISTEN TO ME, COURTNEY. THERE'S SOMETHING I NEED YOU TO DO FOR ME. DO YOU KNOW WHAT THE SCARABAEUS IS?
THAT WEIRD BEETLE THINGAMAJIG MORDRU RIPPED OUT OF SCARAB?
THAT'S RIGHT. YOU NEED TO RETRIEVE IT, WHILE THERE'S STILL TIME. YOU HAVE TO PLACE IT ON THE BABY'S CHEST.
THE SCARABAEUS IS THE KEY, COURTNEY...

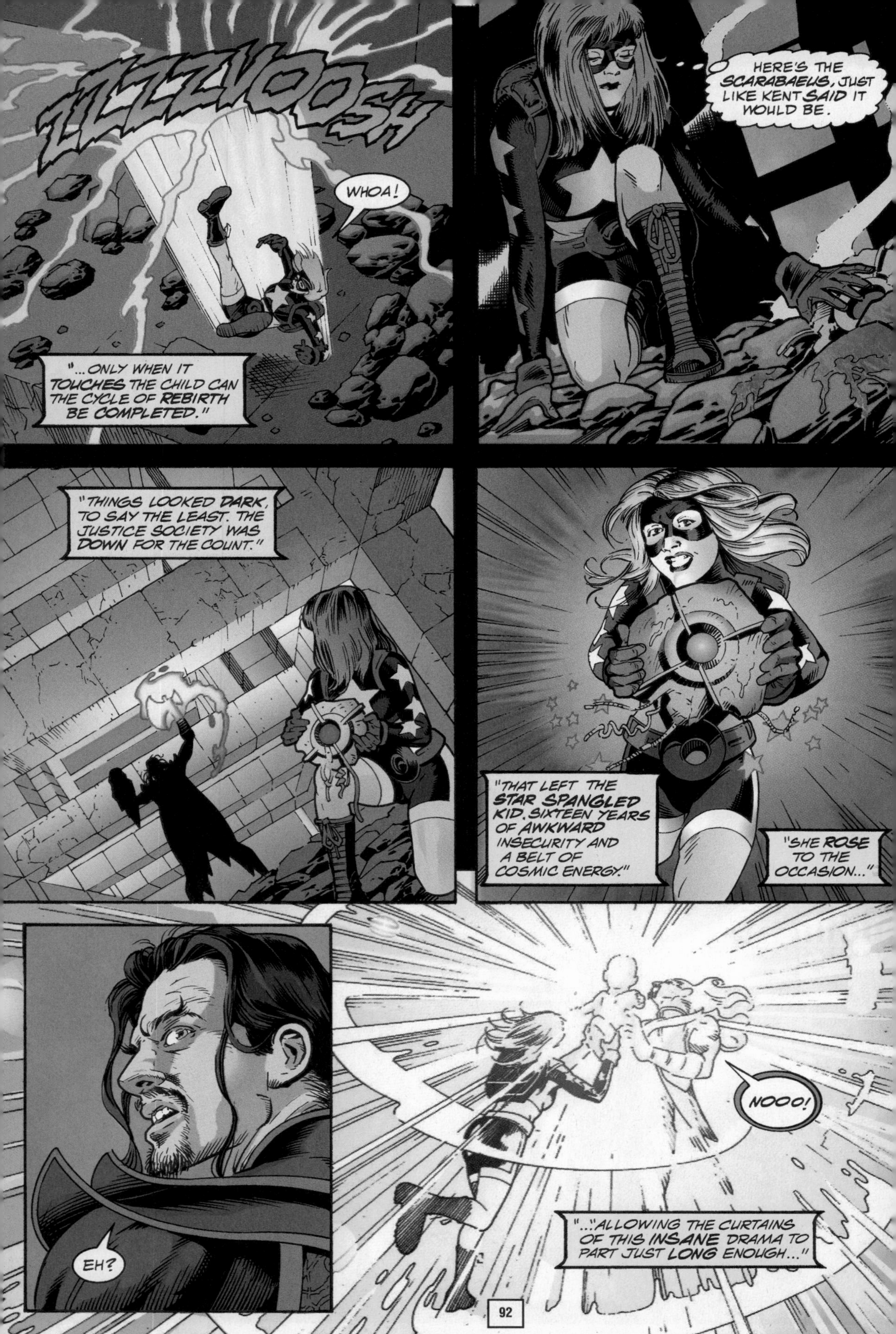
ZZZZZVOOOSH
WHOA!
"...ONLY WHEN IT TOUCHES THE CHILD CAN THE CYCLE OF REBIRTH BE COMPLETED."
HERE'S THE SCARABAEUS, JUST LIKE KENT SAID IT WOULD BE.
"THINGS LOOKED DARK, TO SAY THE LEAST. THE JUSTICE SOCIETY WAS DOWN FOR THE COUNT."
"THAT LEFT THE STAR SPANGLED KID, SIXTEEN YEARS OF AWKWARD INSECURITY AND A BELT OF COSMIC ENERGY."
"SHE ROSE TO THE OCCASION..."
EH?
NOOO!
"..."ALLOWING THE CURTAINS OF THIS INSANE DRAMA TO PART JUST LONG ENOUGH..."

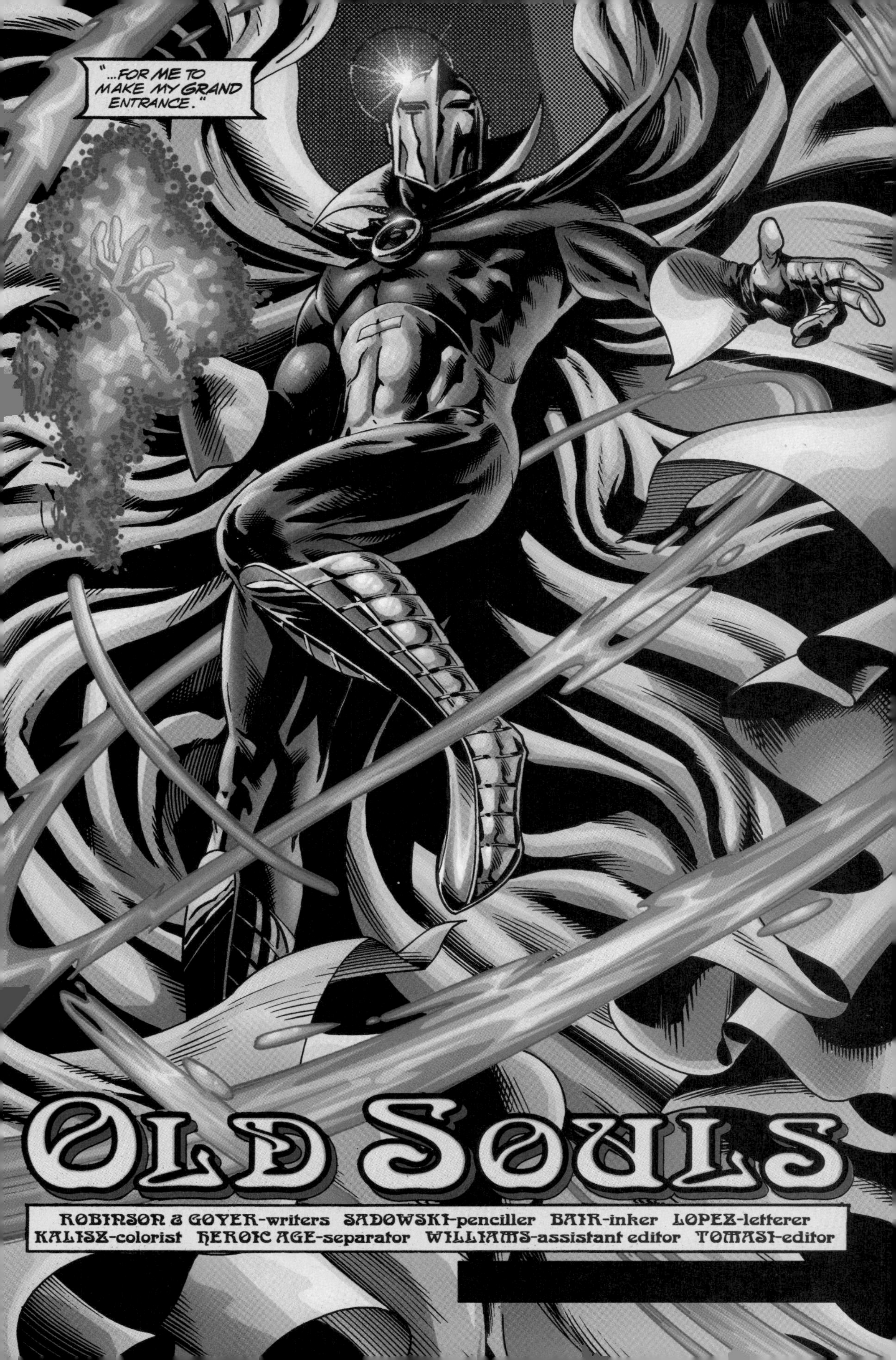
"...FOR ME TO MAKE MY GRAND ENTRANCE."
OLD SOULS
ROBINSON & GOYER-writers SADOWSKI-penciller BAIR-inker LOPEZ-letterer
KALISZ-colorist HEROIC AGE-separator WILLIAMS-assistant editor TOMASI-editor

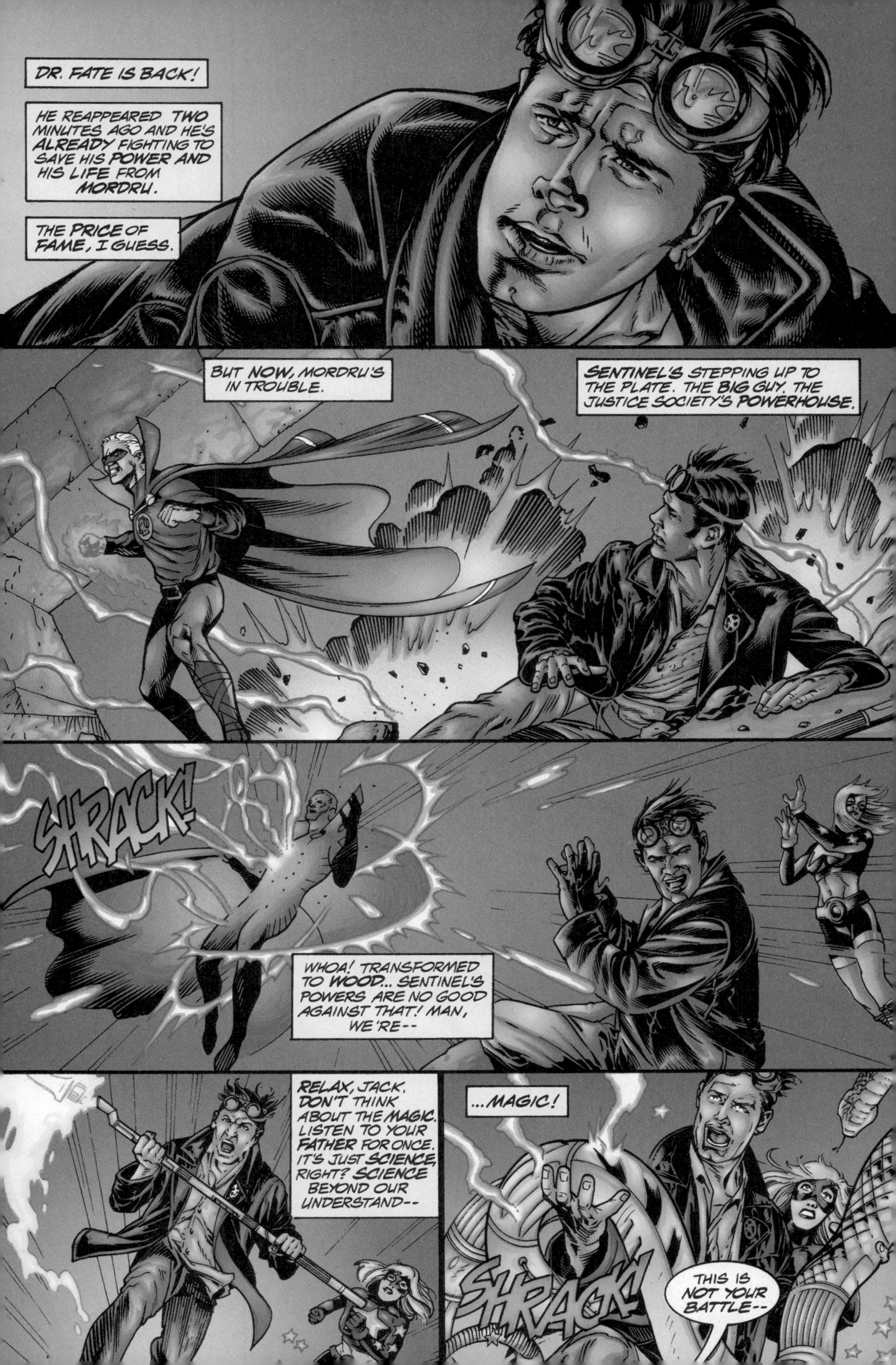
DR. FATE IS BACK!
HE REAPPEARED TWO MINUTES AGO AND HE'S ALREADY FIGHTING TO SAVE HIS POWER AND HIS LIFE FROM MORDRU.
THE PRICE OF FAME, I GUESS.
BUT NOW, MORDRU'S IN TROUBLE.
SENTINEL'S STEPPING UP TO THE PLATE. THE BIG GUY. THE JUSTICE SOCIETY'S POWERHOUSE.
SHRACK!
WHOA! TRANSFORMED TO WOOD... SENTINEL'S POWERS ARE NO GOOD AGAINST THAT! MAN, WE'RE--
RELAX, JACK. DON'T THINK ABOUT THE MAGIC. LISTEN TO YOUR FATHER FOR ONCE. IT'S JUST SCIENCE, RIGHT? SCIENCE BEYOND OUR UNDERSTAND--
...MAGIC!
SHRACK!
THIS IS NOT YOUR BATTLE--

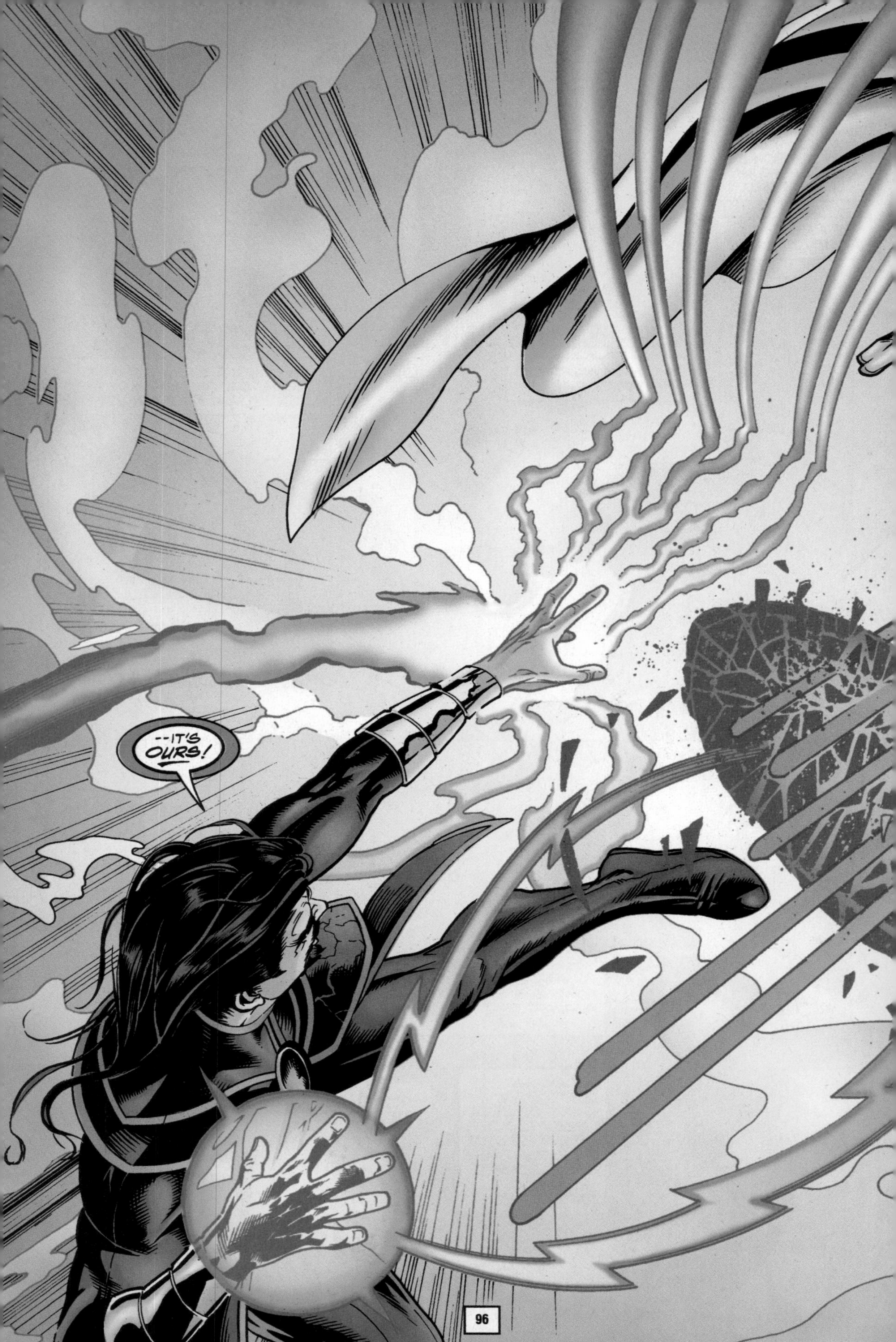
--IT'S OURS!

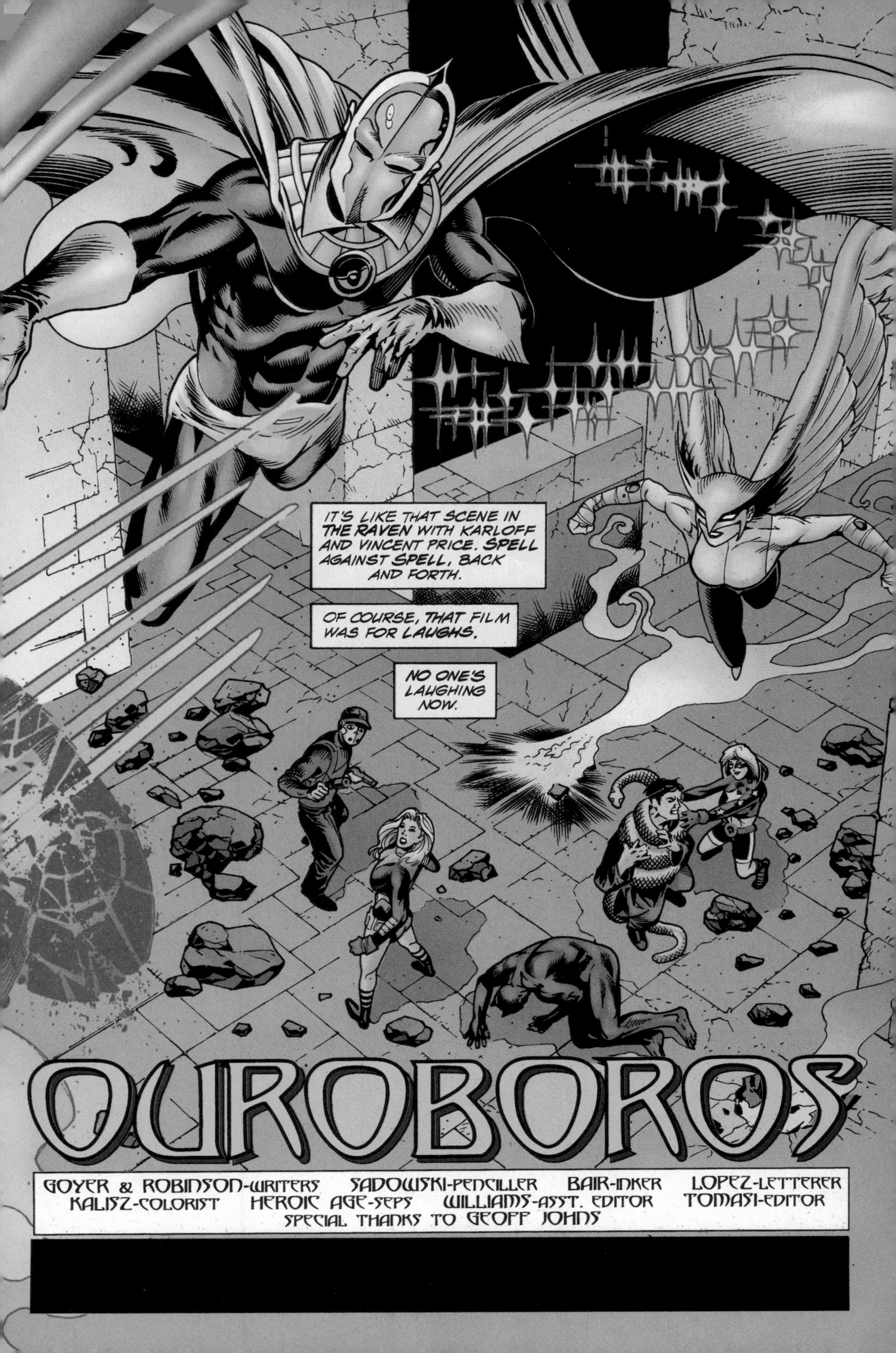
IT'S LIKE THAT SCENE IN THE RAVEN WITH KARLOFF AND VINCENT PRICE. SPELL AGAINST SPELL, BACK AND FORTH.
OF COURSE, THAT FILM WAS FOR LAUGHS.
NO ONE'S LAUGHING NOW.
OUROBOROS
GOYER & ROBINSON-WRITERS SADOWSKI-PENCILLER BAIR-INKER LOPEZ-LETTERER
KALISZ-COLORIST HEROIC AGE-SEPS WILLIAMS-ASST. EDITOR TOMASI-EDITOR
SPECIAL THANKS TO GEOFF JOHNS

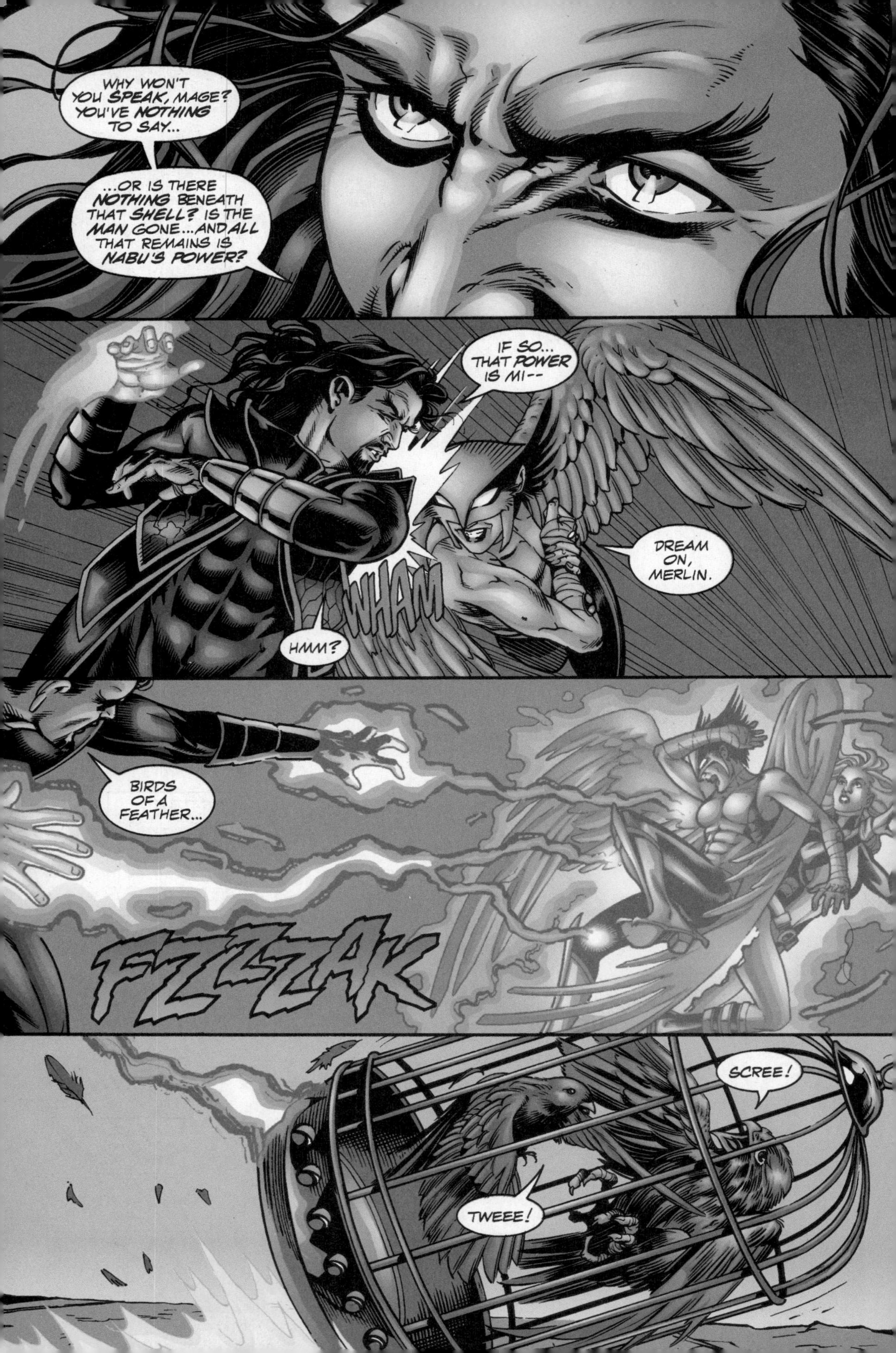

WHY WON'T YOU SPEAK, MAGE? YOU'VE NOTHING TO SAY...
...OR IS THERE NOTHING BENEATH THAT SHELL? IS THE MAN GONE...AND ALL THAT REMAINS IS NABU'S POWER?
IF SO... THAT POWER IS MI--
DREAM ON, MERLIN.
WHAM
HMM?
BIRDS OF A FEATHER...
FZZZAK
SCREE!
TWEEE!

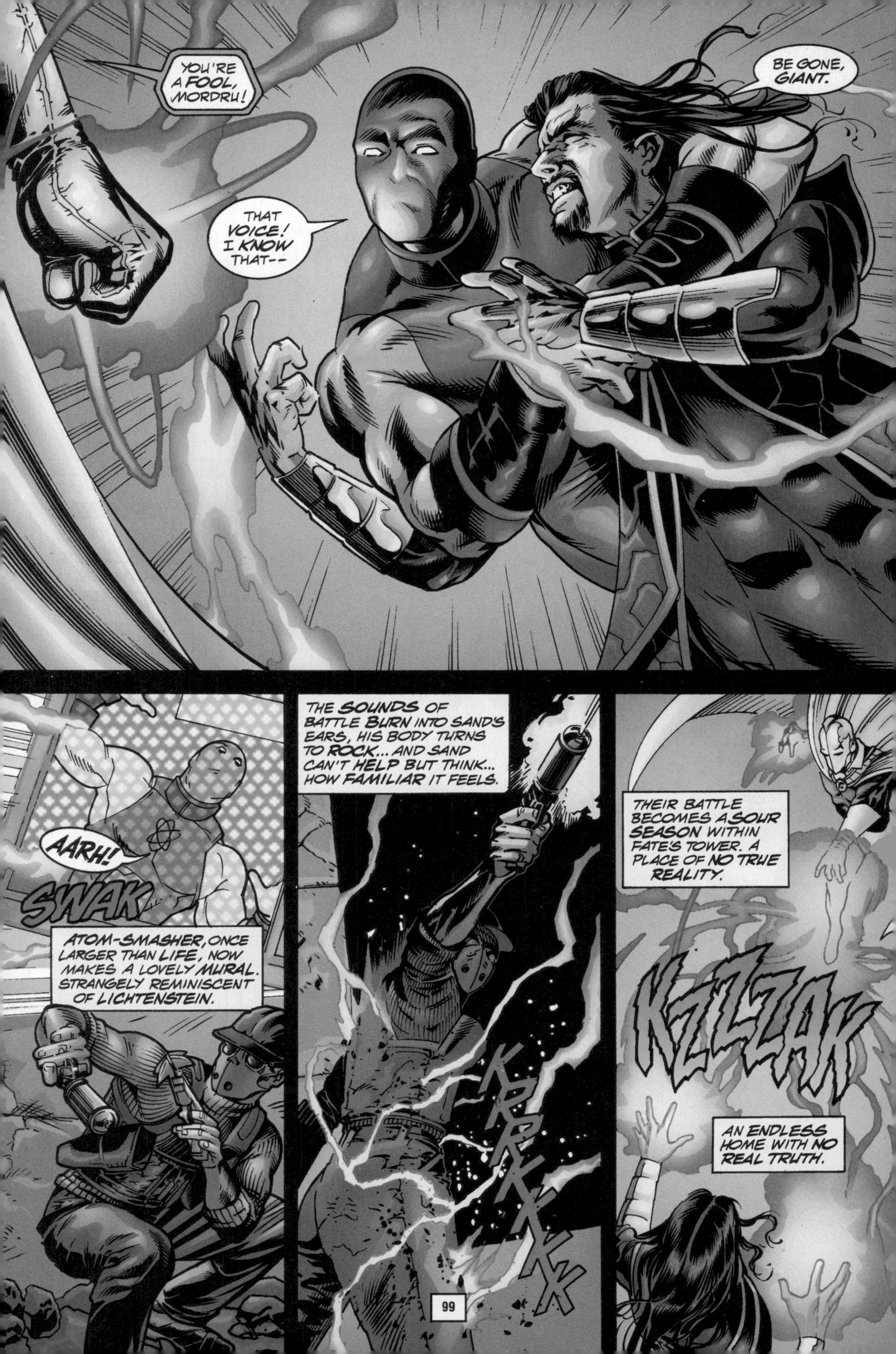
YOU'RE A FOOL, MORDRU!
BE GONE, GIANT.
THAT VOICE! I KNOW THAT--
AARH!
SWAK
ATOM-SMASHER, ONCE LARGER THAN LIFE, NOW MAKES A LOVELY MURAL. STRANGELY REMINISCENT OF LICHTENSTEIN.
THE SOUNDS OF BATTLE BURN INTO SAND'S EARS, HIS BODY TURNS TO ROCK... AND SAND CAN'T HELP BUT THINK... HOW FAMILIAR IT FEELS.
KRRKKK
THEIR BATTLE BECOMES A SOUR SEASON WITHIN FATE'S TOWER. A PLACE OF NO TRUE REALITY.
KZZZAK
AN ENDLESS HOME WITH NO REAL TRUTH.

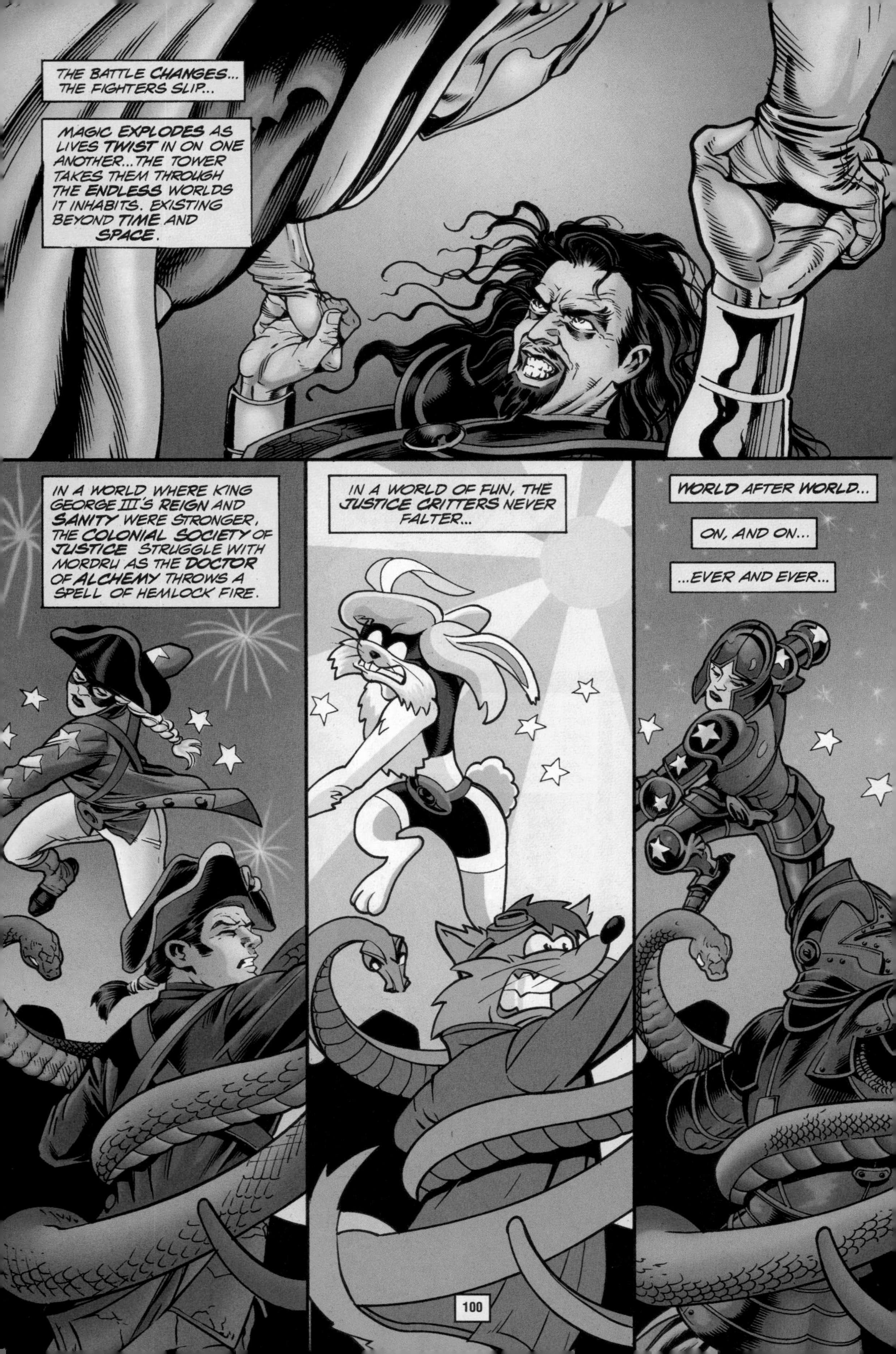
THE BATTLE CHANGES... THE FIGHTERS SLIP...
MAGIC EXPLODES AS LIVES TWIST IN ON ONE ANOTHER...THE TOWER TAKES THEM THROUGH THE ENDLESS WORLDS IT INHABITS. EXISTING BEYOND TIME AND SPACE.
IN A WORLD WHERE KING GEORGE III'S REIGN AND SANITY WERE STRONGER, THE COLONIAL SOCIETY OF JUSTICE STRUGGLE WITH MORDRU AS THE DOCTOR OF ALCHEMY THROWS A SPELL OF HEMLOCK FIRE.
IN A WORLD OF FUN, THE JUSTICE CRITTERS NEVER FALTER...
WORLD AFTER WORLD...
ON, AND ON...
...EVER AND EVER...

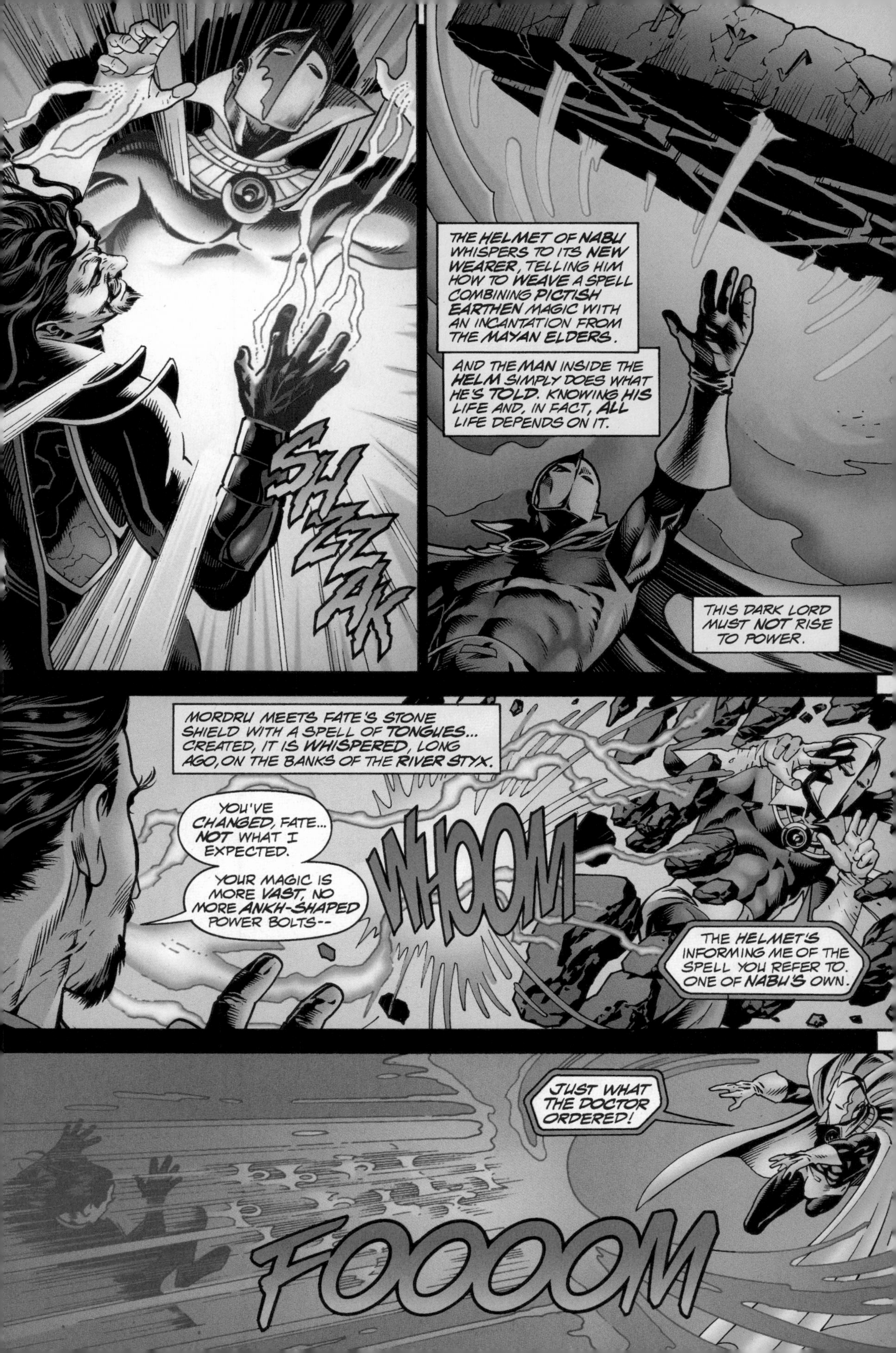

SHZZZAK
THE HELMET OF NABU WHISPERS TO ITS NEW WEARER, TELLING HIM HOW TO WEAVE A SPELL COMBINING PICTISH EARTHEN MAGIC WITH AN INCANTATION FROM THE MAYAN ELDERS.
AND THE MAN INSIDE THE HELM SIMPLY DOES WHAT HE'S TOLD. KNOWING HIS LIFE AND, IN FACT, ALL LIFE DEPENDS ON IT.
THIS DARK LORD MUST NOT RISE TO POWER.
MORDRU MEETS FATE'S STONE SHIELD WITH A SPELL OF TONGUES... CREATED, IT IS WHISPERED, LONG AGO, ON THE BANKS OF THE RIVER STYX.
YOU'VE CHANGED, FATE... NOT WHAT I EXPECTED.
YOUR MAGIC IS MORE VAST, NO MORE ANKH-SHAPED POWER BOLTS--
WHOOM
THE HELMET'S INFORMING ME OF THE SPELL YOU REFER TO. ONE OF NABU'S OWN.
JUST WHAT THE DOCTOR ORDERED!
FOOOOM

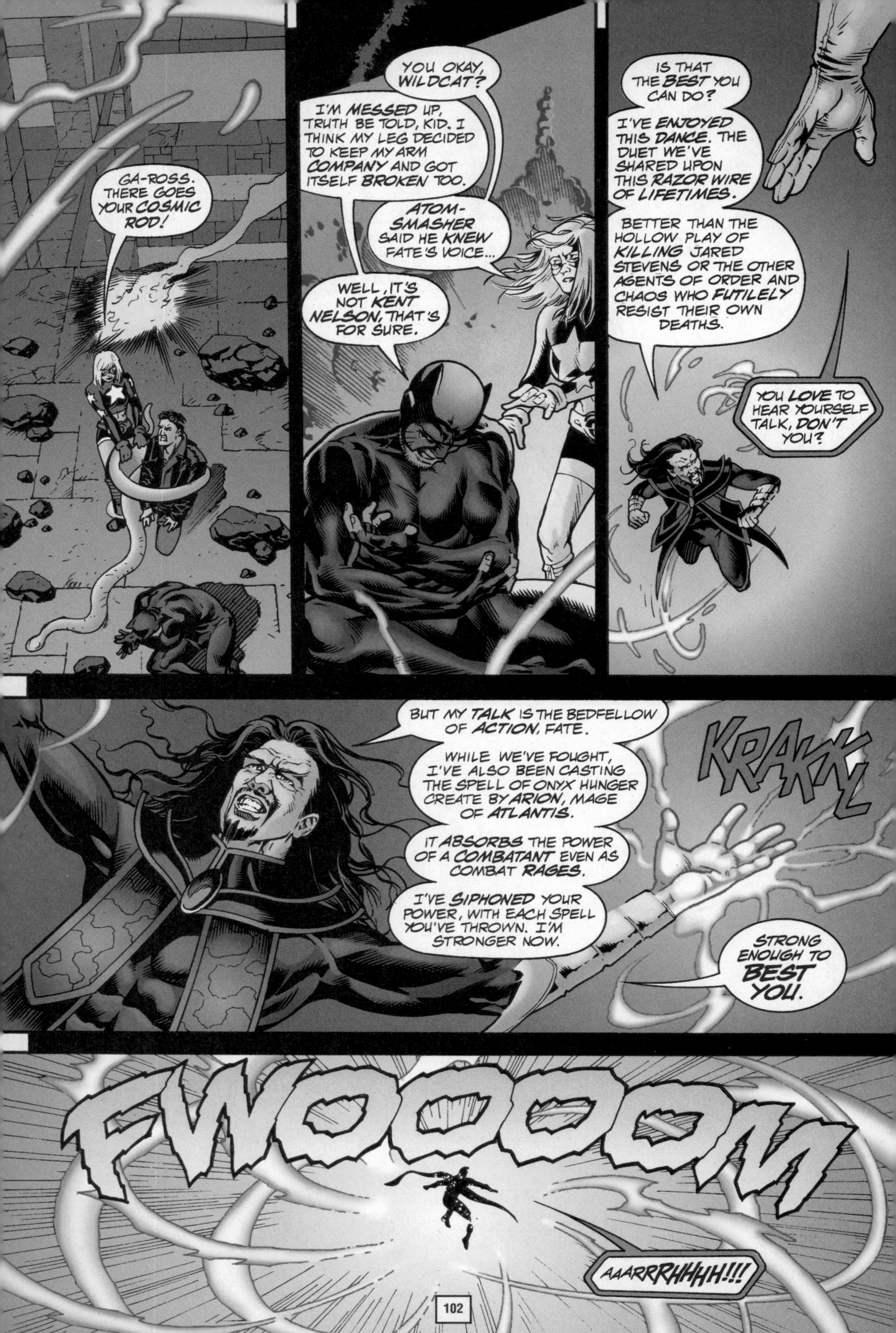
GA-ROSS. THERE GOES YOUR COSMIC ROD!
YOU OKAY, WILDCAT?
I'M MESSED UP, TRUTH BE TOLD, KID. I THINK MY LEG DECIDED TO KEEP MY ARM COMPANY AND GOT ITSELF BROKEN TOO.
ATOM-SMASHER SAID HE KNEW FATE'S VOICE...
WELL, IT'S NOT KENT NELSON, THAT'S FOR SURE.
IS THAT THE BEST YOU CAN DO?
I'VE ENJOYED THIS DANCE. THE DUET WE'VE SHARED UPON THIS RAZOR WIRE OF LIFETIMES.
BETTER THAN THE HOLLOW PLAY OF KILLING JARED STEVENS OR THE OTHER AGENTS OF ORDER AND CHAOS WHO FUTILELY RESIST THEIR OWN DEATHS.
YOU LOVE TO HEAR YOURSELF TALK, DON'T YOU?
BUT MY TALK IS THE BEDFELLOW OF ACTION, FATE.
WHILE WE'VE FOUGHT, I'VE ALSO BEEN CASTING THE SPELL OF ONYX HUNGER CREATE BY ARION, MAGE OF ATLANTIS.
IT ABSORBS THE POWER OF A COMBATANT EVEN AS COMBAT RAGES.
I'VE SIPHONED YOUR POWER, WITH EACH SPELL YOU'VE THROWN. I'M STRONGER NOW.
KRAKKL
STRONG ENOUGH TO BEST YOU.
FWOOOOM
AAARRRHHHH!!!

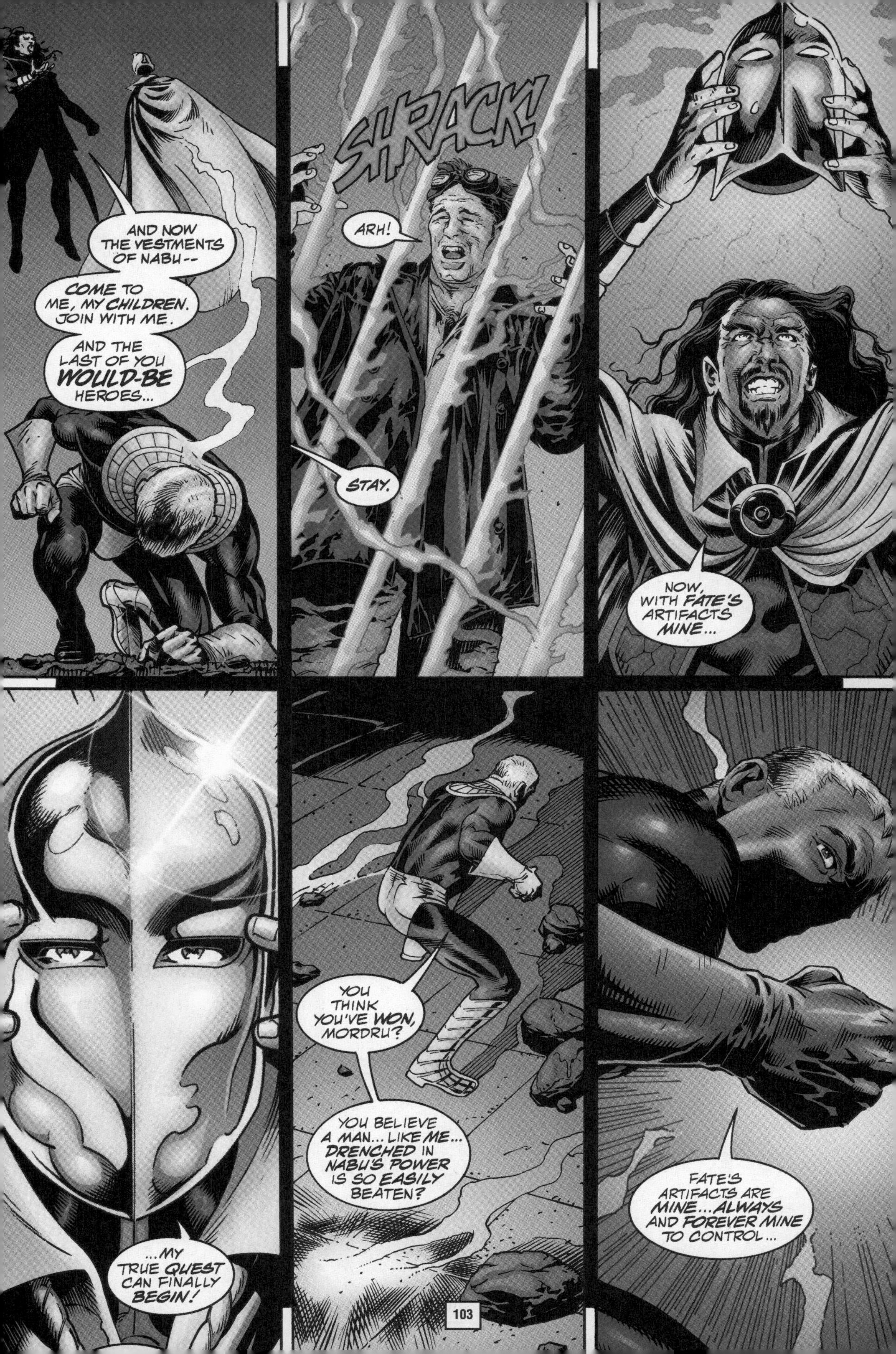

AND NOW THE VESTMENTS OF NABU--
COME TO ME, MY CHILDREN. JOIN WITH ME.
AND THE LAST OF YOU WOULD-BE HEROES...
SHRACK!
ARH!
STAY.
NOW, WITH FATE'S ARTIFACTS MINE...
...MY TRUE QUEST CAN FINALLY BEGIN!
YOU THINK YOU'VE WON, MORDRU?
YOU BELIEVE A MAN... LIKE ME... DRENCHED IN NABU'S POWER IS SO EASILY BEATEN?
FATE'S ARTIFACTS ARE MINE... ALWAYS AND FOREVER MINE TO CONTROL...

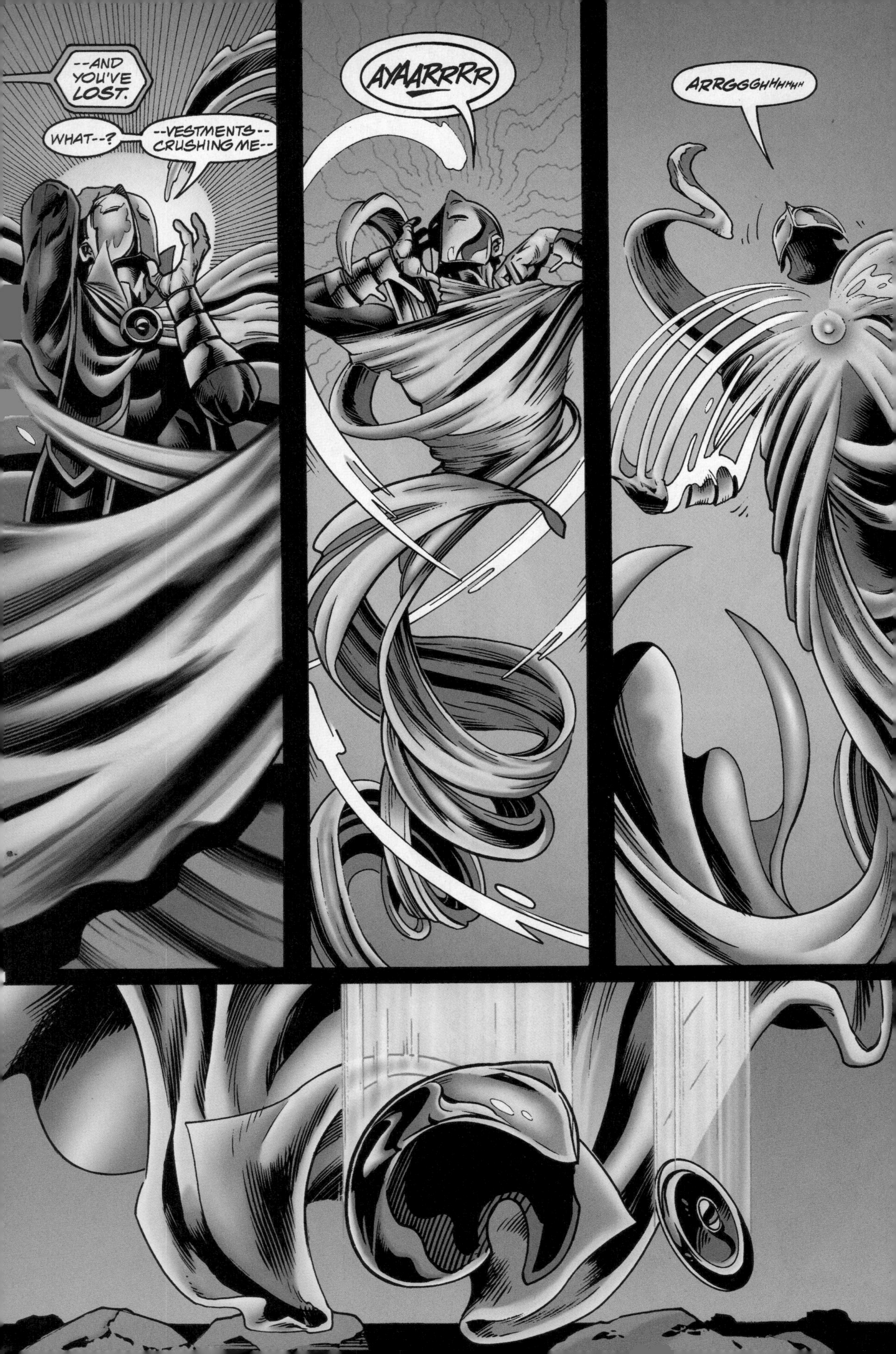
--AND YOU'VE LOST.
WHAT--?
--VESTMENTS-- CRUSHING ME--
AYAARRRR
ARRGGGHHHHHH

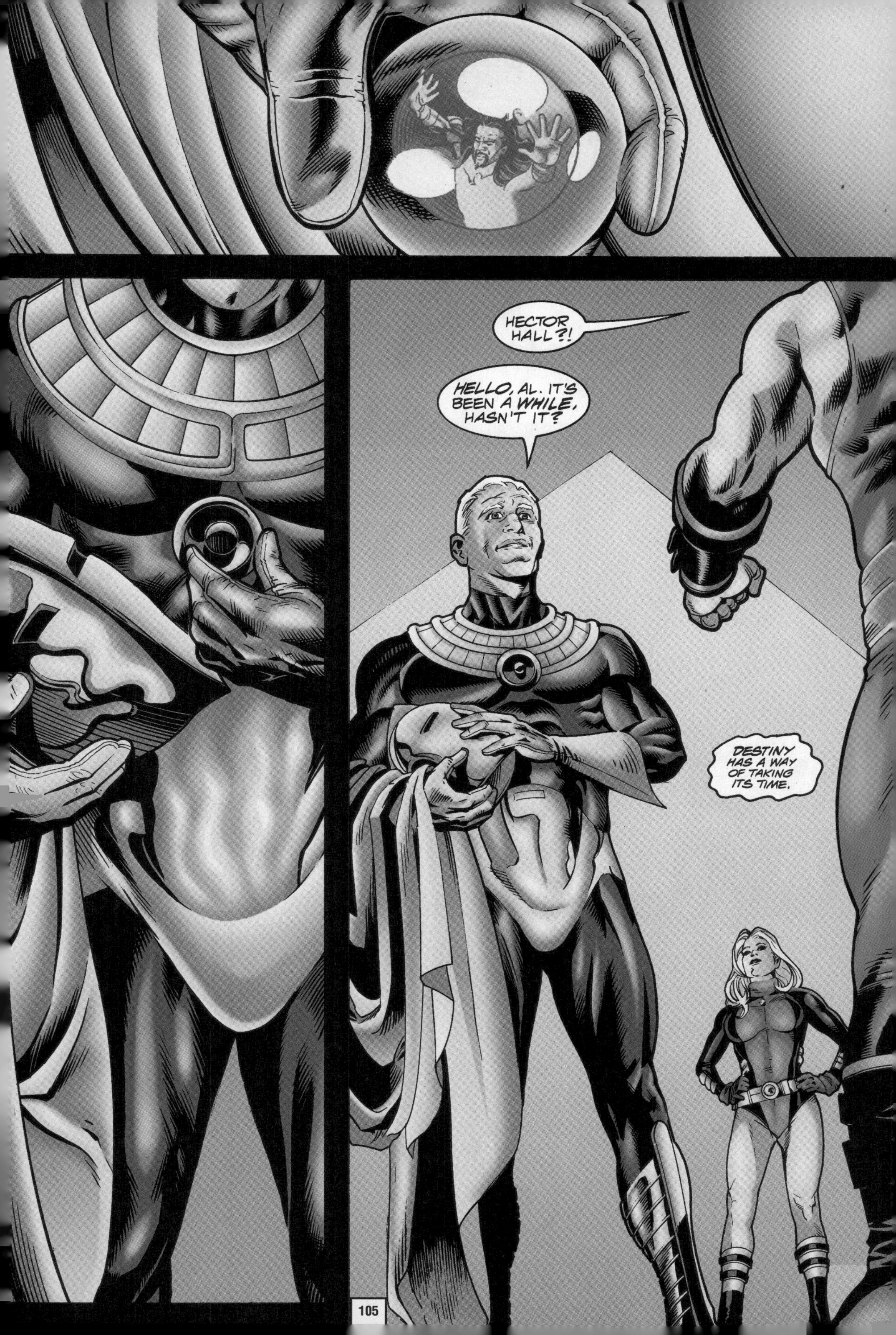
HECTOR HALL?!
HELLO, AL. IT'S BEEN A WHILE, HASN'T IT?
DESTINY HAS A WAY OF TAKING ITS TIME.

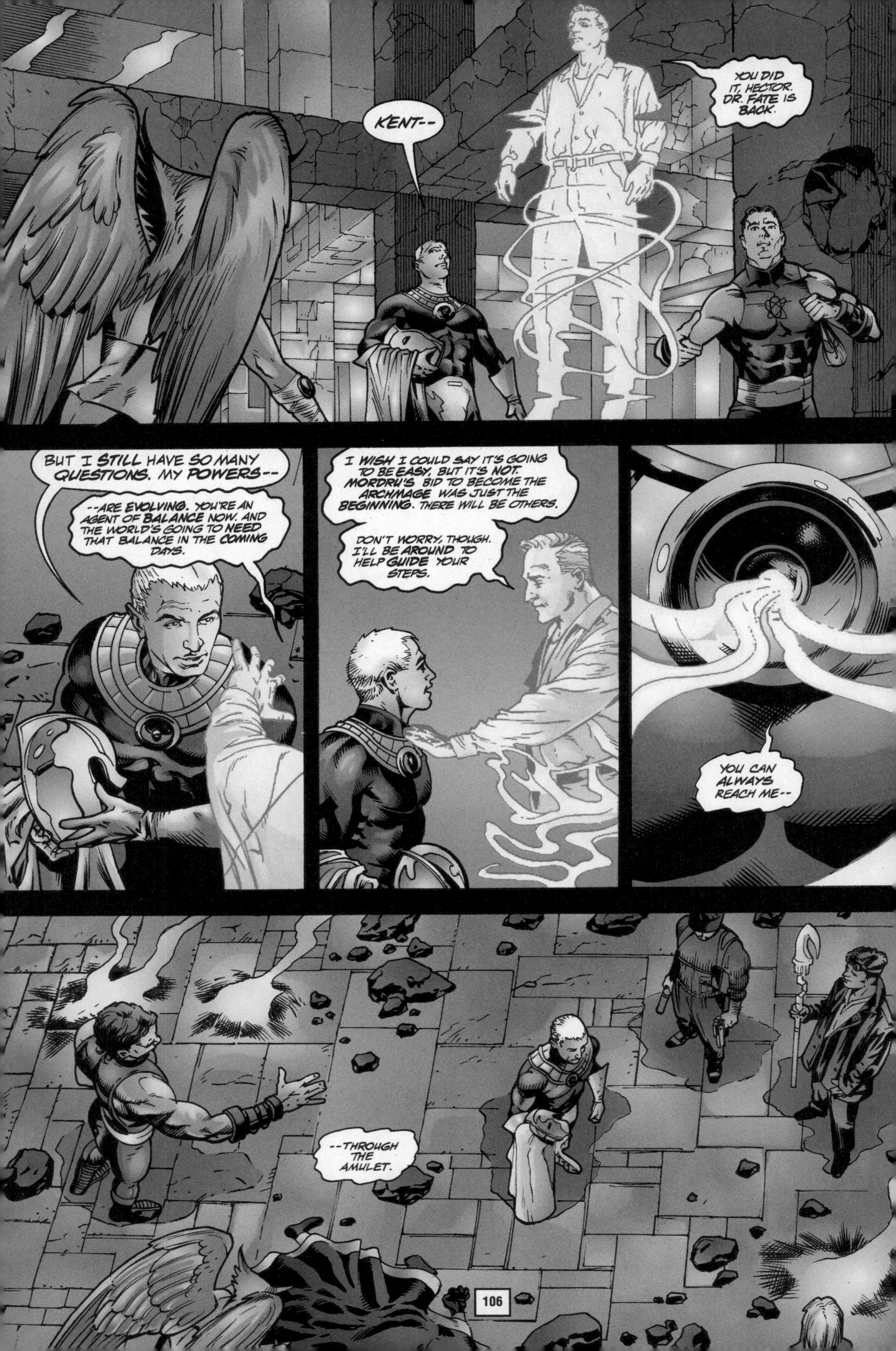
KENT--
YOU DID IT, HECTOR. DR. FATE IS BACK.
BUT I STILL HAVE SO MANY QUESTIONS. MY POWERS--
--ARE EVOLVING. YOU'RE AN AGENT OF BALANCE NOW. AND THE WORLD'S GOING TO NEED THAT BALANCE IN THE COMING DAYS.
I WISH I COULD SAY IT'S GOING TO BE EASY, BUT IT'S NOT. MORDRU'S BID TO BECOME THE ARCHMAGE WAS JUST THE BEGINNING. THERE WILL BE OTHERS.
DON'T WORRY, THOUGH. I'LL BE AROUND TO HELP GUIDE YOUR STEPS.
YOU CAN ALWAYS REACH ME--
--THROUGH THE AMULET.

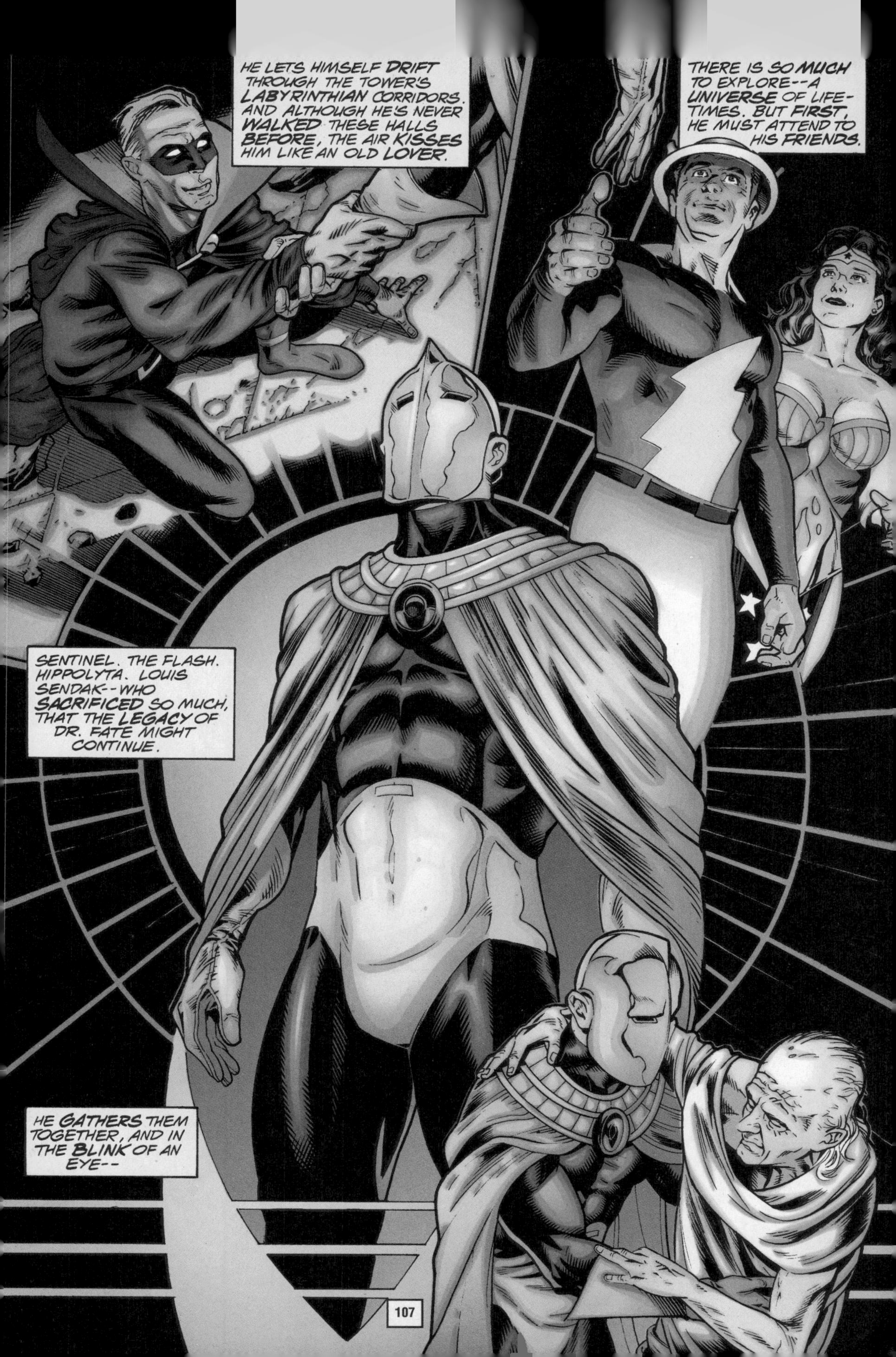
HE LETS HIMSELF DRIFT THROUGH THE TOWER'S LABYRINTHIAN CORRIDORS. AND ALTHOUGH HE'S NEVER WALKED THESE HALLS BEFORE, THE AIR KISSES HIM LIKE AN OLD LOVER.
THERE IS SO MUCH TO EXPLORE--A UNIVERSE OF LIFE-TIMES. BUT FIRST, HE MUST ATTEND TO HIS FRIENDS.
SENTINEL. THE FLASH. HIPPOLYTA. LOUIS SENDAK--WHO SACRIFICED SO MUCH, THAT THE LEGACY OF DR. FATE MIGHT CONTINUE.
HE GATHERS THEM TOGETHER, AND IN THE BLINK OF AN EYE--

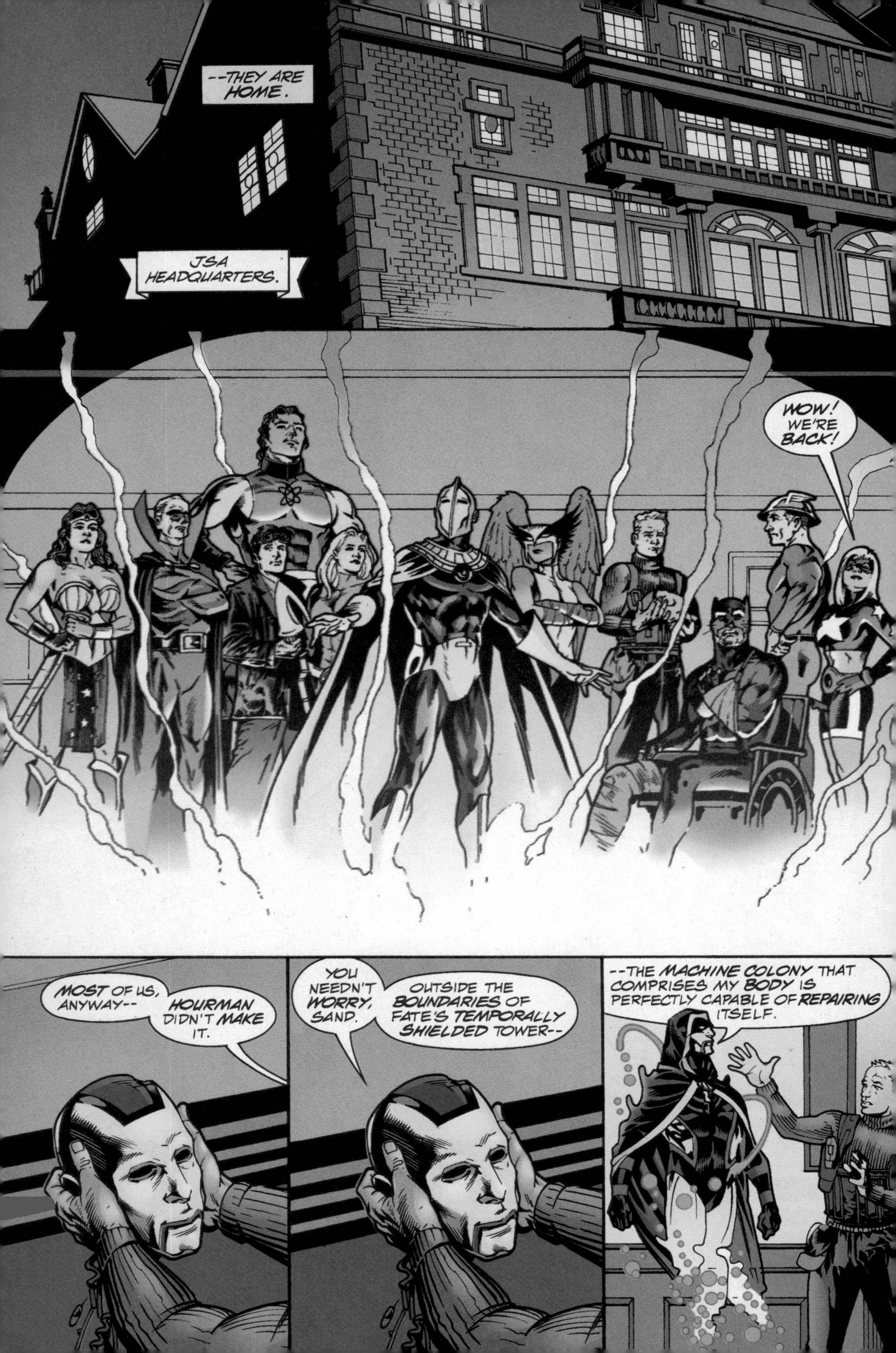

--THEY ARE HOME.
JSA HEADQUARTERS.
WOW! WE'RE BACK!
MOST OF US, ANYWAY--
HOURMAN DIDN'T MAKE IT.
YOU NEEDN'T WORRY, SAND.
OUTSIDE THE BOUNDARIES OF FATE'S TEMPORALLY SHIELDED TOWER--
--THE MACHINE COLONY THAT COMPRISES MY BODY IS PERFECTLY CAPABLE OF REPAIRING ITSELF.

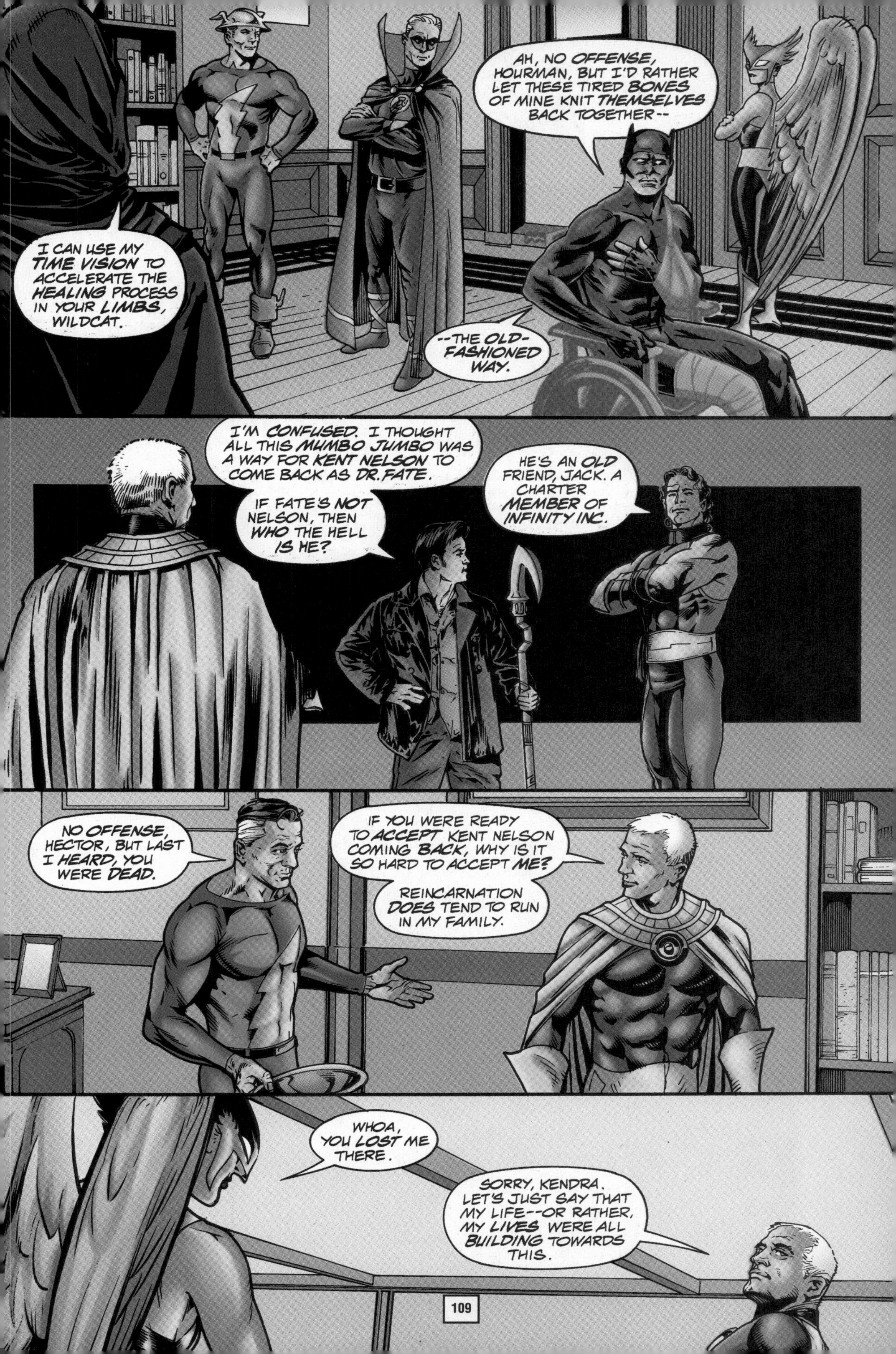
I CAN USE MY TIME VISION TO ACCELERATE THE HEALING PROCESS IN YOUR LIMBS, WILDCAT.
AH, NO OFFENSE, HOURMAN, BUT I'D RATHER LET THESE TIRED BONES OF MINE KNIT THEMSELVES BACK TOGETHER--
--THE OLD-FASHIONED WAY.
I'M CONFUSED. I THOUGHT ALL THIS MUMBO JUMBO WAS A WAY FOR KENT NELSON TO COME BACK AS DR. FATE.
IF FATE'S NOT NELSON, THEN WHO THE HELL IS HE?
HE'S AN OLD FRIEND, JACK. A CHARTER MEMBER OF INFINITY INC.
NO OFFENSE, HECTOR, BUT LAST I HEARD, YOU WERE DEAD.
IF YOU WERE READY TO ACCEPT KENT NELSON COMING BACK, WHY IS IT SO HARD TO ACCEPT ME?
REINCARNATION DOES TEND TO RUN IN MY FAMILY.
WHOA, YOU LOST ME THERE.
SORRY, KENDRA. LET'S JUST SAY THAT MY LIFE--OR RATHER, MY LIVES WERE ALL BUILDING TOWARDS THIS.

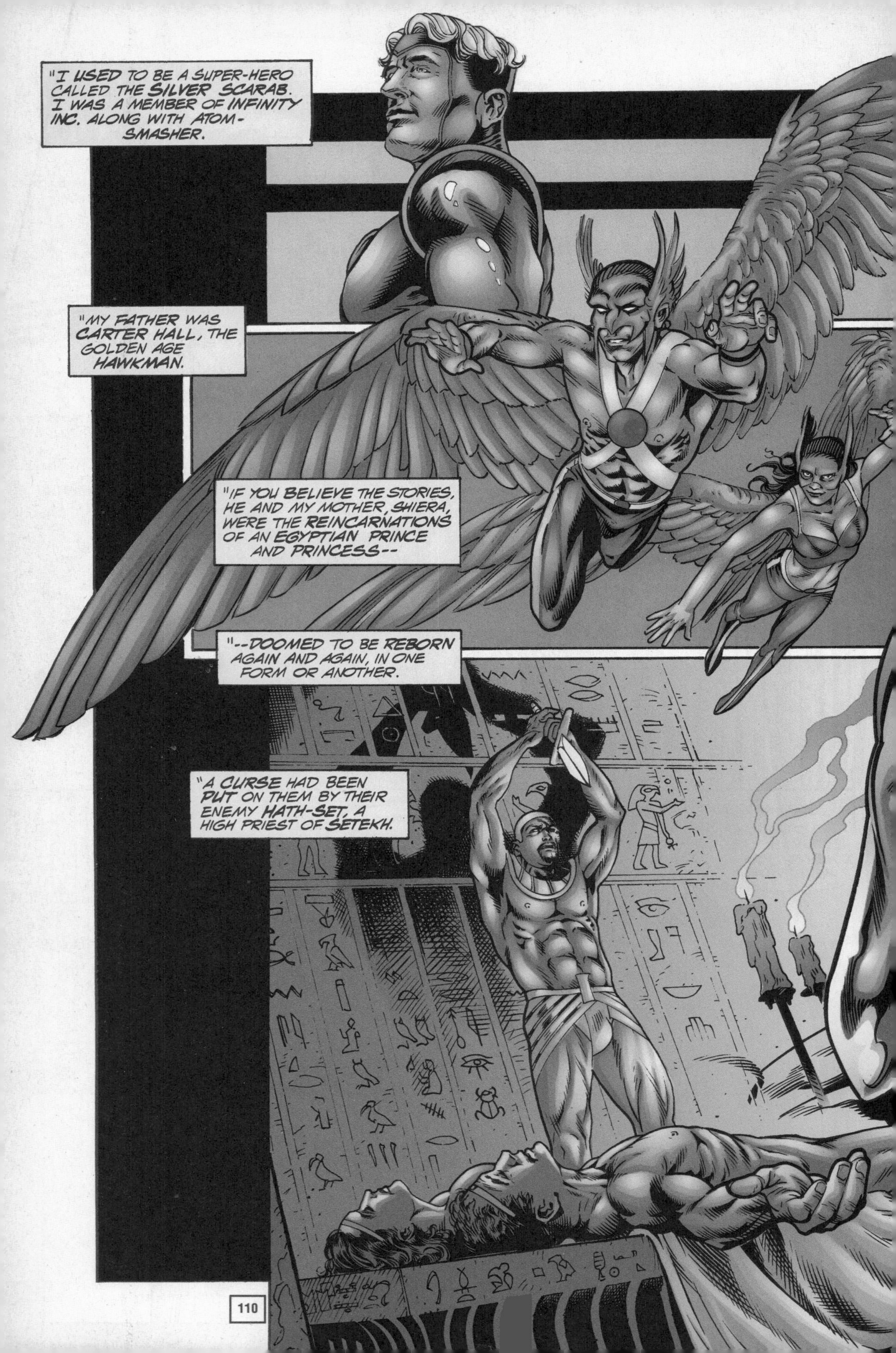
"I USED TO BE A SUPER-HERO CALLED THE SILVER SCARAB. I WAS A MEMBER OF INFINITY INC. ALONG WITH ATOM-SMASHER.
"MY FATHER WAS CARTER HALL, THE GOLDEN AGE HAWKMAN.
"IF YOU BELIEVE THE STORIES, HE AND MY MOTHER, SHIERA, WERE THE REINCARNATIONS OF AN EGYPTIAN PRINCE AND PRINCESS--
"--DOOMED TO BE REBORN AGAIN AND AGAIN, IN ONE FORM OR ANOTHER.
"A CURSE HAD BEEN PUT ON THEM BY THEIR ENEMY HATH-SET, A HIGH PRIEST OF SETEKH.

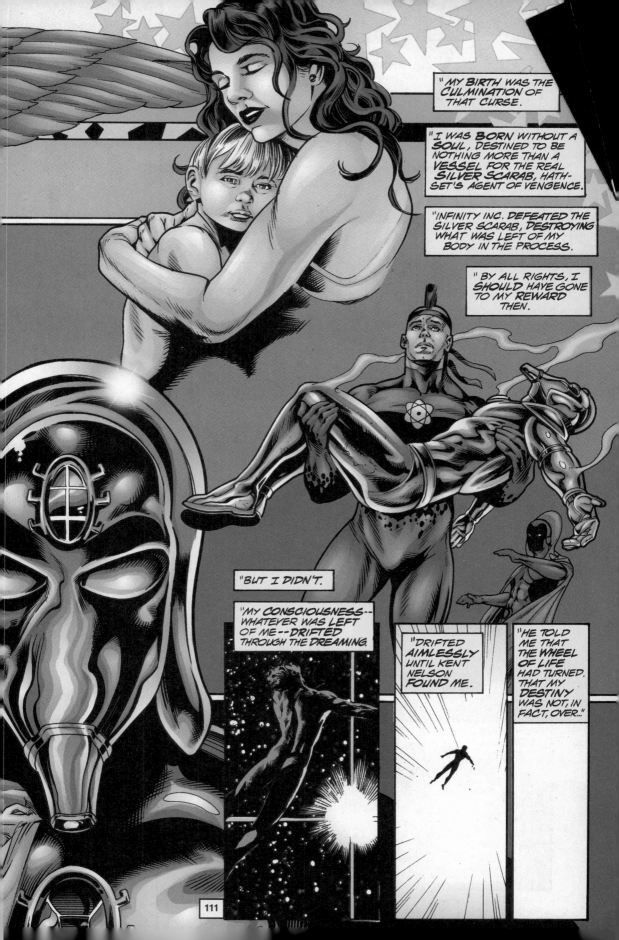

"MY BIRTH WAS THE CULMINATION OF THAT CURSE.

"I WAS BORN WITHOUT A SOUL, DESTINED TO BE NOTHING MORE THAN A VESSEL FOR THE REAL SILVER SCARAB, HATH-SET'S AGENT OF VENGEANCE.

"INFINITY INC. DEFEATED THE SILVER SCARAB, DESTROYING WHAT WAS LEFT OF MY BODY IN THE PROCESS.

" BY ALL RIGHTS, I SHOULD HAVE GONE TO MY REWARD THEN.

"BUT I DIDN'T.

"MY CONSCIOUSNESS-- WHATEVER WAS LEFT OF ME --DRIFTED THROUGH THE DREAMING.

"DRIFTED AIMLESSLY UNTIL KENT NELSON FOUND ME.

"HE TOLD ME THAT THE WHEEL OF LIFE HAD TURNED, THAT MY DESTINY WAS NOT, IN FACT, OVER..."

111

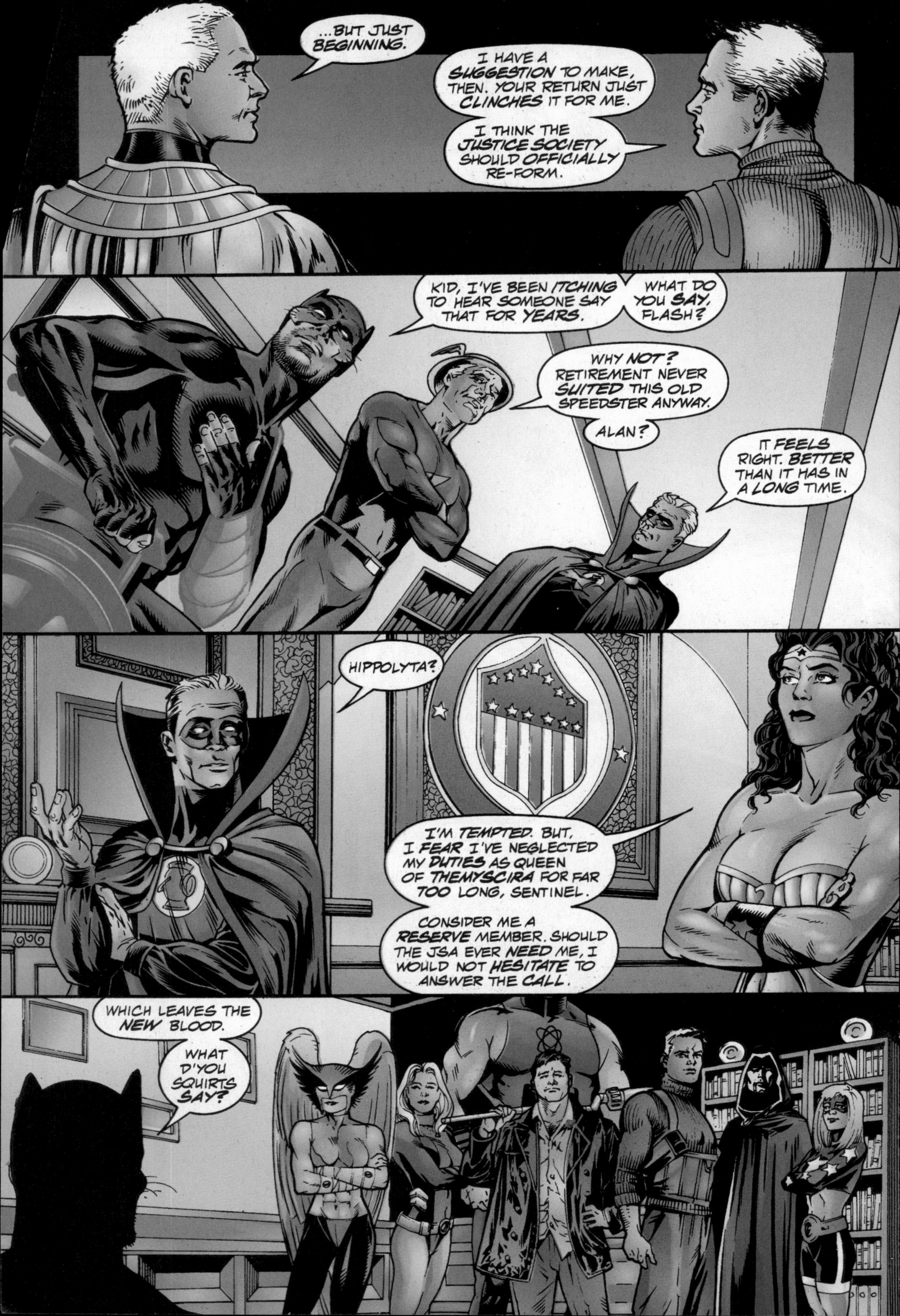
...BUT JUST BEGINNING.
I HAVE A SUGGESTION TO MAKE, THEN. YOUR RETURN JUST CLINCHES IT FOR ME.
I THINK THE JUSTICE SOCIETY SHOULD OFFICIALLY RE-FORM.
KID, I'VE BEEN ITCHING TO HEAR SOMEONE SAY THAT FOR YEARS.
WHAT DO YOU SAY, FLASH?
WHY NOT? RETIREMENT NEVER SUITED THIS OLD SPEEDSTER ANYWAY.
ALAN?
IT FEELS RIGHT. BETTER THAN IT HAS IN A LONG TIME.
HIPPOLYTA?
I'M TEMPTED. BUT, I FEAR I'VE NEGLECTED MY DUTIES AS QUEEN OF THEMYSCIRA FOR FAR TOO LONG, SENTINEL.
CONSIDER ME A RESERVE MEMBER. SHOULD THE JSA EVER NEED ME, I WOULD NOT HESITATE TO ANSWER THE CALL.
WHICH LEAVES THE NEW BLOOD.
WHAT D'YOU SQUIRTS SAY?

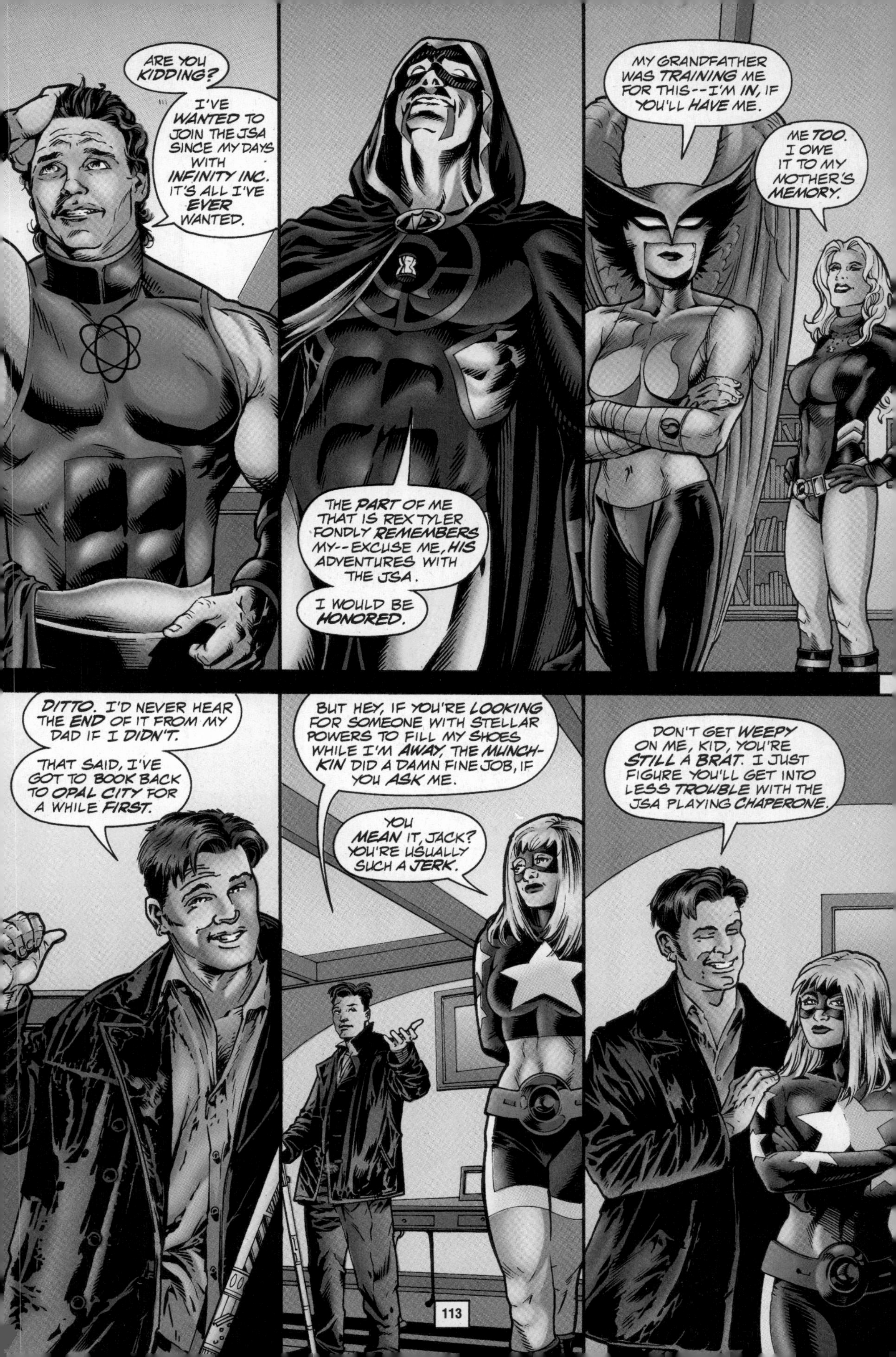
ARE YOU KIDDING?
I'VE WANTED TO JOIN THE JSA SINCE MY DAYS WITH INFINITY INC. IT'S ALL I'VE EVER WANTED.
THE PART OF ME THAT IS REX TYLER FONDLY REMEMBERS MY--EXCUSE ME, HIS ADVENTURES WITH THE JSA.
I WOULD BE HONORED.
MY GRANDFATHER WAS TRAINING ME FOR THIS--I'M IN, IF YOU'LL HAVE ME.
ME TOO. I OWE IT TO MY MOTHER'S MEMORY.
DITTO. I'D NEVER HEAR THE END OF IT FROM MY DAD IF I DIDN'T.
THAT SAID, I'VE GOT TO BOOK BACK TO OPAL CITY FOR A WHILE FIRST.
BUT HEY, IF YOU'RE LOOKING FOR SOMEONE WITH STELLAR POWERS TO FILL MY SHOES WHILE I'M AWAY, THE MUNCH-KIN DID A DAMN FINE JOB, IF YOU ASK ME.
YOU MEAN IT, JACK? YOU'RE USUALLY SUCH A JERK.
DON'T GET WEEPY ON ME, KID, YOU'RE STILL A BRAT. I JUST FIGURE YOU'LL GET INTO LESS TROUBLE WITH THE JSA PLAYING CHAPERONE.

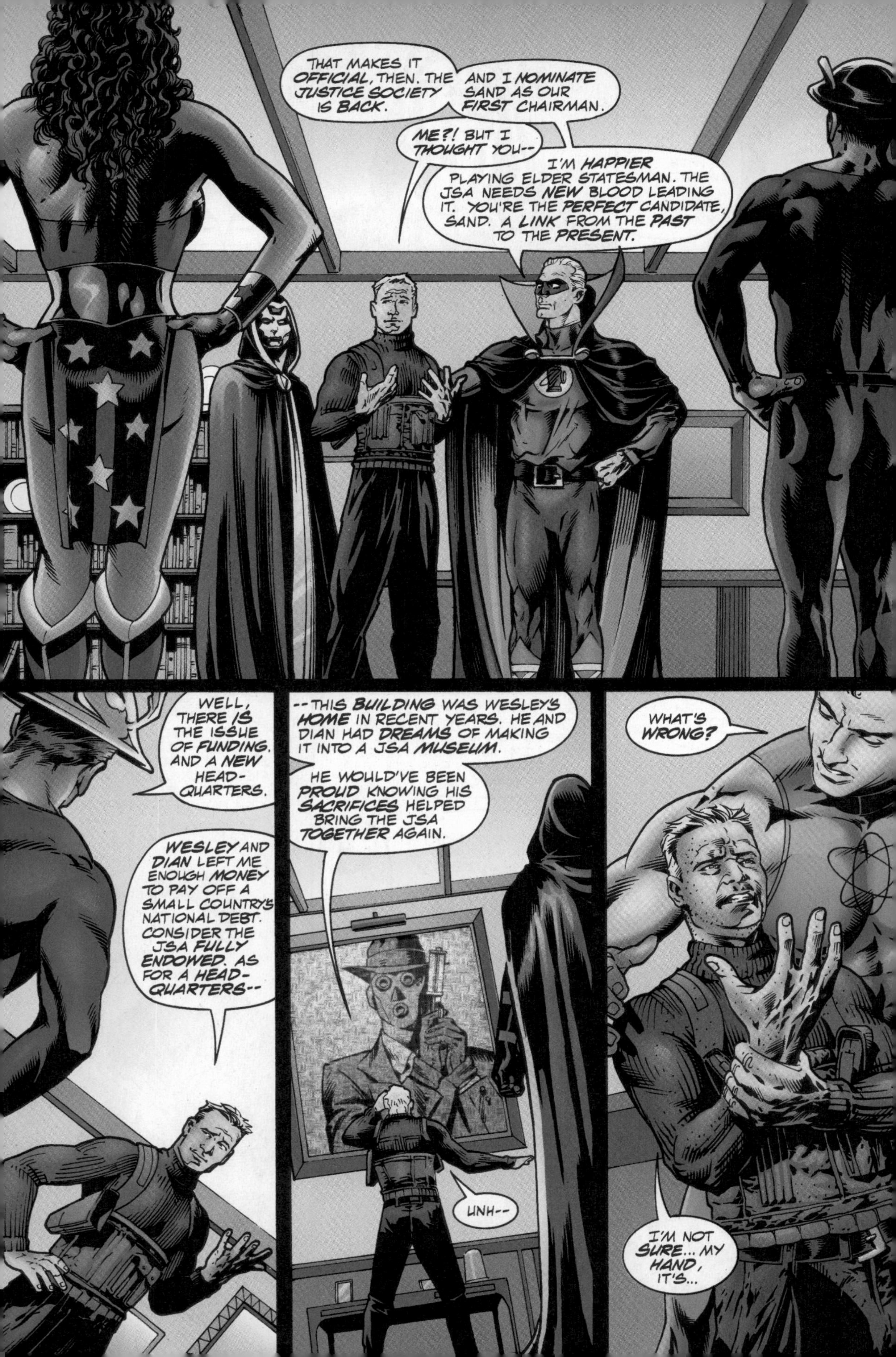
THAT MAKES IT OFFICIAL, THEN. THE JUSTICE SOCIETY IS BACK.
AND I NOMINATE SAND AS OUR FIRST CHAIRMAN.
ME?! BUT I THOUGHT YOU--
I'M HAPPIER PLAYING ELDER STATESMAN. THE JSA NEEDS NEW BLOOD LEADING IT. YOU'RE THE PERFECT CANDIDATE, SAND. A LINK FROM THE PAST TO THE PRESENT.
WELL, THERE IS THE ISSUE OF FUNDING. AND A NEW HEAD-QUARTERS.
WESLEY AND DIAN LEFT ME ENOUGH MONEY TO PAY OFF A SMALL COUNTRY'S NATIONAL DEBT. CONSIDER THE JSA FULLY ENDOWED. AS FOR A HEAD-QUARTERS--
--THIS BUILDING WAS WESLEY'S HOME IN RECENT YEARS. HE AND DIAN HAD DREAMS OF MAKING IT INTO A JSA MUSEUM.
HE WOULD'VE BEEN PROUD KNOWING HIS SACRIFICES HELPED BRING THE JSA TOGETHER AGAIN.
UNH--
WHAT'S WRONG?
I'M NOT SURE... MY HAND, IT'S...

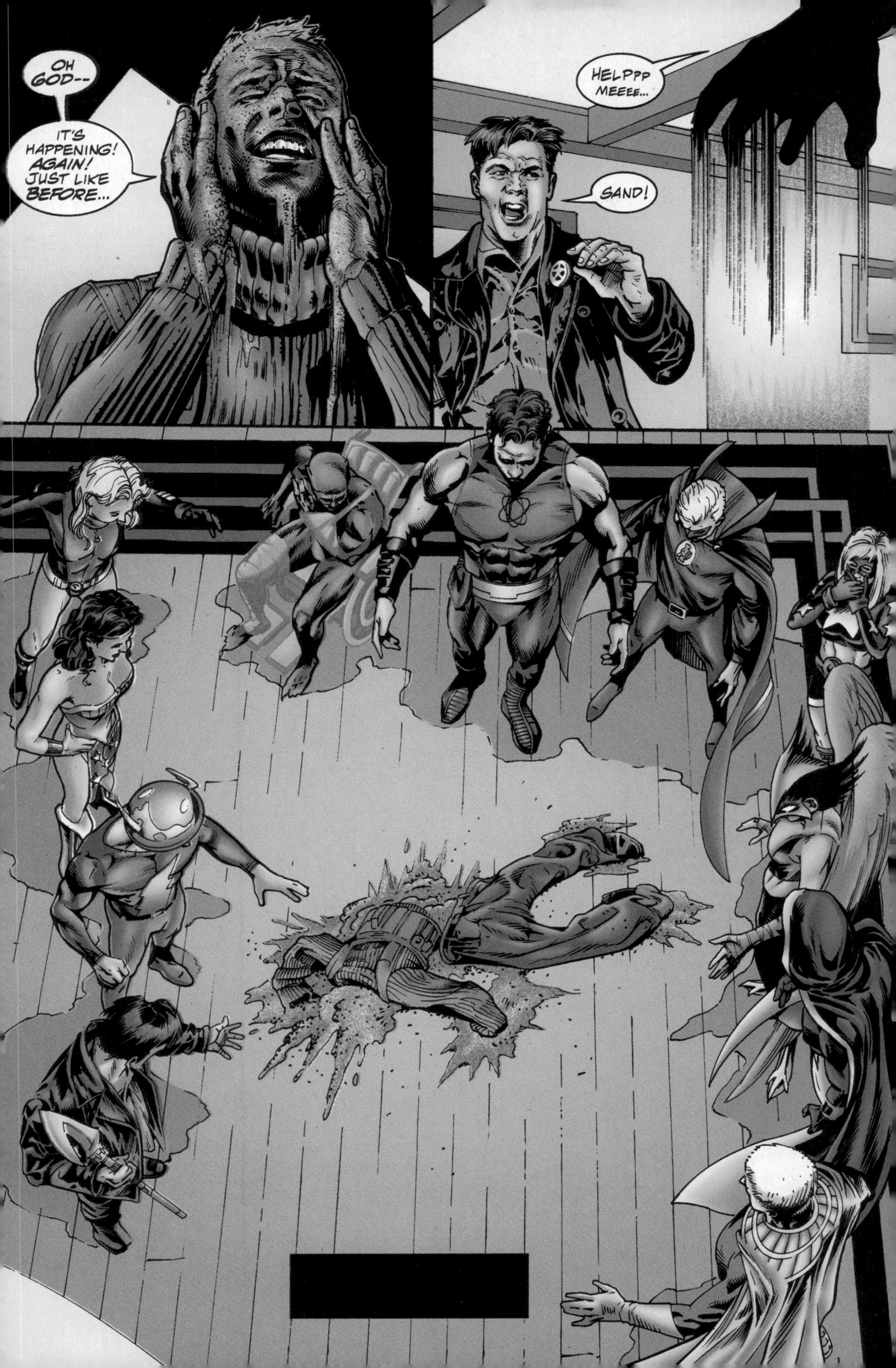
OH GOD--
IT'S HAPPENING! AGAIN! JUST LIKE BEFORE...
HELPPP MEEEE...
SAND!
[redacted]

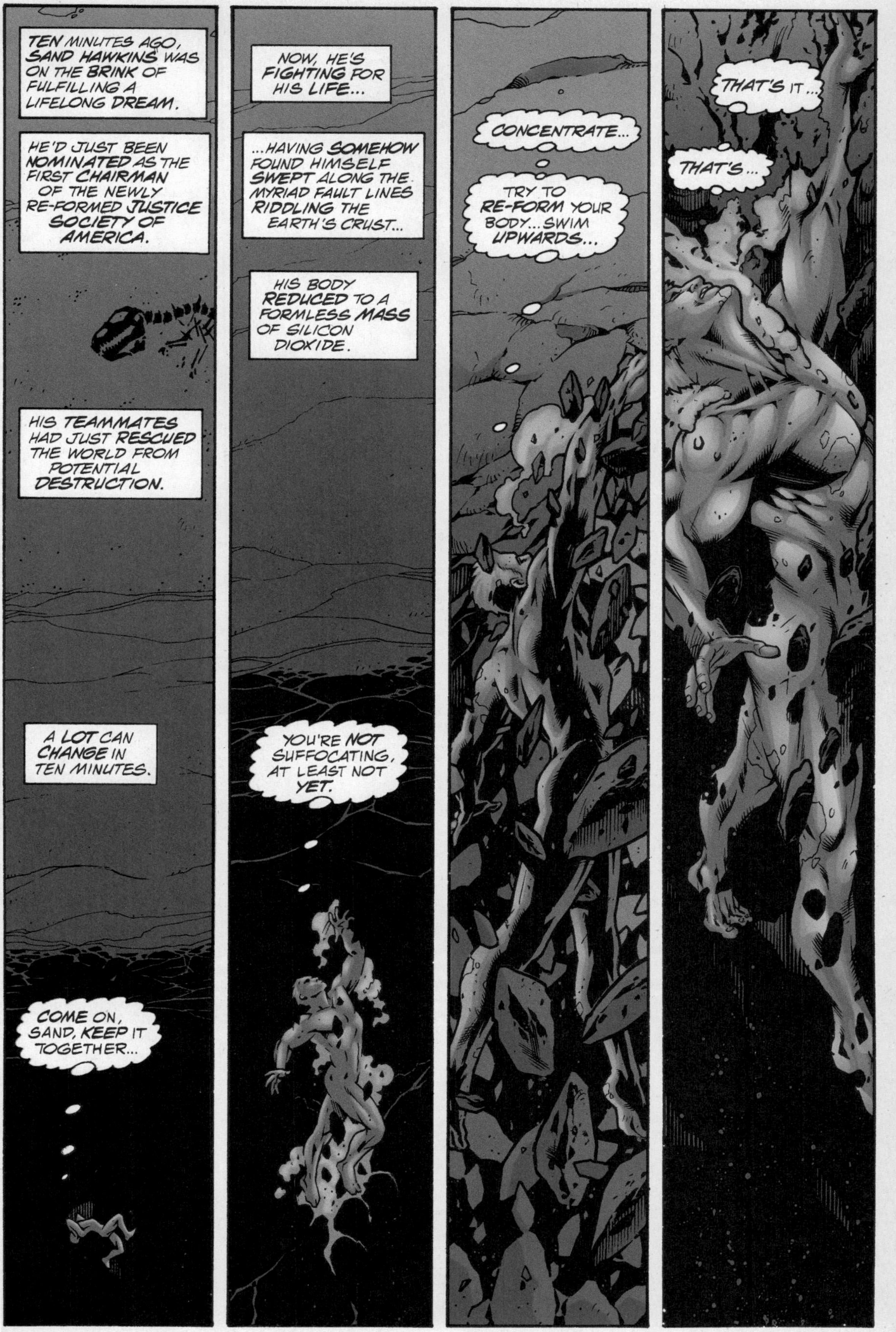
TEN MINUTES AGO, SAND HAWKINS WAS ON THE BRINK OF FULFILLING A LIFELONG DREAM.
HE'D JUST BEEN NOMINATED AS THE FIRST CHAIRMAN OF THE NEWLY RE-FORMED JUSTICE SOCIETY OF AMERICA.
HIS TEAMMATES HAD JUST RESCUED THE WORLD FROM POTENTIAL DESTRUCTION.
A LOT CAN CHANGE IN TEN MINUTES.
COME ON, SAND, KEEP IT TOGETHER...
NOW, HE'S FIGHTING FOR HIS LIFE...
...HAVING SOMEHOW FOUND HIMSELF SWEPT ALONG THE MYRIAD FAULT LINES RIDDLING THE EARTH'S CRUST...
HIS BODY REDUCED TO A FORMLESS MASS OF SILICON DIOXIDE.
YOU'RE NOT SUFFOCATING, AT LEAST NOT YET.
CONCENTRATE...
TRY TO RE-FORM YOUR BODY...SWIM UPWARDS...
THAT'S IT...
THAT'S...

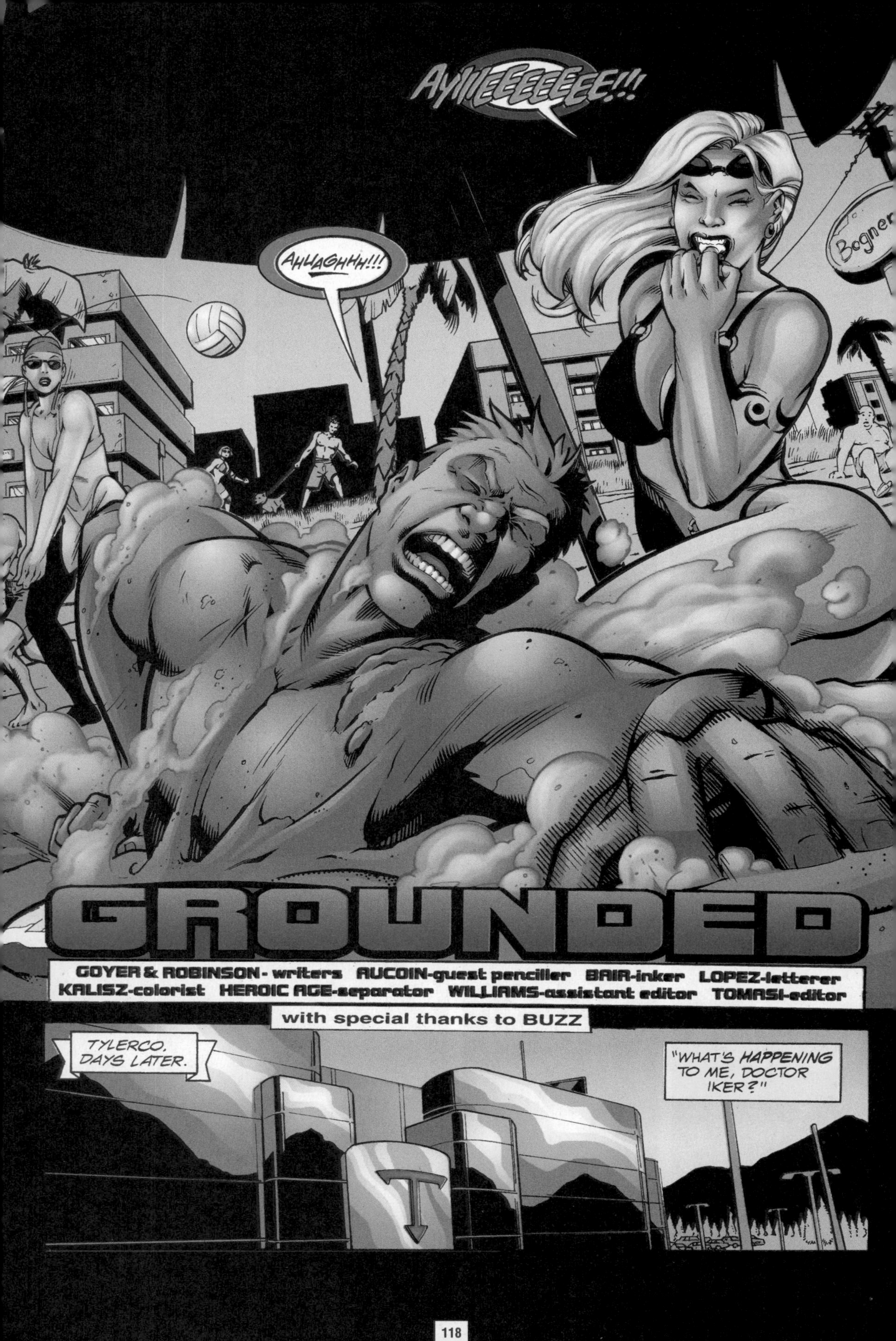
AyIIIEEEEEEEE!!!
AHHAGHHH!!!
Bogner
GROUNDED
GOYER & ROBINSON - writers AUCOIN-guest penciller BAIR-inker LOPEZ-letterer
KALISZ-colorist HEROIC AGE-separator WILLIAMS-assistant editor TOMASI-editor
with special thanks to BUZZ
TYLERCO. DAYS LATER.
"WHAT'S HAPPENING TO ME, DOCTOR IKER?"

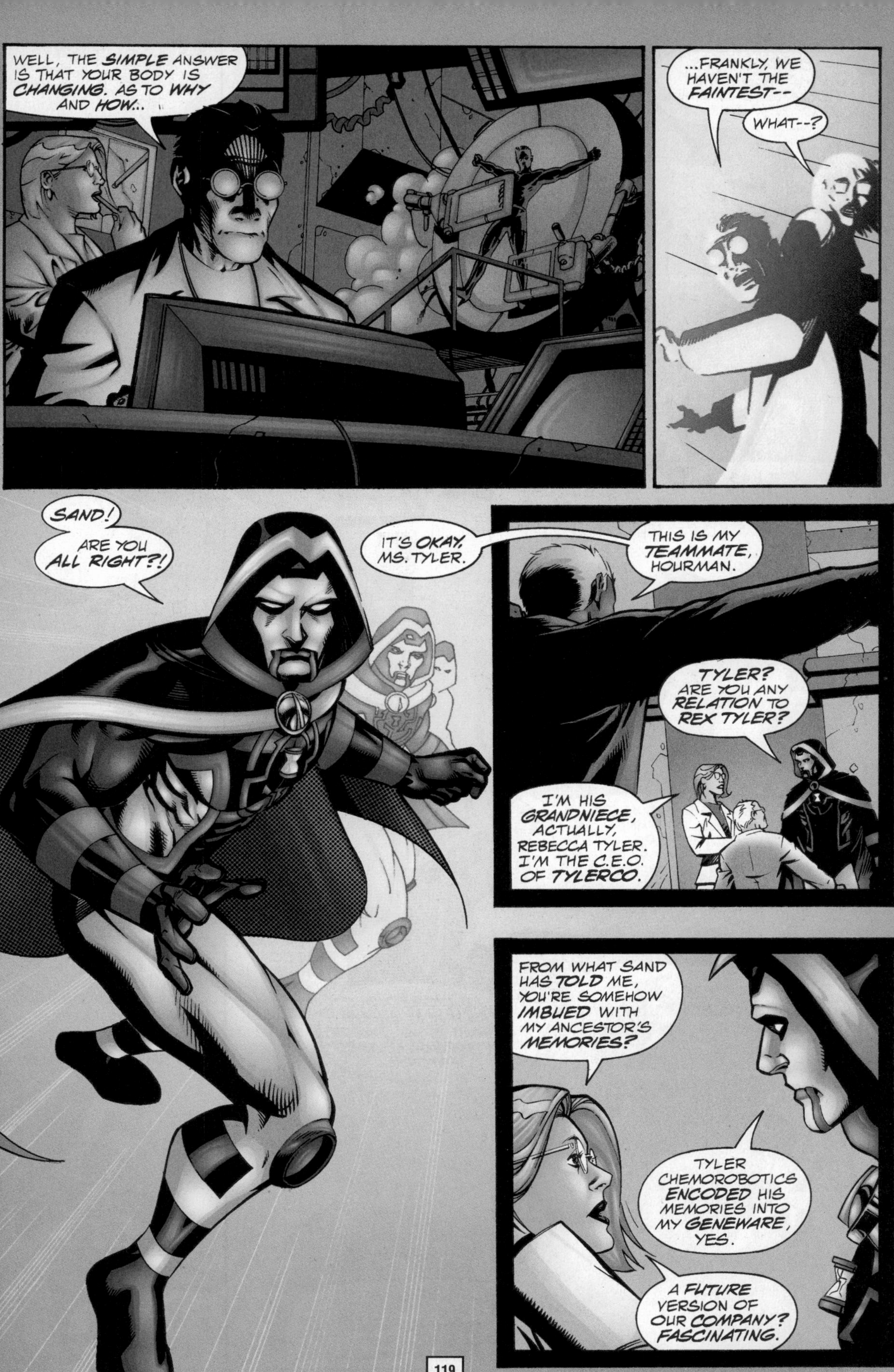
WELL, THE SIMPLE ANSWER IS THAT YOUR BODY IS CHANGING. AS TO WHY AND HOW...
...FRANKLY, WE HAVEN'T THE FAINTEST--
WHAT--?
SAND! ARE YOU ALL RIGHT?!
IT'S OKAY, MS. TYLER.
THIS IS MY TEAMMATE, HOURMAN.
TYLER? ARE YOU ANY RELATION TO REX TYLER?
I'M HIS GRANDNIECE, ACTUALLY, REBECCA TYLER. I'M THE C.E.O. OF TYLERCO.
FROM WHAT SAND HAS TOLD ME, YOU'RE SOMEHOW IMBUED WITH MY ANCESTOR'S MEMORIES?
TYLER CHEMOROBOTICS ENCODED HIS MEMORIES INTO MY GENEWARE, YES.
A FUTURE VERSION OF OUR COMPANY? FASCINATING.

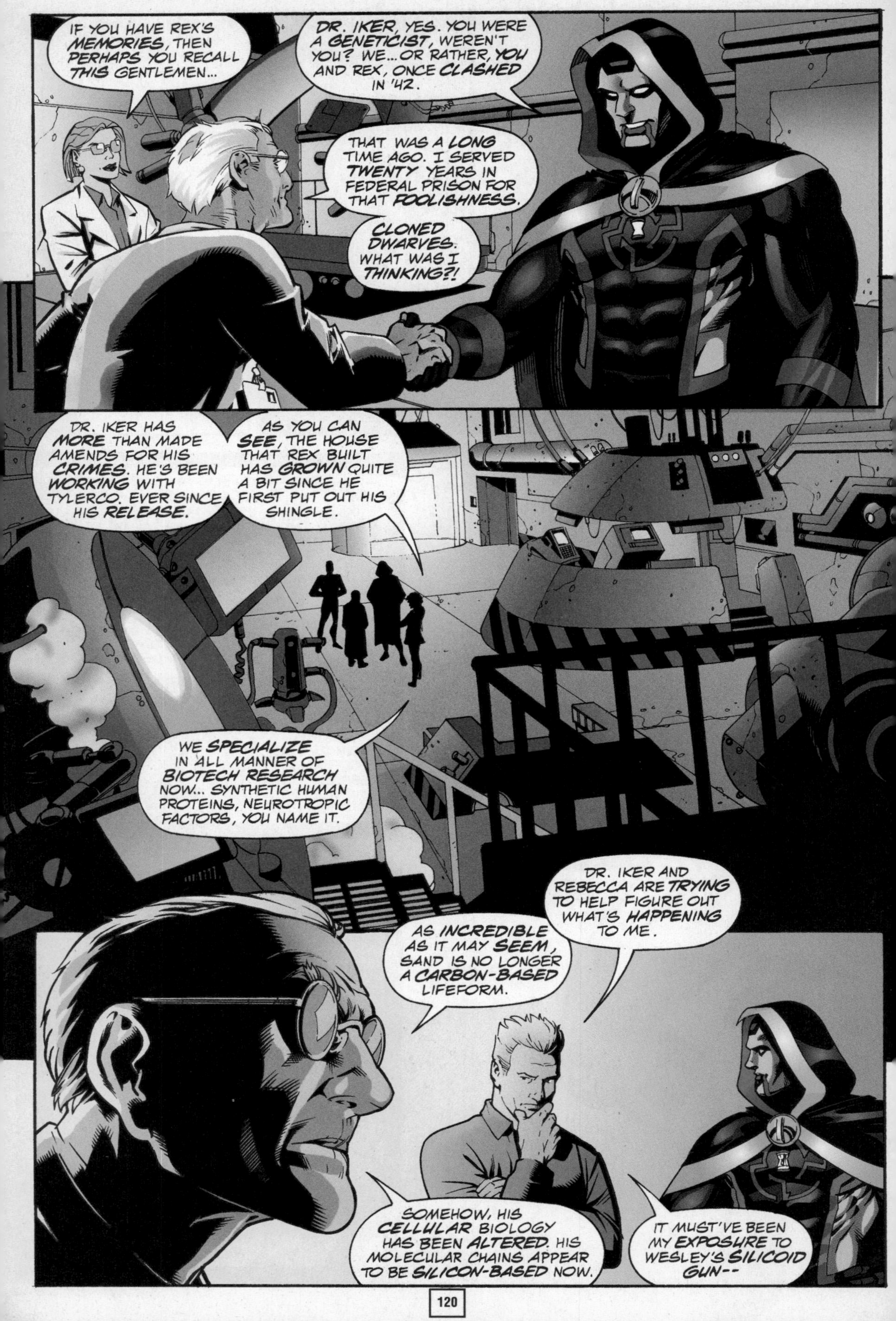
IF YOU HAVE REX'S MEMORIES, THEN PERHAPS YOU RECALL THIS GENTLEMEN...
DR. IKER, YES. YOU WERE A GENETICIST, WEREN'T YOU? WE...OR RATHER, YOU AND REX, ONCE CLASHED IN '42.
THAT WAS A LONG TIME AGO. I SERVED TWENTY YEARS IN FEDERAL PRISON FOR THAT FOOLISHNESS.
CLONED DWARVES. WHAT WAS I THINKING?!
DR. IKER HAS MORE THAN MADE AMENDS FOR HIS CRIMES. HE'S BEEN WORKING WITH TYLERCO. EVER SINCE HIS RELEASE.
AS YOU CAN SEE, THE HOUSE THAT REX BUILT HAS GROWN QUITE A BIT SINCE HE FIRST PUT OUT HIS SHINGLE.
WE SPECIALIZE IN ALL MANNER OF BIOTECH RESEARCH NOW... SYNTHETIC HUMAN PROTEINS, NEUROTROPIC FACTORS, YOU NAME IT.
DR. IKER AND REBECCA ARE TRYING TO HELP FIGURE OUT WHAT'S HAPPENING TO ME.
AS INCREDIBLE AS IT MAY SEEM, SAND IS NO LONGER A CARBON-BASED LIFEFORM.
SOMEHOW, HIS CELLULAR BIOLOGY HAS BEEN ALTERED. HIS MOLECULAR CHAINS APPEAR TO BE SILICON-BASED NOW.
IT MUST'VE BEEN MY EXPOSURE TO WESLEY'S SILICOID GUN--

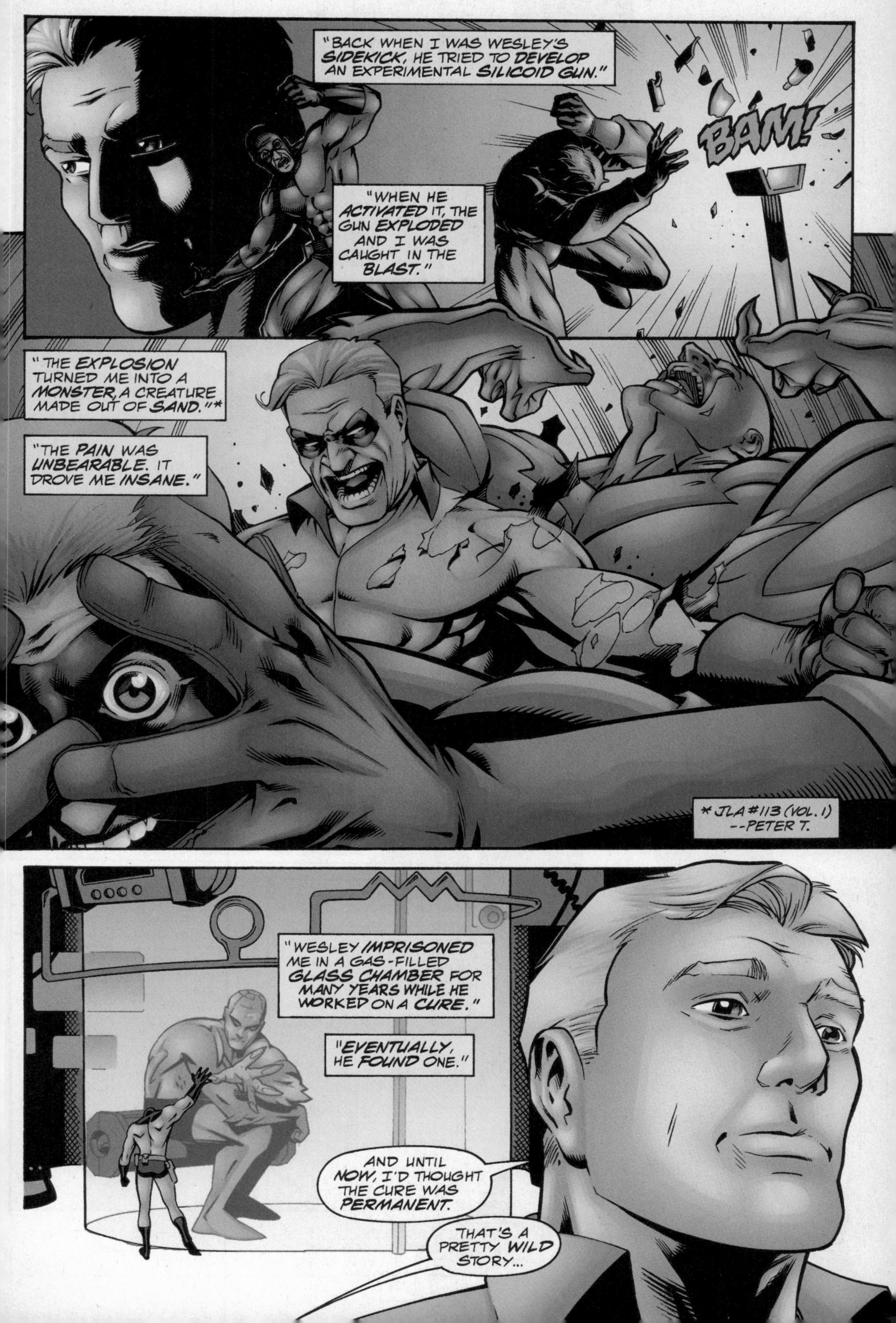
"BACK WHEN I WAS WESLEY'S SIDEKICK, HE TRIED TO DEVELOP AN EXPERIMENTAL SILICOID GUN."
"WHEN HE ACTIVATED IT, THE GUN EXPLODED AND I WAS CAUGHT IN THE BLAST."
BAM!
"THE EXPLOSION TURNED ME INTO A MONSTER, A CREATURE MADE OUT OF SAND."*
"THE PAIN WAS UNBEARABLE. IT DROVE ME INSANE."
*JLA #113 (VOL. 1) --PETER T.
"WESLEY IMPRISONED ME IN A GAS-FILLED GLASS CHAMBER FOR MANY YEARS WHILE HE WORKED ON A CURE."
"EVENTUALLY, HE FOUND ONE."
AND UNTIL NOW, I'D THOUGHT THE CURE WAS PERMANENT.
THAT'S A PRETTY WILD STORY...

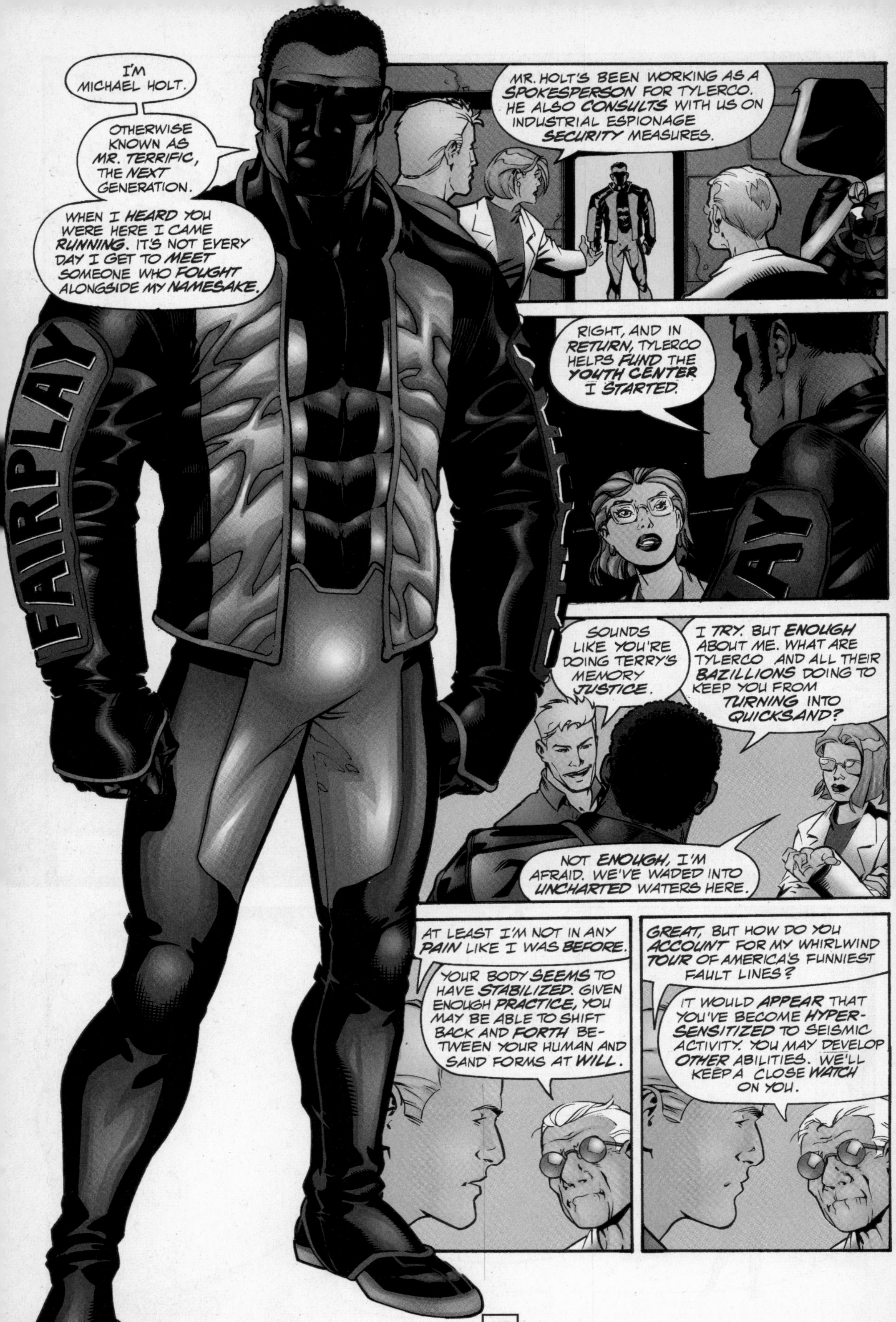
I'M MICHAEL HOLT.
OTHERWISE KNOWN AS MR. TERRIFIC, THE NEXT GENERATION.
WHEN I HEARD YOU WERE HERE I CAME RUNNING. IT'S NOT EVERY DAY I GET TO MEET SOMEONE WHO FOUGHT ALONGSIDE MY NAMESAKE.
FAIRPLAY
MR. HOLT'S BEEN WORKING AS A SPOKESPERSON FOR TYLERCO. HE ALSO CONSULTS WITH US ON INDUSTRIAL ESPIONAGE SECURITY MEASURES.
RIGHT, AND IN RETURN, TYLERCO HELPS FUND THE YOUTH CENTER I STARTED.
SOUNDS LIKE YOU'RE DOING TERRY'S MEMORY JUSTICE.
I TRY. BUT ENOUGH ABOUT ME. WHAT ARE TYLERCO AND ALL THEIR BAZILLIONS DOING TO KEEP YOU FROM TURNING INTO QUICKSAND?
NOT ENOUGH, I'M AFRAID. WE'VE WADED INTO UNCHARTED WATERS HERE.
AT LEAST I'M NOT IN ANY PAIN LIKE I WAS BEFORE.
YOUR BODY SEEMS TO HAVE STABILIZED. GIVEN ENOUGH PRACTICE, YOU MAY BE ABLE TO SHIFT BACK AND FORTH BETWEEN YOUR HUMAN AND SAND FORMS AT WILL.
GREAT, BUT HOW DO YOU ACCOUNT FOR MY WHIRLWIND TOUR OF AMERICA'S FUNNIEST FAULT LINES?
IT WOULD APPEAR THAT YOU'VE BECOME HYPER-SENSITIZED TO SEISMIC ACTIVITY. YOU MAY DEVELOP OTHER ABILITIES. WE'LL KEEP A CLOSE WATCH ON YOU.

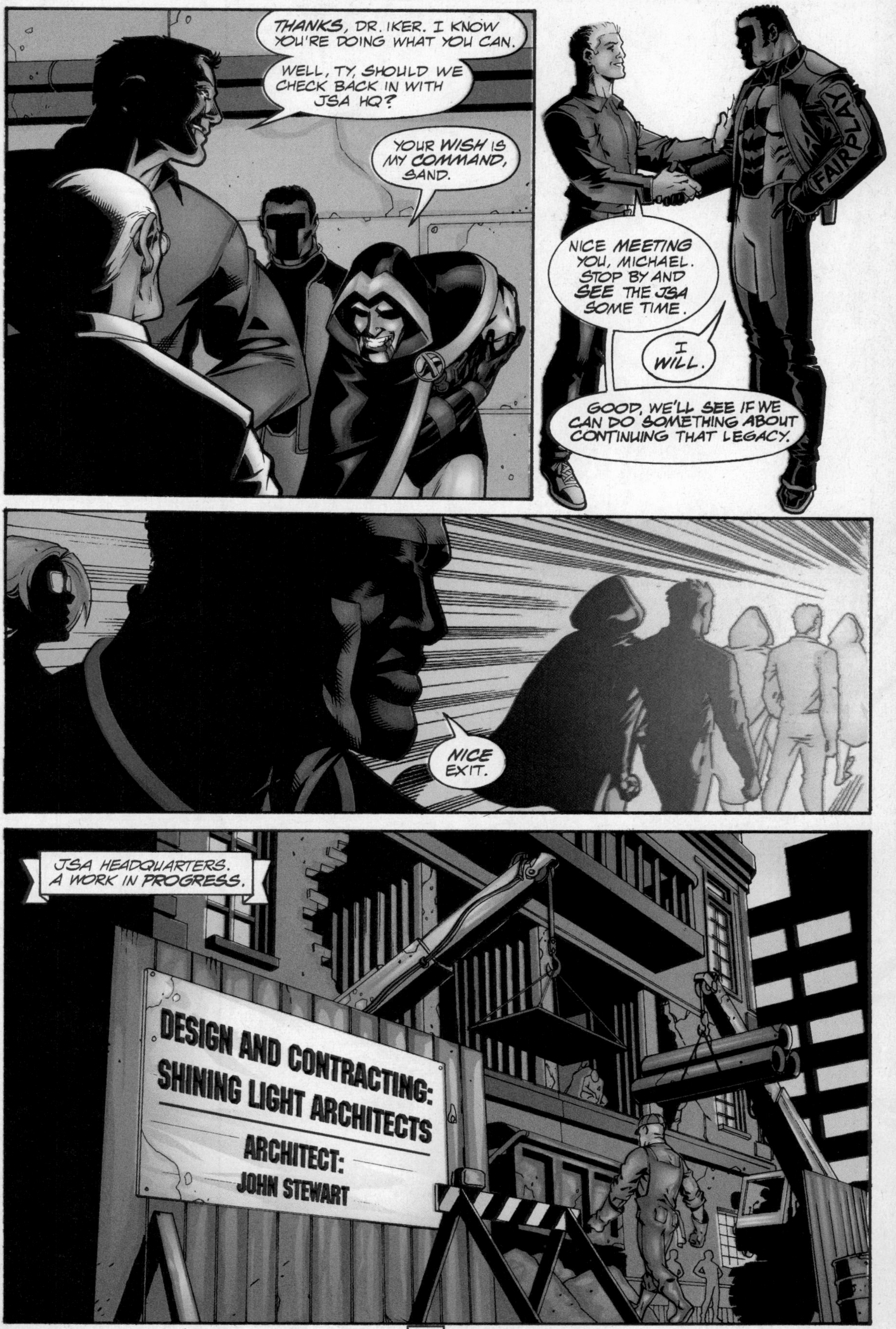
THANKS, DR. IKER. I KNOW YOU'RE DOING WHAT YOU CAN.
WELL, TY, SHOULD WE CHECK BACK IN WITH JSA HQ?
YOUR WISH IS MY COMMAND, SAND.
FAIRPLAY
NICE MEETING YOU, MICHAEL. STOP BY AND SEE THE JSA SOME TIME.
I WILL.
GOOD, WE'LL SEE IF WE CAN DO SOMETHING ABOUT CONTINUING THAT LEGACY.
NICE EXIT.
JSA HEADQUARTERS. A WORK IN PROGRESS.
DESIGN AND CONTRACTING:
SHINING LIGHT ARCHITECTS
ARCHITECT:
JOHN STEWART

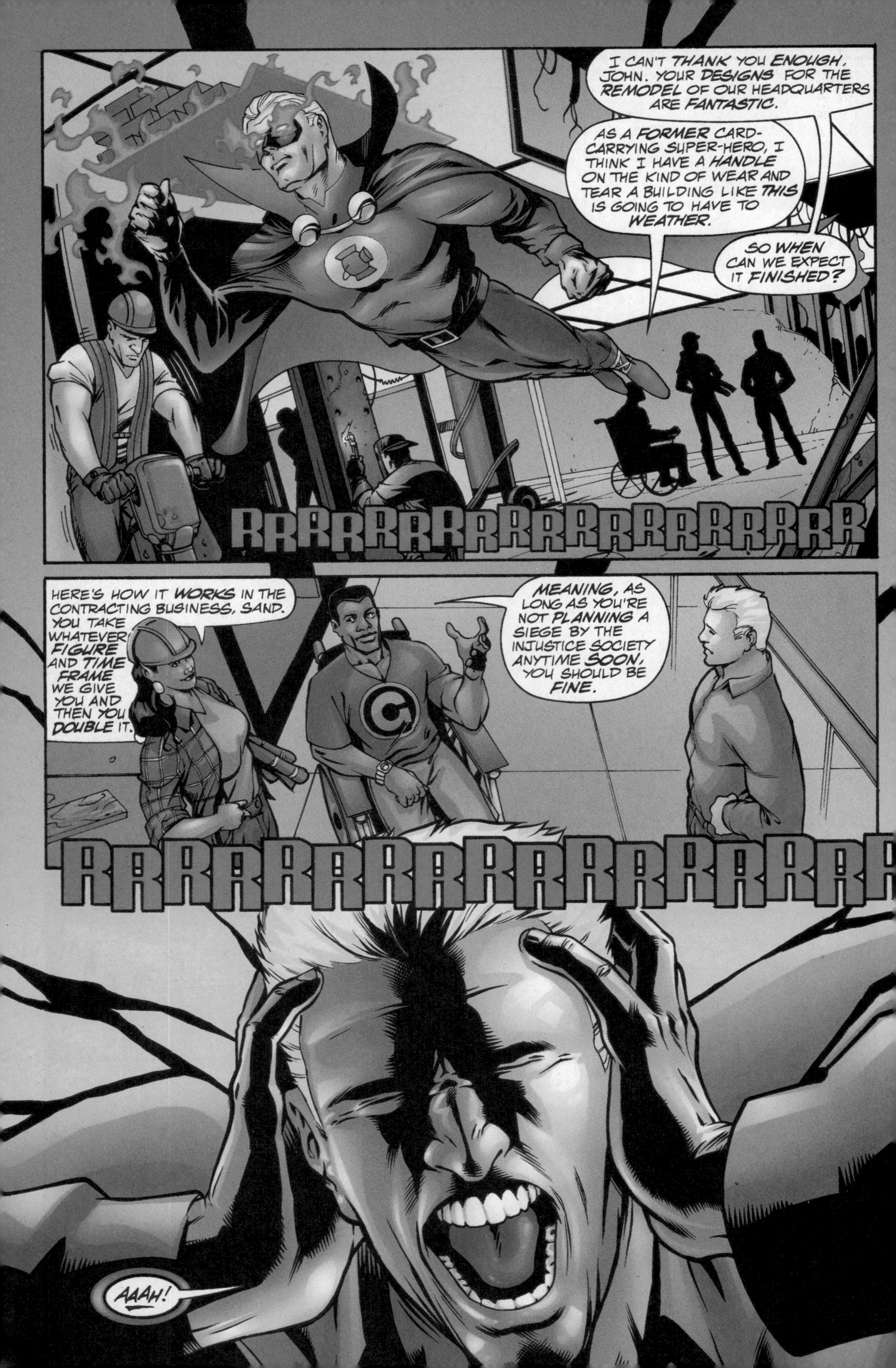
I CAN'T THANK YOU ENOUGH, JOHN. YOUR DESIGNS FOR THE REMODEL OF OUR HEADQUARTERS ARE FANTASTIC.
AS A FORMER CARD-CARRYING SUPER-HERO, I THINK I HAVE A HANDLE ON THE KIND OF WEAR AND TEAR A BUILDING LIKE THIS IS GOING TO HAVE TO WEATHER.
SO WHEN CAN WE EXPECT IT FINISHED?
RRRRRRRRRRRRRRRRRRR
HERE'S HOW IT WORKS IN THE CONTRACTING BUSINESS, SAND. YOU TAKE WHATEVER FIGURE AND TIME FRAME WE GIVE YOU AND THEN YOU DOUBLE IT.
MEANING, AS LONG AS YOU'RE NOT PLANNING A SIEGE BY THE INJUSTICE SOCIETY ANYTIME SOON, YOU SHOULD BE FINE.
RRRRRRRRRRRRRRRRRRRRRRR
AAAH!

ARE YOU *ALL RIGHT*, SAND?

I'M *SENSITIVE* TO SEISMIC VIBRATIONS--IT'S ONE OF THE *SIDE* EFFECTS OF MY *CONDITION*--

PROBABLY JUST THE *JACKHAMMER*. I'LL HAVE THE *FOREMAN* TELL THEM TO STOP--

NO, THIS IS *SOMETHING* ELSE--

SOMEONE IS--UNGH-- MANIPULATING THE EARTH'S *GEOMAGNETIC* FIELDS--

RRRRRRRRRRRRRRRRRRRRR

I'M *SORRY!* I HAVE TO *GO*--

SAND LETS HIMSELF *FALL*, NOT HAPHAZARDLY, LIKE THE *PREVIOUS* TIMES, BUT INTENTIONALLY.

SWAASSHH

HAVE TO DO *SOMETHING* ABOUT THE *CLOTHING* SITUATION. CAN'T HAVE MYSELF *CHARGING* INTO BATTLE EVERY TIME *BUCK-NAKED*.

HE FOCUSES ON THE VIBRATORY PATTERN, *HOMING* IN ON IT LIKE A MOTH TO A FLAME.

FOLLOWING IT BACK TO ITS *POINT OF ORIGIN*--

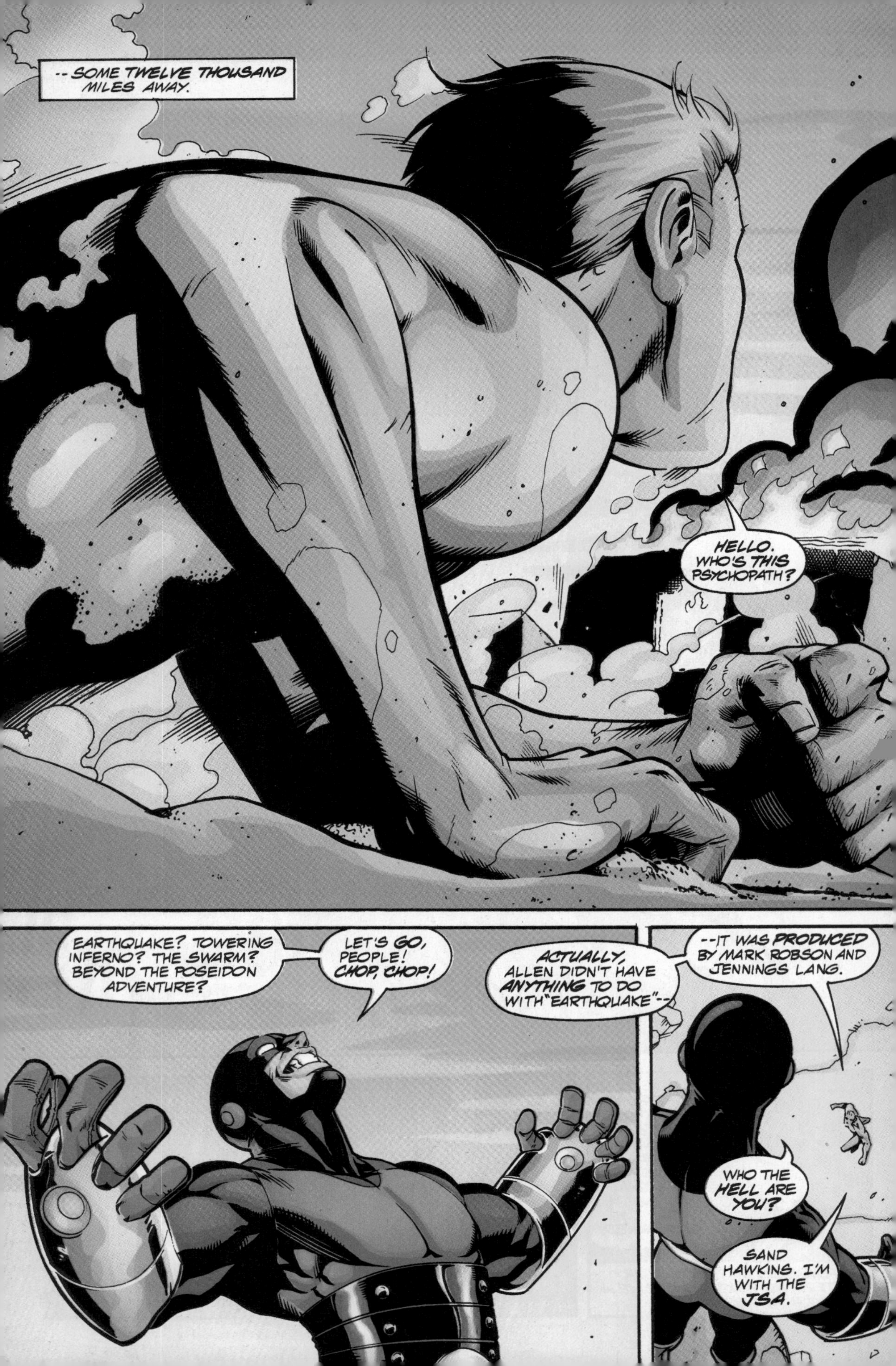

--SOME TWELVE THOUSAND MILES AWAY.
HELLO. WHO'S THIS PSYCHOPATH?
EARTHQUAKE? TOWERING INFERNO? THE SWARM? BEYOND THE POSEIDON ADVENTURE?
LET'S GO, PEOPLE! CHOP, CHOP!
ACTUALLY, ALLEN DIDN'T HAVE ANYTHING TO DO WITH "EARTHQUAKE"--
--IT WAS PRODUCED BY MARK ROBSON AND JENNINGS LANG.
WHO THE HELL ARE YOU?
SAND HAWKING. I'M WITH THE JSA.

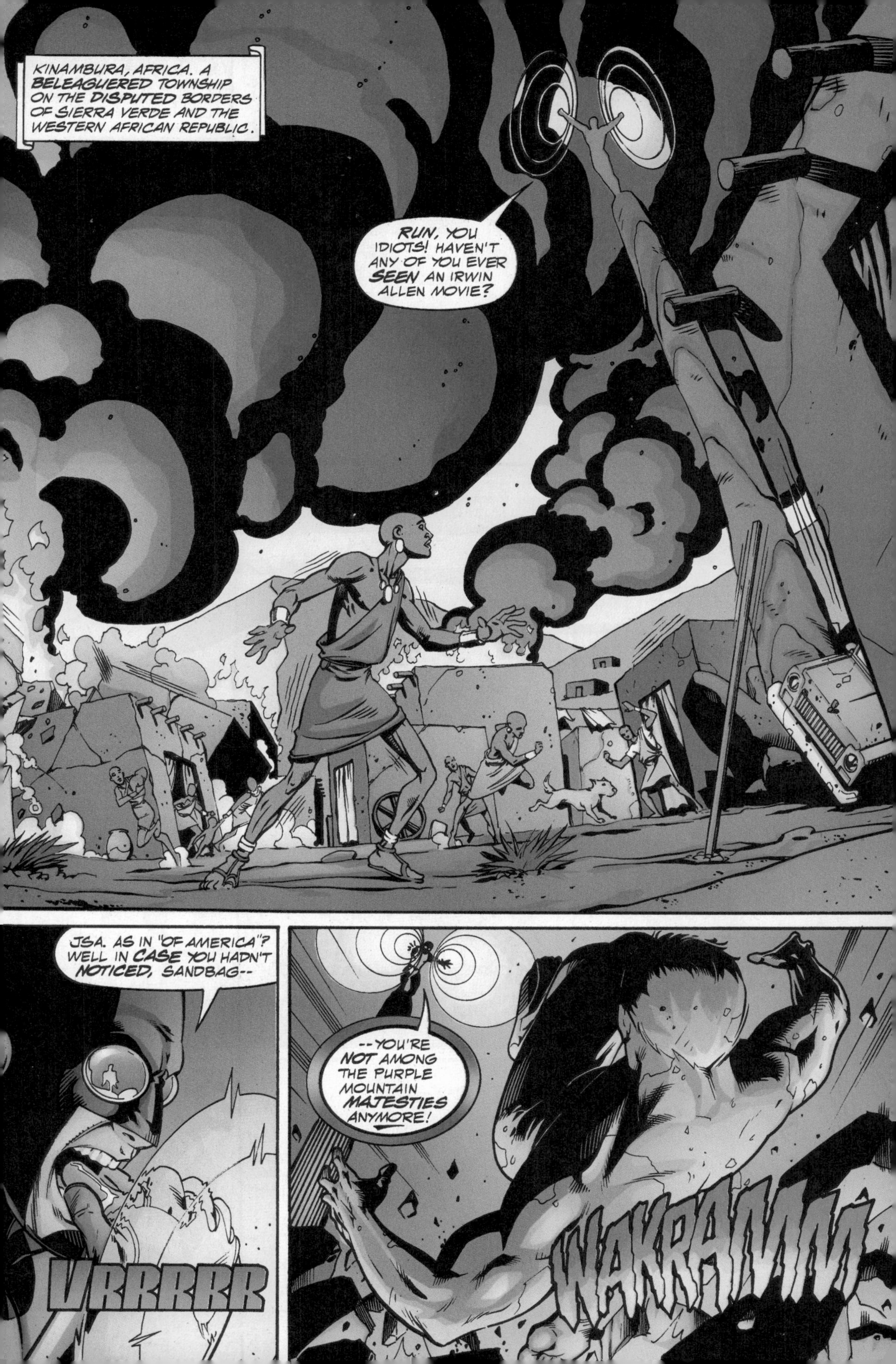
KINAMBURA, AFRICA. A BELEAGUERED TOWNSHIP ON THE DISPUTED BORDERS OF SIERRA VERDE AND THE WESTERN AFRICAN REPUBLIC.
RUN, YOU IDIOTS! HAVEN'T ANY OF YOU EVER SEEN AN IRWIN ALLEN MOVIE?
JSA. AS IN "OF AMERICA"? WELL IN CASE YOU HADN'T NOTICED, SANDBAG--
VRRRRR
--YOU'RE NOT AMONG THE PURPLE MOUNTAIN MAJESTIES ANYMORE!
WAKRAMM

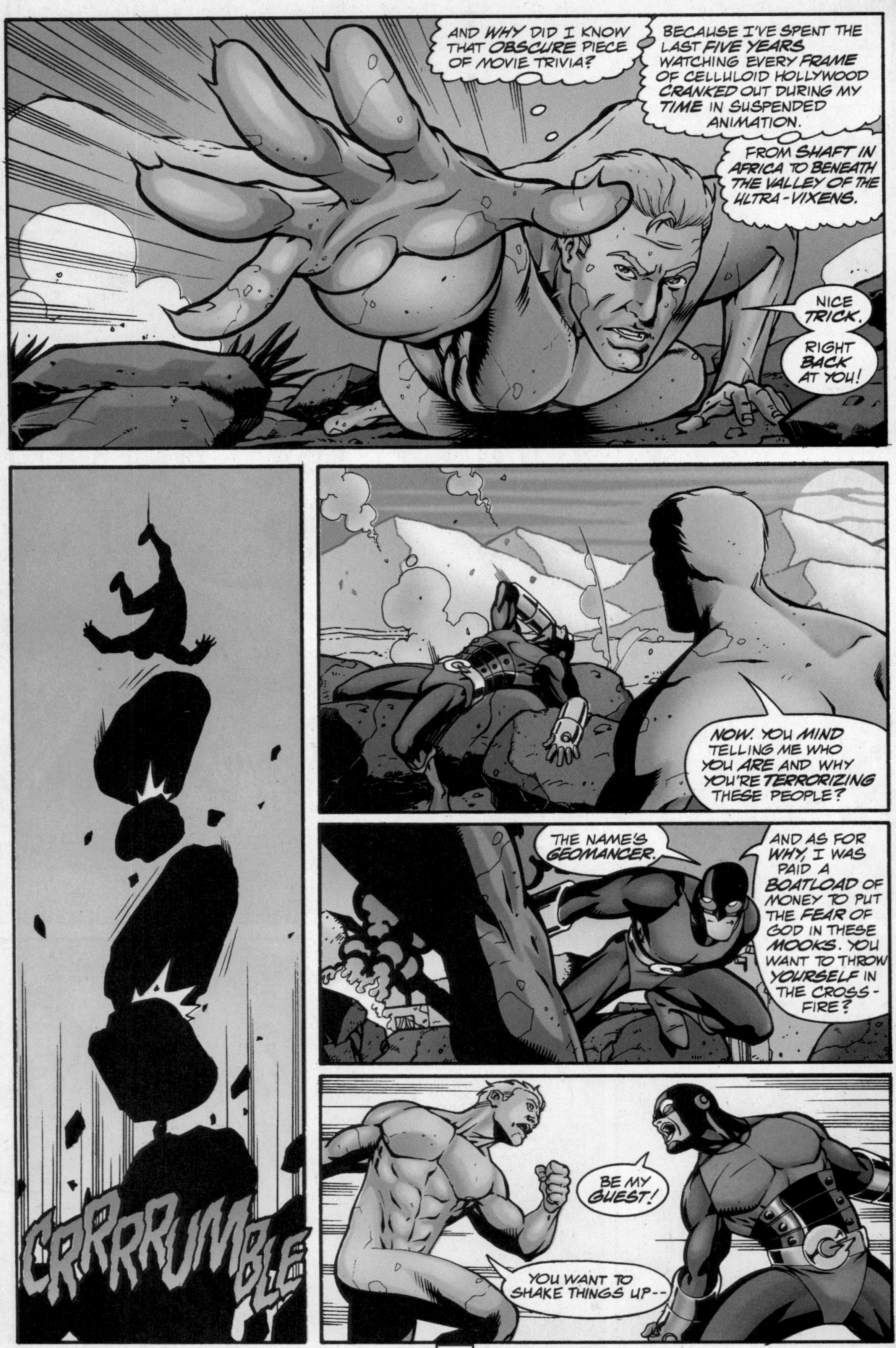
AND WHY DID I KNOW THAT OBSCURE PIECE OF MOVIE TRIVIA?
BECAUSE I'VE SPENT THE LAST FIVE YEARS WATCHING EVERY FRAME OF CELLULOID HOLLYWOOD CRANKED OUT DURING MY TIME IN SUSPENDED ANIMATION.
FROM SHAFT IN AFRICA TO BENEATH THE VALLEY OF THE ULTRA-VIXENS.
NICE TRICK.
RIGHT BACK AT YOU!
CRRRRUMBLE
NOW. YOU MIND TELLING ME WHO YOU ARE AND WHY YOU'RE TERRORIZING THESE PEOPLE?
THE NAME'S GEOMANCER.
AND AS FOR WHY, I WAS PAID A BOATLOAD OF MONEY TO PUT THE FEAR OF GOD IN THESE MOOKS. YOU WANT TO THROW YOURSELF IN THE CROSS-FIRE?
BE MY GUEST!
YOU WANT TO SHAKE THINGS UP--

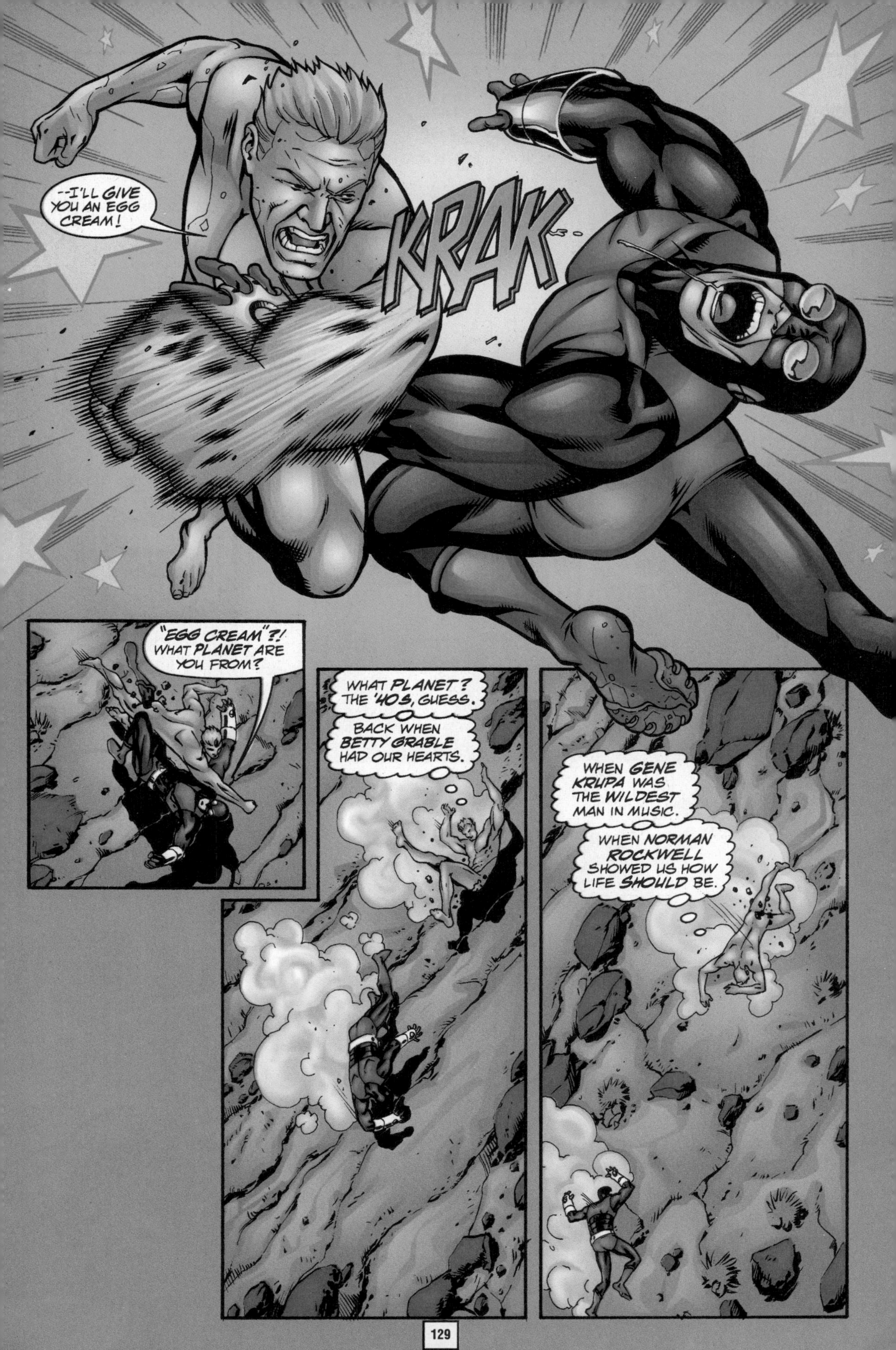
--I'LL GIVE YOU AN EGG CREAM!
KRAK
"EGG CREAM"?! WHAT PLANET ARE YOU FROM?
WHAT PLANET? THE '40s, GUESS.
BACK WHEN BETTY GRABLE HAD OUR HEARTS.
WHEN GENE KRUPA WAS THE WILDEST MAN IN MUSIC.
WHEN NORMAN ROCKWELL SHOWED US HOW LIFE SHOULD BE.

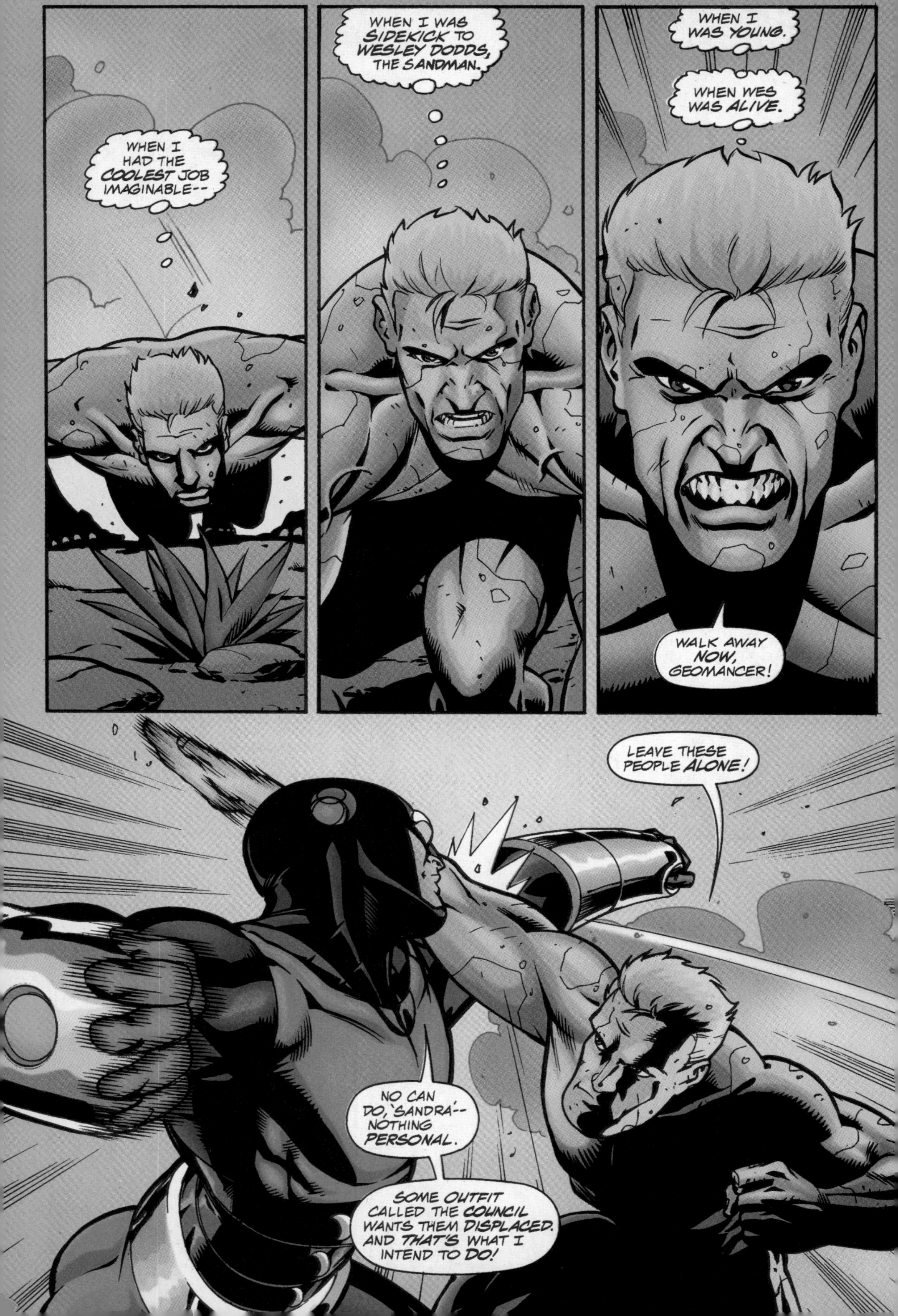

WHEN I HAD THE COOLEST JOB IMAGINABLE--
WHEN I WAS SIDEKICK TO WESLEY DODDS, THE SANDMAN.
WHEN I WAS YOUNG.
WHEN WES WAS ALIVE.
WALK AWAY NOW, GEOMANCER!
LEAVE THESE PEOPLE ALONE!
NO CAN DO, 'SANDRA'-- NOTHING PERSONAL.
SOME OUTFIT CALLED THE COUNCIL WANTS THEM DISPLACED. AND THAT'S WHAT I INTEND TO DO!

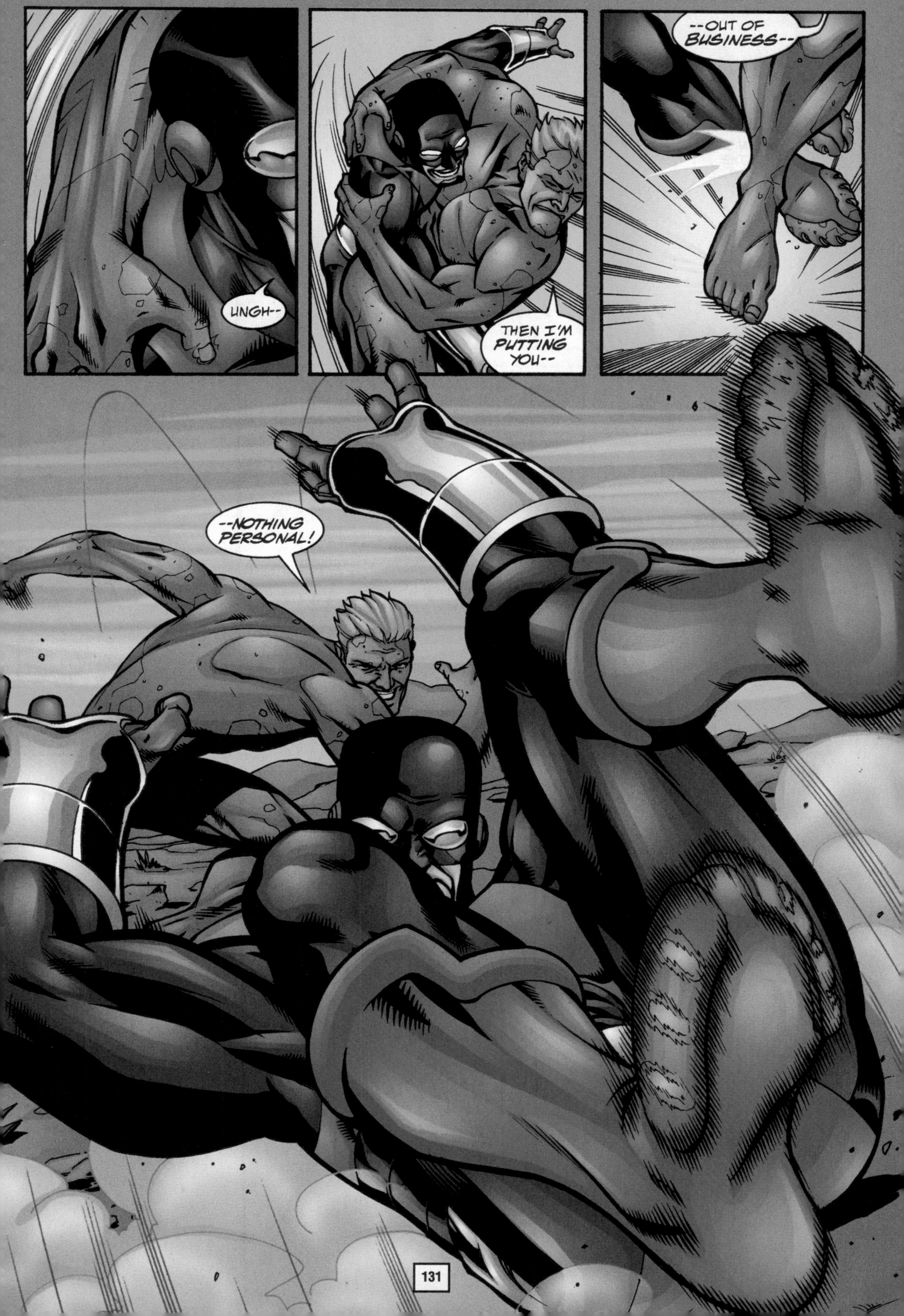
UNGH--
THEN I'M PUTTING YOU--
--OUT OF BUSINESS--
--NOTHING PERSONAL!

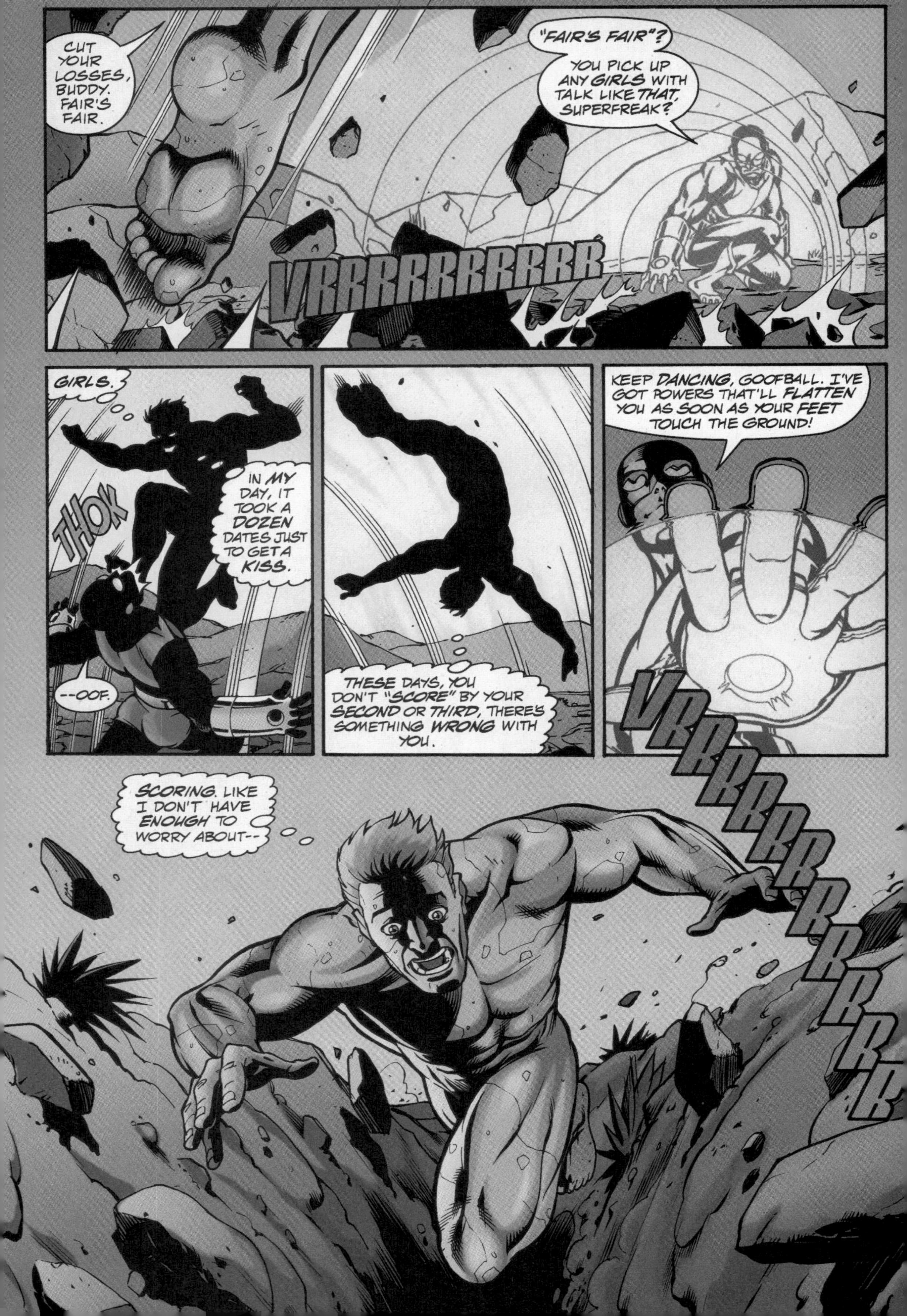
CUT YOUR LOSSES, BUDDY. FAIR'S FAIR.
"FAIR'S FAIR"?
YOU PICK UP ANY GIRLS WITH TALK LIKE THAT, SUPERFREAK?
VRRRRRRRRRRR
GIRLS.
IN MY DAY, IT TOOK A DOZEN DATES JUST TO GET A KISS.
THOK
--OOF.
THESE DAYS, YOU DON'T "SCORE" BY YOUR SECOND OR THIRD, THERE'S SOMETHING WRONG WITH YOU.
KEEP DANCING, GOOFBALL. I'VE GOT POWERS THAT'LL FLATTEN YOU AS SOON AS YOUR FEET TOUCH THE GROUND!
VRRRRRRRRRRRRR
SCORING. LIKE I DON'T HAVE ENOUGH TO WORRY ABOUT--

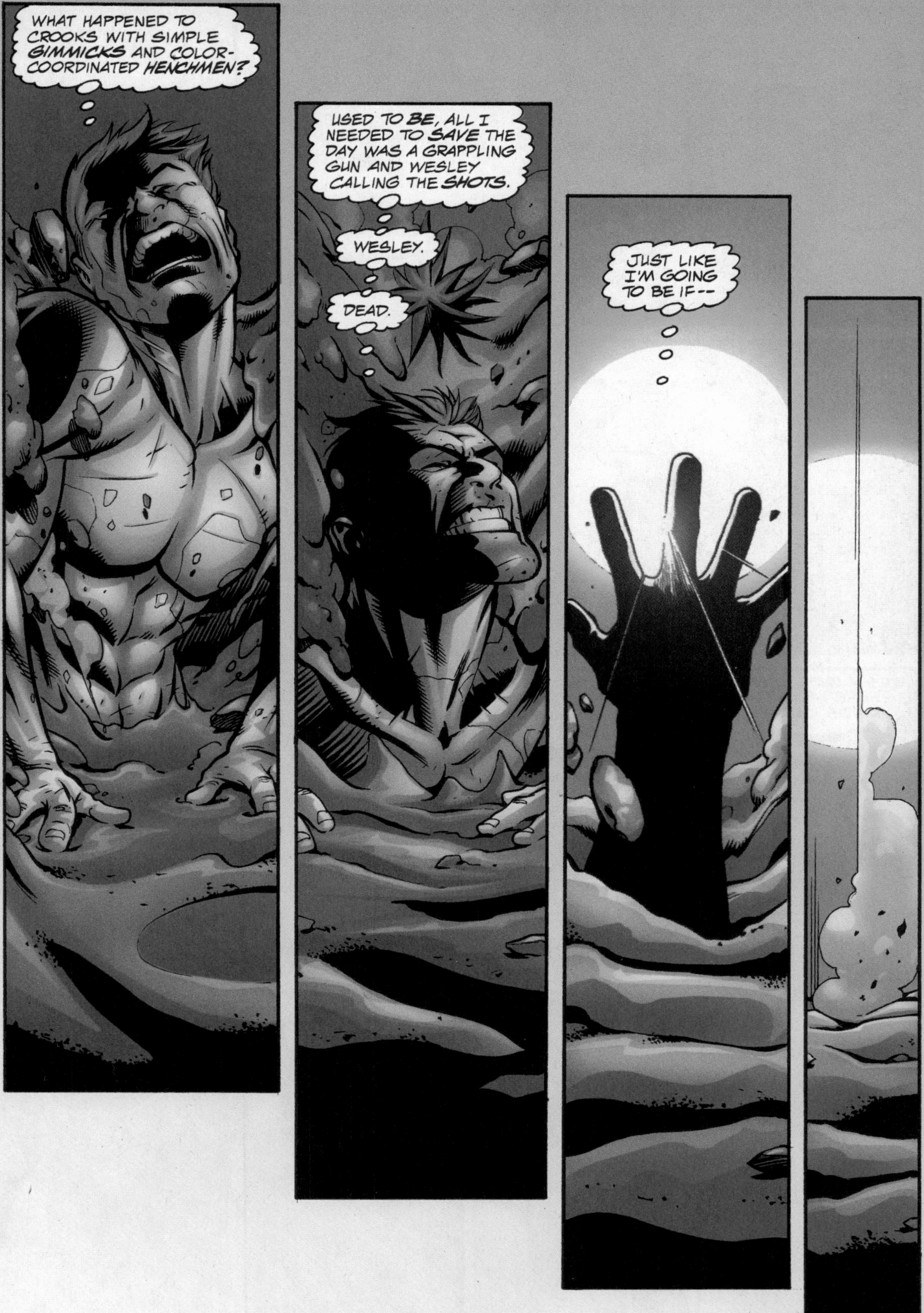
WHAT HAPPENED TO CROOKS WITH SIMPLE GIMMICKS AND COLOR-COORDINATED HENCHMEN?
USED TO BE, ALL I NEEDED TO SAVE THE DAY WAS A GRAPPLING GUN AND WESLEY CALLING THE SHOTS.
WESLEY.
DEAD.
JUST LIKE I'M GOING TO BE IF--

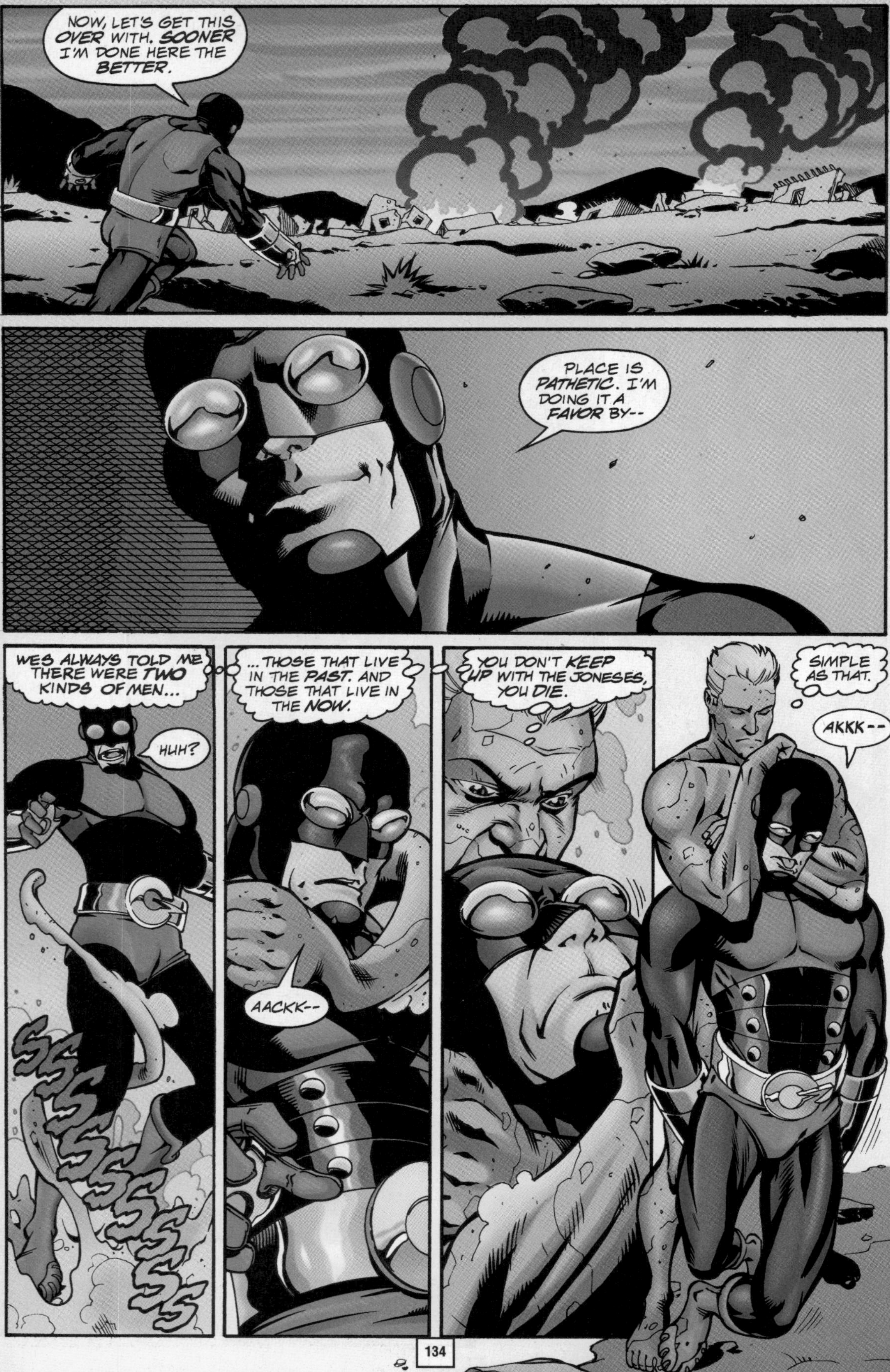
NOW, LET'S GET THIS OVER WITH. SOONER I'M DONE HERE THE BETTER.
PLACE IS PATHETIC. I'M DOING IT A FAVOR BY--
WES ALWAYS TOLD ME THERE WERE TWO KINDS OF MEN...
HUH?
SSSSSSSSSS
...THOSE THAT LIVE IN THE PAST. AND THOSE THAT LIVE IN THE NOW.
AACKK--
YOU DON'T KEEP UP WITH THE JONESES, YOU DIE.
SIMPLE AS THAT.
AKKK--

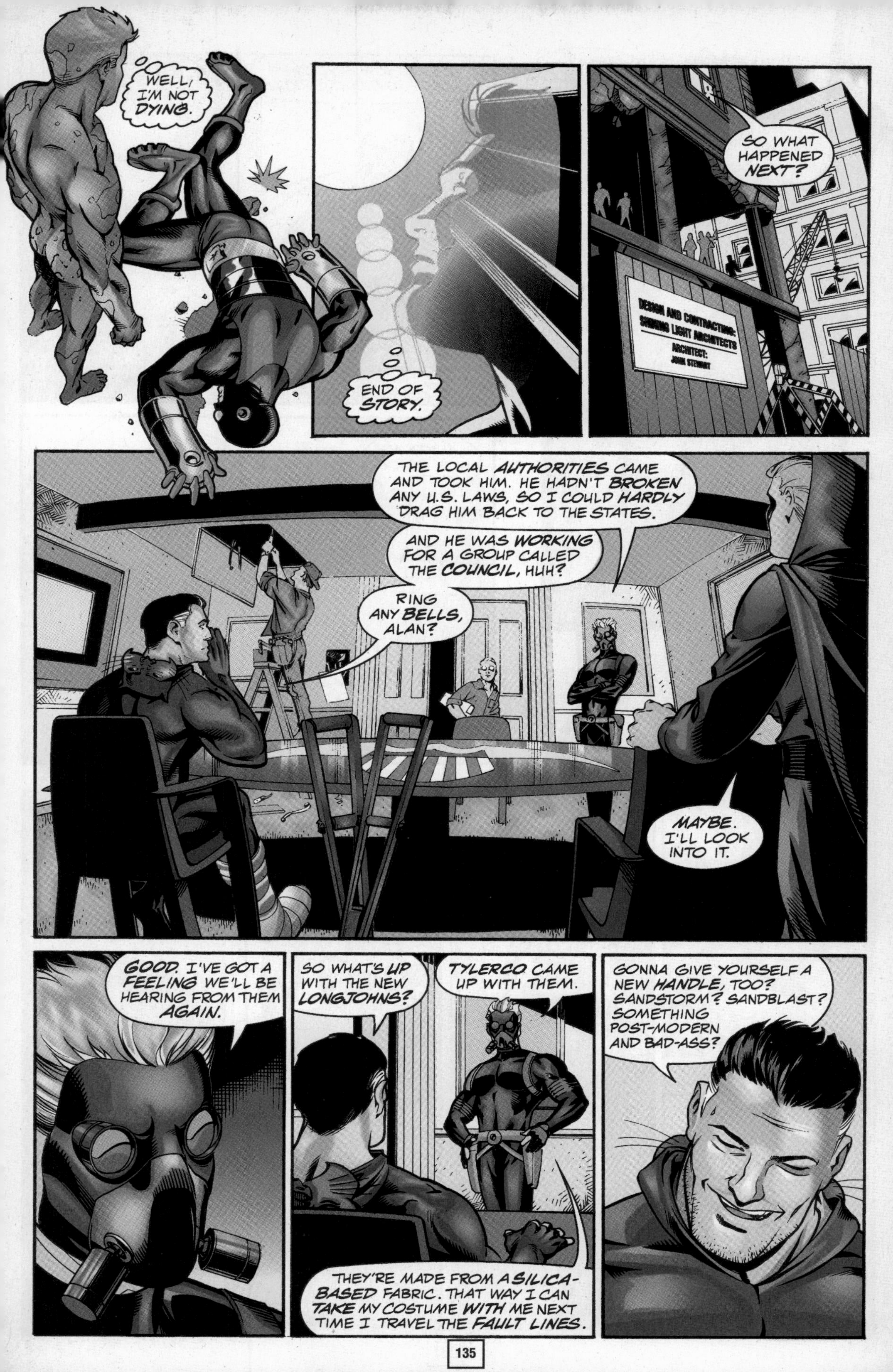
WELL, I'M NOT DYING.
END OF STORY.
SO WHAT HAPPENED NEXT?
DESIGN AND CONTRACTING: SHINING LIGHT ARCHITECTS
ARCHITECT: JOHN STEWART
THE LOCAL AUTHORITIES CAME AND TOOK HIM. HE HADN'T BROKEN ANY U.S. LAWS, SO I COULD HARDLY DRAG HIM BACK TO THE STATES.
AND HE WAS WORKING FOR A GROUP CALLED THE COUNCIL, HUH?
RING ANY BELLS, ALAN?
MAYBE. I'LL LOOK INTO IT.
GOOD. I'VE GOT A FEELING WE'LL BE HEARING FROM THEM AGAIN.
SO WHAT'S UP WITH THE NEW LONGJOHNS?
TYLERCO CAME UP WITH THEM.
THEY'RE MADE FROM A SILICA-BASED FABRIC. THAT WAY I CAN TAKE MY COSTUME WITH ME NEXT TIME I TRAVEL THE FAULT LINES.
GONNA GIVE YOURSELF A NEW HANDLE, TOO? SANDSTORM? SANDBLAST? SOMETHING POST-MODERN AND BAD-ASS?

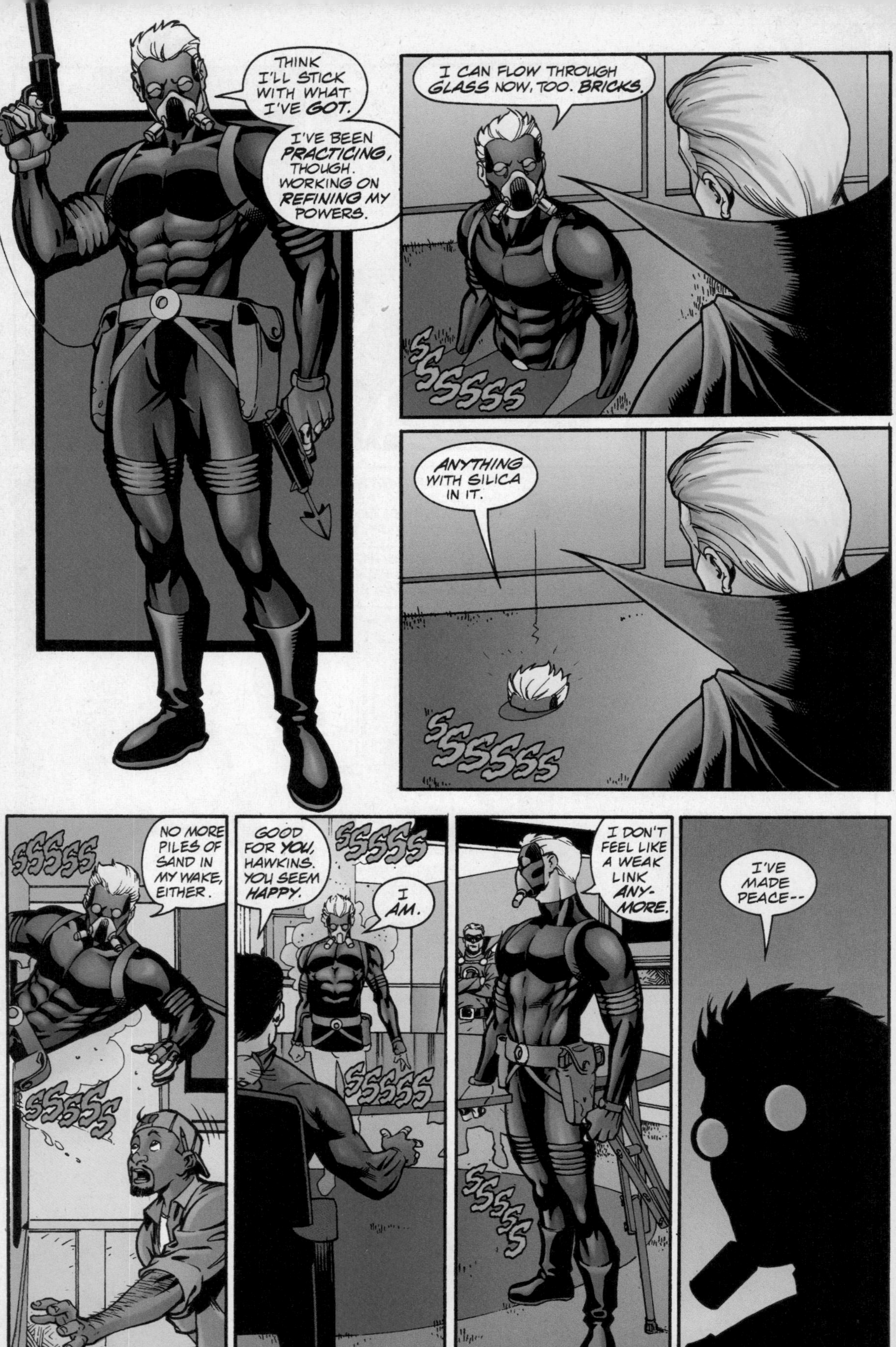

THINK I'LL STICK WITH WHAT I'VE GOT.
I'VE BEEN PRACTICING, THOUGH. WORKING ON REFINING MY POWERS.
I CAN FLOW THROUGH GLASS NOW, TOO. BRICKS.
SSSSSSS
ANYTHING WITH SILICA IN IT.
SSSSSSSS
SSSSSS
NO MORE PILES OF SAND IN MY WAKE, EITHER.
SSSSSS
GOOD FOR YOU, HAWKINS. YOU SEEM HAPPY.
SSSSS
I AM.
SSSSSS
I DON'T FEEL LIKE A WEAK LINK ANY-MORE.
SSSSS
I'VE MADE PEACE--

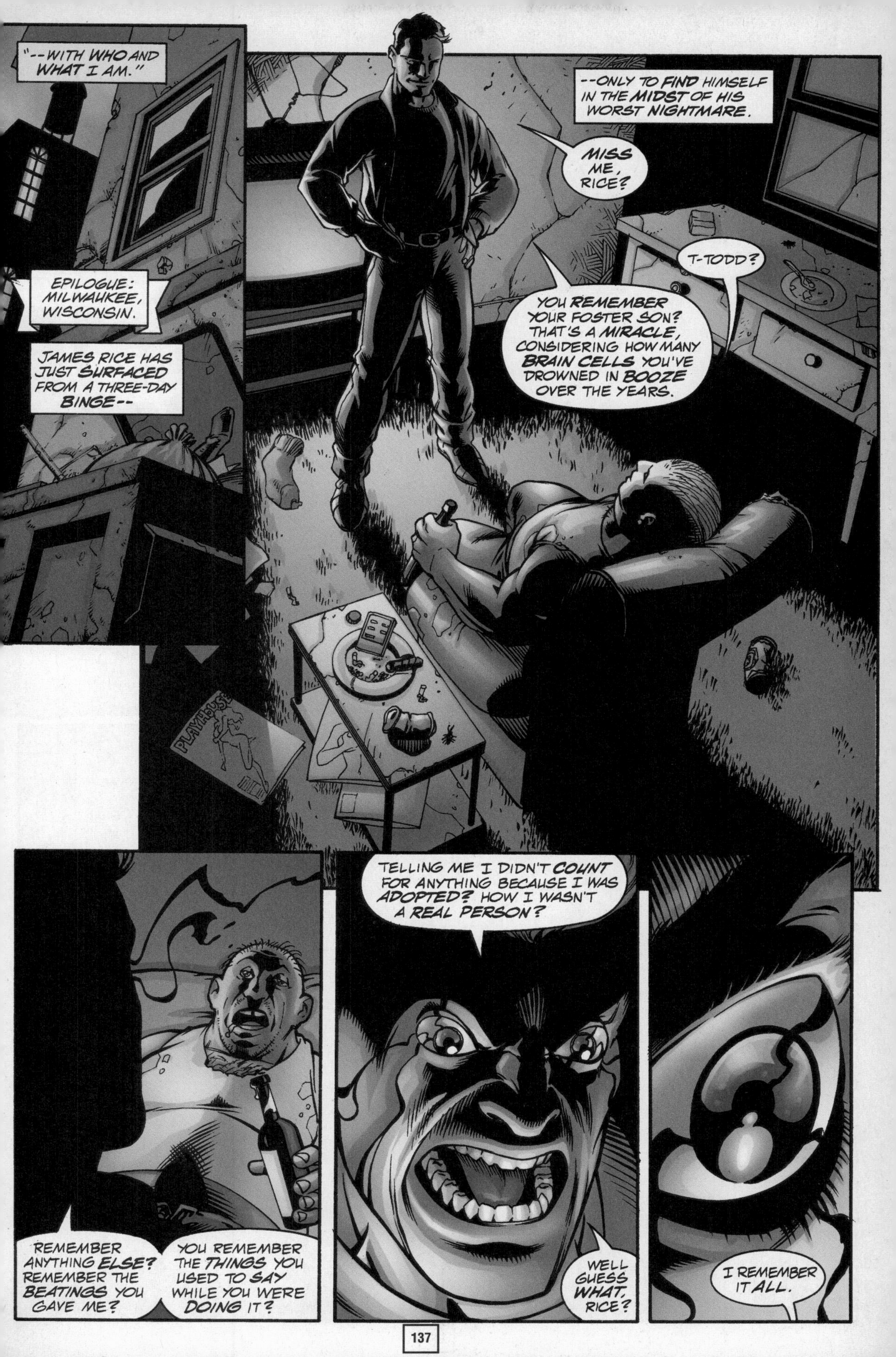
"--WITH WHO AND WHAT I AM."
EPILOGUE: MILWAUKEE, WISCONSIN.
JAMES RICE HAS JUST SURFACED FROM A THREE-DAY BINGE--
--ONLY TO FIND HIMSELF IN THE MIDST OF HIS WORST NIGHTMARE.
MISS ME, RICE?
T-TODD?
YOU REMEMBER YOUR FOSTER SON? THAT'S A MIRACLE, CONSIDERING HOW MANY BRAIN CELLS YOU'VE DROWNED IN BOOZE OVER THE YEARS.
PLAYHOUSE
REMEMBER ANYTHING ELSE? REMEMBER THE BEATINGS YOU GAVE ME?
YOU REMEMBER THE THINGS YOU USED TO SAY WHILE YOU WERE DOING IT?
TELLING ME I DIDN'T COUNT FOR ANYTHING BECAUSE I WAS ADOPTED? HOW I WASN'T A REAL PERSON?
WELL GUESS WHAT, RICE?
I REMEMBER IT ALL.

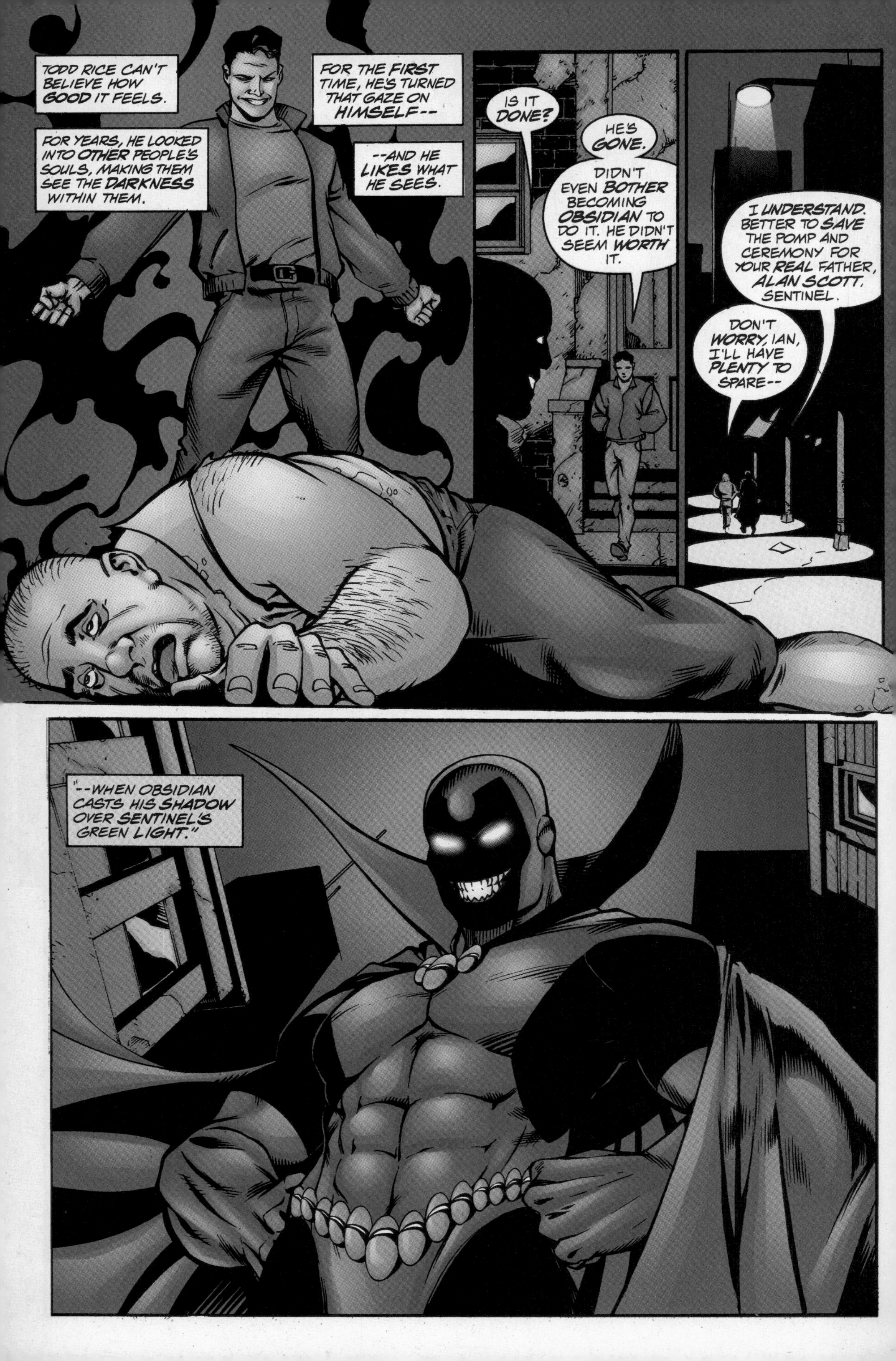
TODD RICE CAN'T BELIEVE HOW GOOD IT FEELS.
FOR YEARS, HE LOOKED INTO OTHER PEOPLE'S SOULS, MAKING THEM SEE THE DARKNESS WITHIN THEM.
FOR THE FIRST TIME, HE'S TURNED THAT GAZE ON HIMSELF--
--AND HE LIKES WHAT HE SEES.
IS IT DONE?
HE'S GONE.
DIDN'T EVEN BOTHER BECOMING OBSIDIAN TO DO IT. HE DIDN'T SEEM WORTH IT.
I UNDERSTAND. BETTER TO SAVE THE POMP AND CEREMONY FOR YOUR REAL FATHER, ALAN SCOTT, SENTINEL.
DON'T WORRY, IAN, I'LL HAVE PLENTY TO SPARE--
"--WHEN OBSIDIAN CASTS HIS SHADOW OVER SENTINEL'S GREEN LIGHT."

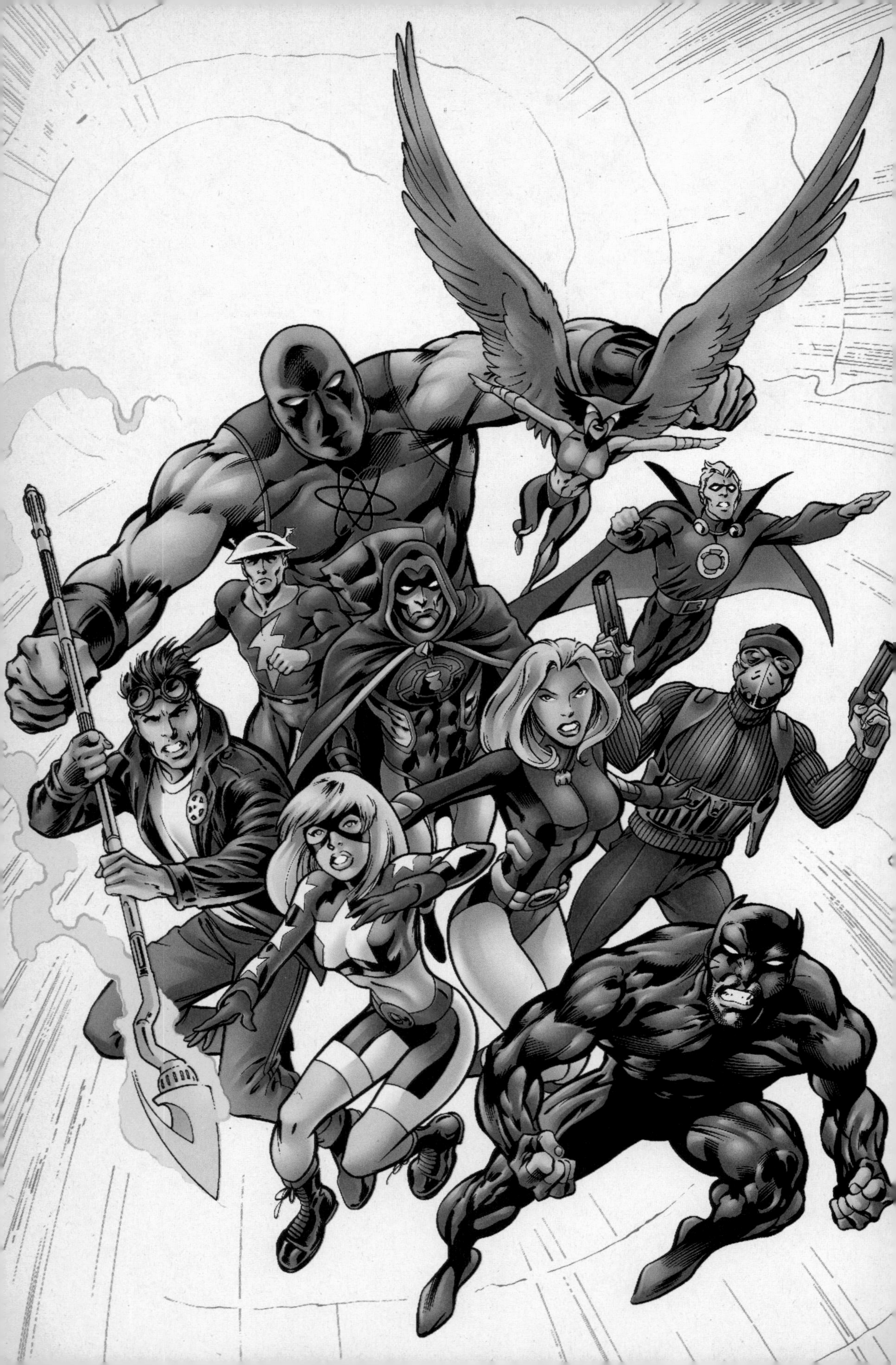

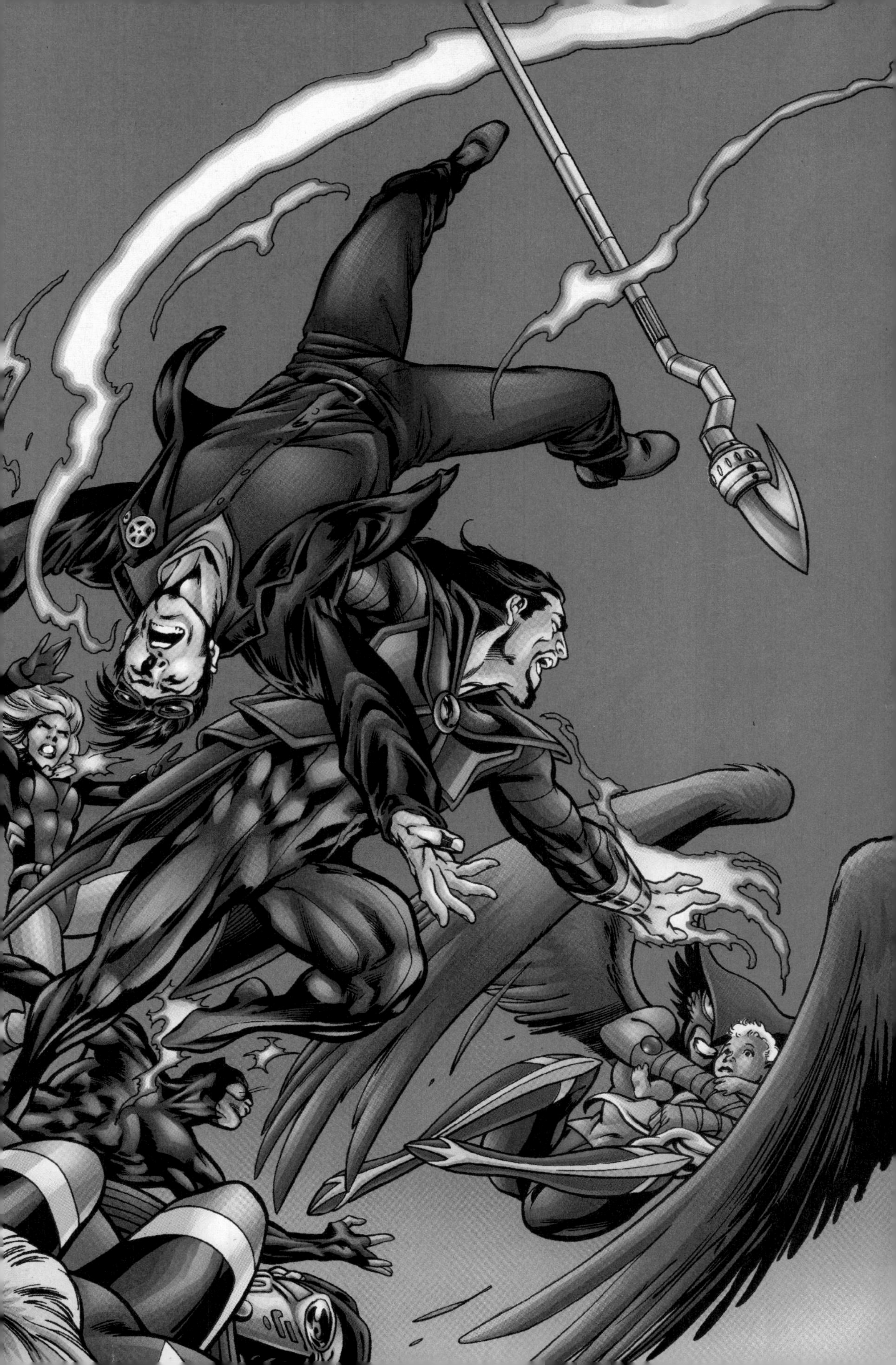

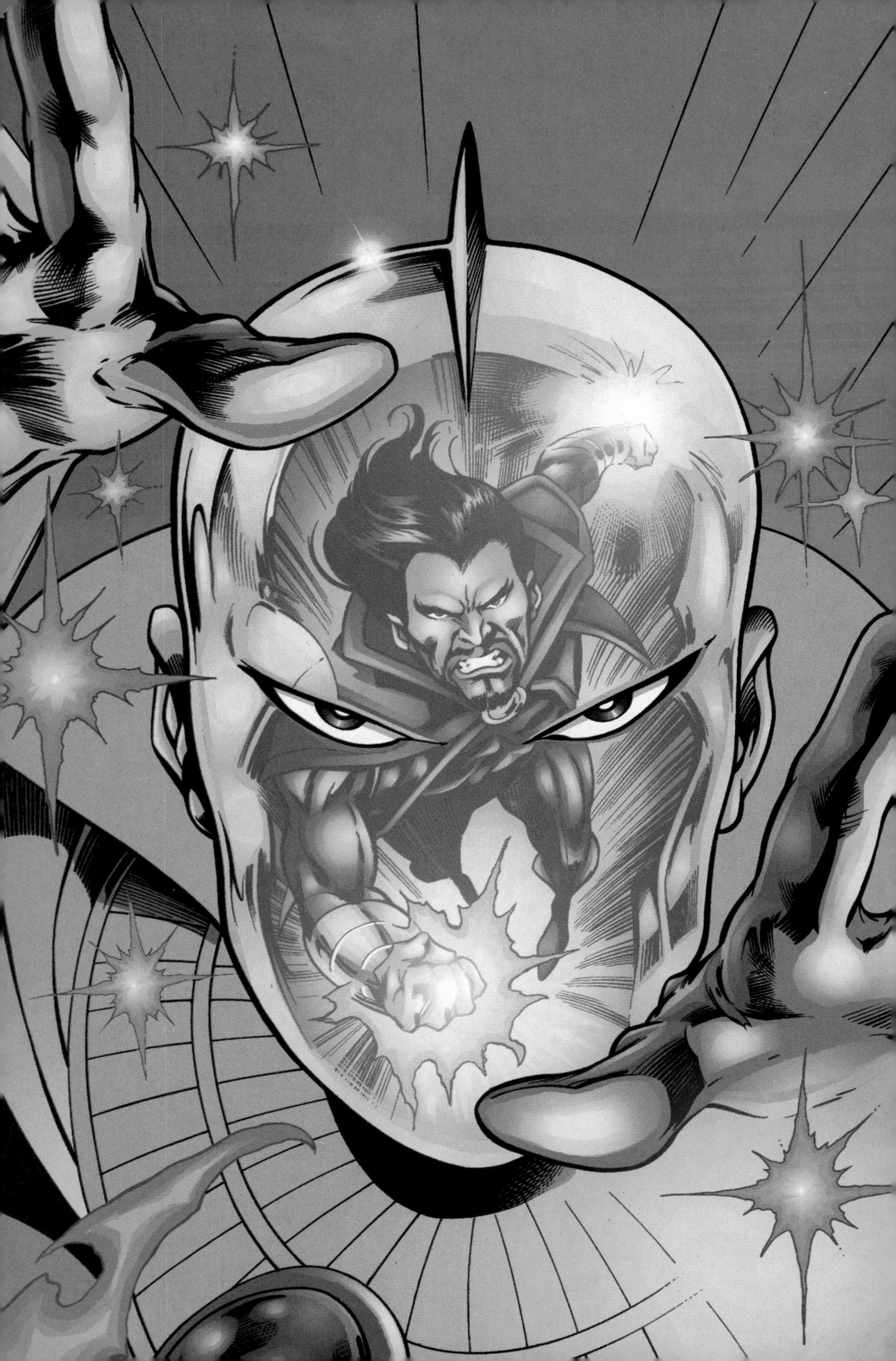